Running for Their Lives

Running for Their Lives

Girls, Cultural Identity, and Stories of Survival

edited by
Sherrie A. Inness

ROWMAN & LITTLEFIELD PUBLISHERS, INC.
Lanham • Boulder • New York • Oxford

ROWMAN & LITTLEFIELD PUBLISHERS, INC.

Published in the United States of America
by Rowman & Littlefield Publishers, Inc.
4720 Boston Way, Lanham, Maryland 20706
http://www.rowmanlittlefield.com

12 Hid's Copse Road
Cumnor Hill, Oxford OX2 9JJ, England

British Library Cataloguing in Publication Information Available

Library of Congress Cataloging-in-Publication Data
Running for their lives : girls, cultural identity, and stories of survival / edited
by Sherrie A. Inness.
    p.   cm.
    Includes bibliographical references and index.
    ISBN 0-8476-9850-5 (cloth : alk. paper)—ISBN 0-8476-9851-3 (paper :
    alk. paper)
        1. Girls—Social conditions—Case studies.   2. Minority youth—Social
conditions—Case studies.   3. Racism—Case studies.   4. Marginality,
Social—Case studies.   I. Inness, Sherrie A.
HQ777.R86   2000
305.23—dc21   99-056025

Printed in the United States of America

♾ ™ The paper used in this publication meets the minimum requirements of
American National Standard for Information Sciences—Permanence of Paper
for Printed Library Materials, ANSI Z39.48-1992.

"What is 'Real'?" asked the Rabbit one day. . . . "Does it mean having things that buzz inside you and a stick-out handle?"

"It doesn't happen all at once," said the Skin Horse. "You become. It takes a long time. That's why it doesn't happen to people who break easily, or have sharp edges, or who have to be carefully kept. Generally, by the time you are Real, most of your hair has been loved off, and your eyes drop out and you get loose in the joints and very shabby. But these things don't matter at all, because once you are Real you can't be ugly, except to people who don't understand."

—Margery Williams, *The Velveteen Rabbit*

Contents

Acknowledgments

I appreciate all the work that my contributors, both young and old, have done to make this book a reality. Their efforts were Herculean, especially under often difficult circumstances. I am honored to work with all of them. I am also privileged to work with Jill Rothenberg, Janice Braunstein, Christine Gatliffe, and Kathleen Silloway, and everyone at Rowman & Littlefield; they have contributed significantly to the book's success. Jill is a "dream" editor—working with her is a delight. I always appreciate her as both a professional and a friend.

I also wish to thank Faye Parker Flavin, someone I feel privileged to know. It is impossible to fit her character into a few slender lines. It will have to suffice to say that she is a rare individual, someone with a genuine good heart. Maybe it would be easier to capture Faye's personality by mentioning that she is someone who, very much like the Velveteen Rabbit in the story by Margery Williams, is Real—a difficult feat for anyone to achieve. This book is dedicated to Parker.

I can never express how much the support of my students and friends means to me. A few of the people I would thank include Alice Adams, Martina Barash, Barbara Emison, Darrell Gordon, Stephanie Levine, Michele Lloyd, Lisa Somer, Barbara Spaulding, Paige Wheeler, Liz Wilson, and my colleagues at Miami University. A special thank you goes to Allison Chandler George, a fellow writer. I also want to thank Ruth Ebelke Inness (1920–1998). Ruth, my mom and my best friend, even though she is no longer with me in person, influences everything I do, especially my writing. Her thoughts and ideals shape my writing and my life.

Introduction

Girl Problems

Sherrie A. Inness

$\mathcal{G}$irls are outsiders. Because of their age and gender, girls are ignored or overlooked in many societies around the world. Due to their gender, girls are often given little authority, prestige, or voice in cultures that privilege sons over daughters. They are rarely allowed to govern themselves because society views them as immature, not capable of making informed, thoughtful decisions; they must let others govern their actions. Many societies assume that girls are frivolous, empty-headed. Adults often perceive girls as lost in fantasy worlds, chock-full of Barbies driving around in canary-yellow Corvette roadsters and Kens sporting never-fail tans and pearly white iron-on smiles. Girls are associated with everything inane and frivolous.

For many reasons, *all* the world's girls are placed in the margins of existence. But how much infintely more complex and perilous this situation is when girls are doubly or triply marginalized by socioeconomic class, race, ethnicity, and a host of other factors. If life is complex for middle-class white girls growing up in U.S. suburbs, life is ten times more difficult for girls growing up without such privileges. Think about a young Thai teenage girl who, after being abandoned by her husband, must work in a button factory in order to earn enough money to feed and support her daughter and herself. Think about a poverty-stricken young girl who is raped in rural Pakistan, and whose rapist is never brought to trial, leaving her brutally battered, mentally and physically. Reflect on an African girl who is adopted and brought to the United States, yet discovers that she is not accepted there because of her cultural background. These stories and other equally painful sagas are the ones I want you to hear; I hope the chapters in this collection will give these

girls and other disenfranchised young women a place to be heard, a place
to express some of the pain—emotional and physical—that is felt by
these girls and millions of others.

These disenfranchised girls' voices are seldom heard, their plights
rarely told. A reason for this silence is that researchers interested in studying and writing about contemporary girlhood often focus on relatively
privileged girls. One of the most influential studies in recent decades
about girlhood, Carol Gilligan's book *Making Connections: The Relational
Worlds of Adolescent Girls at Emma Willard School* (1990), focuses primarily
on affluent white girls at an elite, private boarding school. This emphasis
is not uncommon. For instance, Mary Pipher in her best-selling book
Reviving Ophelia: Saving the Selves of Adolescent Girls (1994) writes princi-
pally about white middle-class U.S. girls. Similarly, Peggy Orenstein's
Schoolgirls: Young Women, Self-Esteem, and the Confidence Gap (1994) focuses on middle-class girls, studying how they are shortchanged by an
educational system that implicitly and explicitly sets up girls to fail. After
spending a year as a participant and observer in two different school systems, Orenstein writes a firsthand account about the realities of today's
girls. Even though one of the schools is not financially well-off, however, Orenstein still focuses on girls who are privileged to attend school
and on U.S. girls in California—a relatively affluent group in the world's
economy. These three books are but a few of the most prominent ones
in girls' studies that look at relatively well-off American girls, often white
ones. Although these girls have important stories to tell, their stories tend
to obscure the life stories of less privileged girls—girls who could never
afford to attend Emma Willard or any school at all, a situation that holds
true for millions of girls today. Girls' studies need to become more inclusive, to embrace these millions absent from the field of girls' cultural
studies.[1] This is also true in the field of youth studies, which focuses
largely on middle-class white boys and girls.[2] This anthology tries to
bring at least a few of the inadequately represented girls into the picture
of youth studies, creating a more realistic and comprehensive vision of
the lives of girls around the globe.[3]

Along with focusing on primarily white middle-class girls, girls'
studies also has another shortcoming: the "real" experiences of "real"
girls are either left out entirely or given only fleeting consideration by
scholars interested in girls' lives. It is difficult, after all, for scholars to talk
to girls. These girls may have parents who do not wish them to speak to
strangers about painful issues in their private family lives. Girls may also

be swept up in their own lives, unwilling to give time to talk to researchers interested in better understanding girlhood, and many girls view adults with suspicion, disdain, or hostility. Why would such girls share their life stories with adults who seem to inhabit a different world? For numerous reasons, "girls" are often left out of girls' studies, but it is essential that girls—the subject of girls' cultural studies—not be left voiceless. After all, girls are the ones who truly understand the problems they face in the world and what it means to be made into social outcasts for a plethora of reasons. This anthology seeks to give girls a place to write about the painful difficulties and realities facing them.[4]

Fortunately, a few authors in recent years have started to make an effort to record the thoughts of disenfranchised youth throughout the world. For example, Anthony Allison's book, *Hear These Voices: Youth at the Edge of the Millennium* (1999), includes reflections from children. Allison's work, however, is more generally about girls and boys; he does not deal exclusively with gender-related issues facing girls today, including only a few chapters that focus on four different girls and their concerns. Needless to say, this is a small sampling of the girls' stories that remain to be told. I hope that *Running for Their Lives* will provide a broader understanding of girls living in the margins of global society.[5]

This anthology is focused not only on telling girls' stories but also on making sure readers understand the different cultural contexts in which girls exist. To achieve this goal, I chose not to focus the book purely on academics and their meditations on girlhood. I wanted to make sure that the girls' voices in this collection were in the forefront, not shunted aside, so that the words of scholars were in the limelight. I have also recognized that having chapters that were written solely by young girls could make it difficult for readers to understand the larger social contexts in which these girls (and other similar ones) operate. Thus, I thought it best to combine the words of younger girl writers and academics. Together, the girl writers and the academics create a stronger, more nuanced, more fully rounded vision of girlhood today.

Despite my attempts to make this an anthology that represents a broad variety of girls from different backgrounds and cultures, I know that inevitable gaps will exist in any such collection. For instance, I have thought about what it means that, as a writer and editor, I am white and middle class and that most of the girls are not. I have never suffered the tremendous hardships that many of the girls whose voices are included in this anthology have confronted. I have not wondered from where my next meal would come or had to drop out of school to go to work so my family could survive. I have not been taunted because my skin color was different from that of the majority's. My mother was not unavailable to help me with my homework due to her mental illness. I have also never lived in many of the cultures described in this book. Thus, there is a chasm between the lives of the girls represented and my own life—plus the lives of many of my academic contributors. As academics, we struggle to record experiences that might be foreign to us as often relatively privileged individuals. In the process of translation, no matter how sensitive we are to a girl's words and her culture's mores, it is difficult not to lose something.

This anthology addresses the life stories of only the smallest handful of girls. No collection could cover the complexity of experiences that is girlhood today for girls around the globe. We are left with a few stories of girls who have been lucky or fortunate enough to have their stories told—to have someone who cared enough to work with them to record their stories or encourage them to write down their experiences. This is an unusual situation for the majority of the world's girls. Indeed, there are many cultures in this world where talking to a young girl and recording her story, especially if it expresses rebellion, could result in the girl's injury or death.

Even though I recognize that, as a middle-class white academic living in the United States, I have not lived the same experience as many of these girls, and even though I know that not all girls' stories can be told in this collection, I still think that creating a space in which *some* of these girls' words may be heard is valuable. These words, no matter how few, offer readers a vivid look at girlhood, revealing not only the tragedies that girls face in their daily lives but also the triumphs. I hope these chapters will leave readers with a better understanding of the demands and difficulties facing today's girls. These chapters will also show the many ways that girls cope with impossible situations, ways of coping that should draw admiration, respect, and compassion from us all. These girls are survivors.

The book is divided into two sections. The chapters in the first part address the racism that girls must face in different situations and different cultural contexts. The common thread is that all of these girls face persecution from others due to the color of their skin and their different cultural mores. The collection begins with three chapters that explore the racism faced by four different black immigrant girls. Already a marginalized group in the United States due to the color of their skin, these girls must also cope with the discrimination they face as Africans. For all the girls, the move from Africa to the United States has been a troubling one. In the first chapter, Palesa Kendall, Manko Kendall, and K. Lima-katso Kendall confront racism in Louisiana after the young girls, Palesa and Manko, move from South Africa to New Orleans, where they are subjected to suspicion and hostility from schoolmates due to their cultural differences. Palesa and Manko tell a sobering story about what it means to discover that the United States is *not* the promised land it is touted to be by popular movies and television shows; instead, America is a place where Palesa and Manko need to deal with hatred because they are "different."

Bosson Caroline Kouassiaman and Susan Frazier-Kouassi explore the life of an African girl who has traveled and lived in a number of African countries before she moves to the United States. Teenager Bosson Caroline Kouassiaman writes about what it means to be a teenage girl whose background springs from a multitude of different cultures. Similarly, Joy Ekema-Agbaw and Vivian Yenika-Agbaw reflect on the difficulties of being a young black American girl who has emigrated from another country, Cameroon. For Joy, a young girl who only wants to "fit in," life in rural Pennsylvania means learning to live with her difference, acknowledging that her experiences are going to be different from those of her native-born friends. This is a cruel and painful lesson, as Joy struggles with the expectations of her friends and her assumptions about what it means to be American.

But it is not only immigrant girls who are marginalized in the United States, as the next chapter shows. Wendy M. Thompson and Lisa B. Thompson describe the experiences of a young bicultural girl growing up in the United States, who doesn't feel accepted fully by either of her cultures. With an Asian mother and an African American father, Wendy grew up in two different worlds. She reflects on coping with the cultural stereotypes that society associates with being Asian or black. She writes about the sense of not belonging in either culture, examining the ways that, while a young teen, she expressed her rebellion against a society that seemed to offer her no home. Ultimately, her story is one of triumph, as she learns to understand that coming from two cultures only enriches her life; this is a lesson, however, that she learns only after much emotional and physical pain.

Wendy's story as a bicultural girl is similar to that of Mah-Rukh Ali, even though the girls grew up thousands of miles apart and come from different cultural backgrounds. Mah-Rukh Ali and Elisabeth Sandberg explore what it means to grow up as a Pakistani–Norwegian girl. Mah-Rukh writes about the racism and persecution she faces; she reflects on how painful it is to be made to feel an outsider in her home country of Norway. Mah-Rukh creates a biting, bitter account of the racism that troubles that nation, known for its homogenous population. Mah-Rukh's story, however, is also one of survival, as she learns to fight the discrimination she must endure, eventually writing a book about the persecution she encounters. This chapter points out the ubiquity of racism and the tremendous pain that confronts any girl who is persecuted by others due to the color of her skin. Mah-Rukh's story destroys any preconceived ideas that the reader might have that some more "civilized" countries escape the burdens of racism that are so visible in the United States.

The next chapter is also about a "civilized" nation, Canada, which is supposed to be free—at least in our popular imagination—of the scourge of racism. As we discover, quite the opposite is true for one young woman, Ayanna. Ayanna Anamoor—a pseudonym—and Merlinda Weinberg describe the discrimination that Ayanna must face as an immigrant from Somali to Canada and as a single teenage mother—a plight faced by many young women around the world. As an immigrant and a single teenage mother, she is an outcast in mainstream Canadian society. She finds no succor, however, from her Muslim family, for whom having a baby out of wedlock is taboo. Forced to flee her family, she finds no friendly home in the outer world; she shares the fate of millions of girls and young women, rejected by both society at large and their families. Ayanna's story is more sobering because her real name cannot be used, since her family members could choose to persecute, perhaps even murder, her.

The chapters in the first section focus on how girls confront racism regularly, the chapters in the second section share an interest in other hardships that girls must endure, including poverty, war, or a parent's mental instability. The section begins with a chapter by Ariana-Sophia Kartsonis that examines the lives of a group of poverty-stricken girls living in India. The chapter combines fiction and fact as Kartsonis struggles to tell the story of a group of girls she has never met face-to-face; introduced to the young girls Preeti, Priya, Pratibha, Kamala, and Lalitha through the e-mail messages of a friend in India, Kartsonis herself was thousands of miles away in the United States. This narrative isn't only a story of the girls' survival against tremendous economic odds, it is also a reflection on how difficult it is truly to "know" someone else, particularly someone from a different cultural background. Kartsonis reflects on the impossibility of ever really knowing others' experiences, especially the experiences of young girls, who are taught not to talk to strangers and not to reveal too much of their lives.

Like Kartsonis's chapter, the next two chapters address the difficulties of telling girls' stories when the girls come from economic or cultural backgrounds that are different from that of the writers working with them. Najma Habib and Rebecca Sultana, both from Bangladesh, discover that their high-class status both economically and socially makes it awkward to talk to young working girls in the factories of Bangladesh, who view the outsiders with suspicion. After Najma meets Afia Begum, a teenage female worker in a garment factory, Najma must strive to gain the young woman's trust in order to share her story. In a similar fashion, trust between social classes is an issue in the next chapter, in which Tahera Aftab writes about the lives of poor rural girls living in Pakistan. As Aftab comments, telling the stories of Mithi, Pomi, and Nasima is a difficult feat because few Pakistani girls from rural areas are allowed to talk with strangers, particularly educated ones. The stories of Mithi, Pomi, and Nasima must inevitably be told in scraps and pieced together like a patchwork quilt.

The next chapter can also be imagined as a patchwork quilt, sewn together out of Ajla Hodzic's memories of what life was like in Sarajevo before war ripped her country apart. Ajla's journey takes her from Sarajevo, to Turkey, to the United States, and to many other places. Her odyssey is the plight of countless other girls (and boys), young people whose homes are destroyed due to a war that youth cannot completely comprehend. Ajla poignantly describes what happens when a girl's life is destroyed. Never can she go back to the Sarajevo she knew as a small girl; it is as foreign, as strange, as alien as any other place she visits.

Finally, Charley Lauren Ortman and Patricia E. Ortman conclude the book with an exploration of one of the most invisible ways that girls are marginalized: by the mental illness of a parent. The United States has a culture built on the assumption that parents or guardians are "naturally" not suffering from any severe mental problems. Thus, an educational culture is built on parents who come to awards banquets and teacher meetings, band performances, sports events, and a host of other activities. The assumption of parents' mental normalcy appears in a hundred other areas. Students are assumed to have parents who are willing and able to help with homework and supportive of their children's quest to grow into responsible and capable young adults. Parents are expected to donate something to the annual bake sale. They are called upon to be chaperones to the class dance or a field trip to the local zoo. Little or no consideration is given to the fact that mental illness might make some of these tasks impossible for a mother or father. Charley Lauren writes about what it means for a young girl to have a mentally ill mother, a mother so ill that she is incapable of performing many of the acts of parenthood that we take for granted. Mental illness is one of the least acknowledged forms of marginalization that girls must endure, as mental illness is rarely acknowledged in schools, seldom mentioned by teachers. By bringing this taboo subject out into the open, Charley Lauren and Patricia E. Ortman make readers cognizant of an issue that affects the lives of millions of girls.

This book should leave its readers disturbed—disturbed about how many girls around the world suffer simply because they are female. The physical and emotional pain is compounded by many other reasons, too, including the color of their skin, poverty, and lack of education. Since they often cannot speak out due to their age and gender, girls must suffer in silence. This silence is still something with which many girls, especially those who exist in the margins of the world's societies, must struggle; ensuring that girls are actually heard in the world and listened to as carefully as any other group is a monumental task.

This anthology is also about hope. It is about girls who endure tremendous suffering and manage to overcome it. This book is about girls who make the best of their lives in seemingly impossible situations. It is about girls who manage to maintain their dignity, despite the indignities heaped upon them. Although these girls suffer, they also show their ability to overcome tremendous hardships. There is a lesson about the dignity of the human spirit that all of us should carry away from reading these girls' stories.

NOTES

1. For more information on girls' cultural studies, see Formanek-Brunell (1993); Leadbeater and Way (1996); Mitchell (1995); Nelson and Vallone (1994); Prowelier (1998); and Vallone (1995).

2. General sources on youth culture include Austin and Willard (1998); Cote and Allahar (1996); Epstein (1998); Griffin (1993); Jenkins (1998); Kett (1977); Palladino (1996); Springhall (1998); and West and Petrik (1992).

3. For scholarship that focuses specifically on youth culture and issues of ethnicity or race, see Amit-Talai and Wulff (1995); Giroux (1998); and Lipsitz (1989).

4. My past books on girls and their cultures include *Delinquents and Debutantes: Twentieth-Century American Girls' Cultures* (1998a); *Intimate Communities: Representation and Social Transformation in Women's College Fiction, 1895–1910* (1995); *Millennium Girls: Today's Girls Around the World* (1998b); and *Nancy Drew and Company: Culture, Gender, and Girls' Series* (1997).

5. Other works that create a space for girls and their own words include Blake (1997); Carlip (1995); Carroll (1997); Finders (1997); Gaines (1990); Hey (1997); Johnston (1997); Sikes (1997); and Thompson (1995).

WORKS CITED

Allison, Anthony. 1999. *Hear These Voices: Youth at the Edge of the Millennium.* New York: Dutton.

Amit-Talai, Vered, and Helena Wulff, eds. 1995. *Youth Cultures: A Cross-Cultural Perspective.* New York: Routledge.

Austin, Joe, and Michael Nevin Willard, eds. 1998. *Generations of Youth: Youth Cultures and History in Twentieth-Century America.* New York: New York University Press.

Blake, Brett Elizabeth. 1997. *She Say, He Say: Urban Girls Write Their Lives.* Albany: State University of New York Press.

Carlip, Hillary. 1995. *Girl Power.* New York: Warner.

Carroll, Rebecca. 1997. *Sugar in the Raw: Voices of Young Black Girls in America.* New York: Crown.

Cote, James E., and Anton L. Allahar. 1996. *Generation on Hold: Coming of Age in the Late Twentieth Century.* New York: New York University Press.

Epstein, Jon, ed. 1998. *Youth Culture: Identity in a Postmodern World.* Malden, Mass.: Blackwell.

Finders, Margaret J. 1997. *Just Girls: Hidden Literacies and Life in Junior High.* New York: Teachers College Press.

Formanek-Brunell, Miriam. 1993. *Made to Play House: Dolls and the Commercialization of American Girlhood, 1830–1930.* New Haven: Yale University Press.

Gaines, Donna. 1990. *Teenage Wasteland: Suburbia's Dead End Kids*. New York: Pantheon.

Gilligan, Carol, Nona P. Lyons, and T. J. Hanmer. 1990. *Making Connections: The Relational Worlds of Adolescent Girls at Emma Willard School*. Cambridge: Harvard University Press.

Giroux, Henry A. 1998. *Channel Surfing: Racism, the Media, and the Destruction of Today's Youth*. New York: St. Martin's.

Griffin, Christine. 1993. *Representations of Youth: The Study of Youth and Adolescence in Britain and America*. Cambridge, England: Polity Press.

Hey, Valerie. 1997. *The Company She Keeps: An Ethnography of Girls' Friendships*. Philadelphia: Open University Press.

Inness, Sherrie A. 1995. *Intimate Communities: Representation and Social Transformation in Women's College Fiction, 1895–1910*. Bowling Green, Oh.: Bowling Green State University Popular Press.

———. 1998b. *Millennium Girls: Today's Girls Around the World*. Lanham, Md.: Rowman & Littlefield.

———, ed. 1998a. *Delinquents and Debutantes: Twentieth-Century American Girls' Cultures*. New York: New York University Press.

———, ed. 1997. *Nancy Drew and Company: Culture, Gender, and Girls' Series*. Bowling Green, Oh.: Bowling Green State University Popular Press.

Jenkins, Henry, ed. 1998. *The Children's Culture Reader*. New York: New York University Press.

Johnston, Andrea. 1997. *Girls Speak Out: Finding Your True Self*. New York: Scholastic.

Kett, Joseph F. 1977. *Rites of Passage: Adolescence in America, 1790 to the Present*. New York: Basic Books.

Leadbeater, Bonnie J. Ross, and Niobe Way, eds. 1996. *Urban Girls: Resisting Stereotypes, Creating Identities*. New York: New York University Press.

Lipsitz, George. 1989. "Land of a Thousand Dances: Youth, Minorities, and the Rise of Rock and Roll." In *Recasting America: Culture and Politics in the Age of Cold War,* ed. Lary May. Chicago: University of Chicago Press, 267–84.

Mitchell, Sally. 1995. *The New Girl: Girls' Culture in England, 1880–1915*. New York: Columbia University Press.

Nelson, Claudia, and Lynne Vallone, eds. 1994. *The Girls' Own: Cultural Histories of the Anglo-American Girl, 1830–1915*. Athens: University of Georgia Press.

Orenstein, Peggy. 1994. *Schoolgirls: Young Women, Self-Esteem, and the Confidence Gap*. New York: Doubleday.

Palladino, Grace. 1996. *Teenagers: An American History*. New York: Basic Books.

Pipher, Mary. 1994. *Reviving Ophelia: Saving the Selves of Adolescent Girls*. New York: Putnam.

Prowelier, Amira. 1998. *Constructing Female Identities: Meaning Making in an Upper Middle Class Youth Culture*. Albany: State University of New York Press.

Sikes, Gini. 1997. *8 Ball Chicks: A Year in the Violent World of Girl Gangsters*. New York: Doubleday.

Springhall, John. 1998. *Youth, Popular Culture and Moral Panics: Penny Gaffs to Gangsta-Rap, 1830–1996*. New York: St. Martin's.

Thompson, Sharon. 1995. *Going All the Way: Teenage Girls' Tales of Sex, Romance, and Pregnancy*. New York: Hill and Wang.

Vallone, Lynne. 1995. *Disciplines of Virtue: Girls' Culture in the Eighteenth and Nineteenth Centuries*. New Haven: Yale University Press.

West, Eliot, and Paula Petrik, eds. 1992. *Small Worlds: Children and Adolescents in America, 1850–1950*. Lawrence: University of Kansas Press.

· Part I ·

Dancing the *Bashenga:*
Girls Confront Racism

· 1 ·

Coming to America
Not the Movie by Eddie Murphy

Palesa and Manko Kendall

INTRODUCTION

K. Limakatso Kendall, adoptive mother of Palesa and Manko

Palesa, born in 1986, and Manko, born in 1988, were both living in the village of Mafikeng, in the Roma Valley of Lesotho, when I met them in 1992 and 1994, respectively.[1] I was in Lesotho as a Senior Fulbright Scholar, creating theater for development and teaching English courses at the National University of Lesotho.[2] Palesa's mother was ill and unable to care for her or her little sister; Palesa had never attended school, had no clothes, and was severely malnourished.[3] A number of children in their village were in the same condition, but Palesa and I bonded soon after my arrival in Lesotho, and I took a special interest in her. I bought clothes and a school uniform for Palesa, enrolled her in Roma Primary School, the local Roman Catholic elementary school, and began supplementing her diet. I also provided clothes and food for Palesa's little sister, who was too young to attend school. When Palesa contracted typhoid in 1993 and had to be hospitalized, I took over as Palesa's primary caregiver, with her mother's permission. Palesa's mother said she would be happy for me to adopt Palesa if I wanted to, but I postponed making that decision. I enrolled Palesa in St. Rose Primary School, a boarding school in the town of Peka, Lesotho, about an hour and a half from Mafikeng by car, and I would fetch her during school holidays and bring her back to stay with me and play with her old friends.

In 1994, when Palesa was with me during her holidays from boarding school, she brought Manko to me. Manko lived in Mafikeng and

3

had long been a friend of Palesa's. Manko was an orphan, then living with an impoverished elderly woman she called her "granny," though the woman was not actually related to Manko. This "granny" was unable to feed and support Manko, and although Manko, as an orphan, was granted free admission to the nearby Roma Primary School and was given free uniforms, she had no other clothing and was severely malnourished. Manko had not only suffered deep grief when her mother died, she had also been mauled by a dog and abused by some village boys, and Palesa feared that without a stable home and care, Manko would die. Rape statistics are not available for Lesotho, but neighboring South Africa is called "the rape capital of the world."[4] I sought placement in foster homes or an orphanage for both children, but Palesa's mother was not willing for Palesa to be placed in an orphanage, and Lesotho was not able to provide foster homes or an orphanage for either child.[5] I was by then deeply attached to Palesa, and I was so moved by Manko's situation that I determined after some deliberation to adopt both children. This was not a decision I made easily or lightly. My second child had just matured and moved away to live on his own, and I had been looking forward to a long-postponed career as a writer and to the solitude and simplicity of life that might make that possible. I had no property or savings, and I was about to turn fifty. According to U.S. immigration regulations, in order to bring the children into the United States, given my financial situation, I would have to adopt them in Lesotho and live with them for at least two years outside the States, and that meant I would have to seek employment in Africa—not an easy prospect.

Palesa asked me to adopt her little sister as well, but Palesa's mother was not willing to allow that. I knew Palesa was more deeply bonded with her little sister than with anyone else, and I knew that separation from her sister, her mother, her village, and her culture would be very difficult for her. This has certainly proved true. Manko had not bonded closely with anyone since her mother's death, though she was fond of the "granny" who cared for her. She had endured a great deal of trauma. Separation from her culture and her language would not be easy for her, either. It was for all these reasons that I tried desperately to locate a family or an individual in Lesotho that could take one or both girls, and to whom I could perhaps send money from the United States. I was not able to locate anyone willing to take that responsibility. Therefore, the

Palesa, left, and Manko in New Orleans. (Photo by K. Kendall.)

alternatives were for me to move to Africa with the idea that eventually we might all move to the States, or for me to abandon both girls.

I am familiar with debates concerning interracial adoption, and I am in principle opposed to whites adopting black children, because I believe white people cannot provide sufficient survival skills to equip black children for life in a racist society. However, these were extreme circumstances. If I did not take Palesa and Manko, they very likely would both die. Both were so severely malnourished before I began caring for them that they had already been permanently damaged in a number of ways. Perhaps the most important factor in my decision-making was that I loved them, they wanted me to adopt them, and nothing else I had in mind to do with my life seemed more important at the time. It was also at this time that I decided to ask my good friend, *'M'e* Mpho Nthunya, with whom I had been engaged for two years in the writing of her book, *Singing Away the Hunger* (1997), to live with me, provided I could find work in South Africa.[6] If she would coparent with me, it would be a

Palesa and Manko with their friends in Pietermaritzburg. Back row, left to right: Palesa, Rogini, and Ntobeko; front row, left to right: Pretty, Anna, and Manko. (Photo by K. Kendall.)

way to provide continuity for the children with their language and their culture. She knew their mothers, she had known the children since they were born, and she would be our resident cultural advisor. She agreed, and that was the final piece of the puzzle that needed to be put into place.

I found a job teaching at the University of Natal in Pietermaritzburg, South Africa, about eight hours by car from the girls' home village. Before we could begin our lives there, however, I had to return to the United States and take care of some personal business, resettle myself in Pietermaritzburg, and then reclaim the children. During this period, from July 1994 to June 1995, I left both girls in the boarding school in Peka. They came to Pietermaritzburg for their first visit during Easter break, 1995, and in June 1995 I brought both girls to my new home in South Africa to stay.

In July 1995, they entered first grade at Ridge Junior Primary School, where English was the language of instruction; at that time, neither of the girls had spoken English. They were older by several years than the other first graders, but they were happy to relax in the company of younger children, to occupy themselves learning English, and to experience something of the childhood that their poverty had robbed them of. They learned English quickly and well, and the principal and teachers at Ridge supported them in every possible way. By June 1998, when the adoptions finally made their way through the courts in Lesotho, both girls were speaking English as fluently as many children for whom it is a first language.

Once the adoptions were final, I had to decide whether to stay in Africa or return to the United States. I had been pondering this decision for four years. Many factors went into my decision to return, the most pressing of which were the following: (1) I felt unwelcome as a foreigner in a country with a very high unemployment rate; (2) the falling rand was making my full professor's net salary of roughly $10,000 a year dwindle; and (3) I would be subject to mandatory retirement at age sixty, which was rapidly approaching, and the minuscule retirement fund I was accumulating would not support any of us.

In November 1998, we moved to New Orleans. I chose that city for our resettlement because I had no home or roots anywhere in the United States and had lived in New Orleans in the 1970s and knew it to have a large African American population. I assumed that living among African American children would help my children learn to deal with American life, and I suppose it has, although not in the ways I had imagined.

For six months I tried to find a job in the United States, but being unable to appear for an interview made that impossible. I had a distinguished record before leaving the United States, but six years abroad made me an unknown quantity to potential employers. During this period of uncertainty, Sherrie A. Inness contacted me about this book. I asked Palesa and Manko if they would like to contribute. They said, very clearly, no. I went on trying to sort out our lives. The South African academic year runs from January to November, while the U.S. academic year runs from August to May. I had to resign from my South African post in November, or commit to remain in South Africa another year, but it was unlikely I would find employment in my field before the following August.

I spent nearly everything I had ever saved to support the girls and several other families with whom I have strong personal relationships in Africa. I used my retirement account from the South African university to buy our tickets and to ship my books and our personal effects back to the United States. That meant I arrived here jobless, homeless, and nearly penniless, with two children. Because of immigration regulations, we were not allowed to apply for food stamps or public assistance of any kind. My friends took up a collection and raised nearly $2,000 for us, my dad chipped in another $1,000, and that is what we had to get started on. 'M'e Mpho chose not to join us. She had business to take care of in Lesotho, and she didn't want to be another mouth for me to feed in the United States. I began "temping," doing temporary clerical work, looking for a permanent job, and for months we had no car, nor any of the middle-class conveniences we had grown accustomed to in South Africa. We moved into a double house in what I thought was a good neighborhood, but the house was in a school district that drew from an impoverished part of town. Palesa and Manko have encountered hostility, ridicule, and prejudice or internalized racism from African American children. This hurt and shocked them, and I began to feel that talking about their experiences in the three countries might help them heal from the pain of the rejection they experienced from children in New Orleans.

This time, when I proposed writing their stories for this book, they were interested. I said that people who write stories for books often get paid something for their stories, and if they would do this, I would pay them each $50 when the book was published. Compared to their usual allowance of $1 a week, this was an exciting prospect. Palesa agreed with enthusiasm, Manko a bit reluctantly. We began with Palesa's story. Palesa sat in a chair near my computer table and just began to talk, and I transcribed her words exactly as she spoke them. Her story poured out of her, and she laughed and gestured and seemed stronger and brighter as she went on talking. The whole process took only an hour and a half. That night Manko hesitated, said she was too tired, and put off telling her story for several days.

During those days, Manko seemed depressed. Finally, I said we *must* do this if we are going to do it at all, the deadline is already past. I told Manko she didn't have to do it; we could just send Palesa's story. But that didn't please Manko, so she resolved to tell her story. She sat in the same chair Palesa had used and began to cry. She couldn't speak. I suggested we try something different. Manko and I cuddled up on the couch, and I put one arm around her and held a notebook on my lap and wrote in speedwriting with my free arm and hand. I sensed it was the memories of her life in Lesotho that were making it difficult for her, and I told her she didn't have to begin there. She could begin with South Africa. She brightened somewhat at that idea, and gradually she began.

Her story came out haltingly, in jagged bits and pieces. She would often fall silent, and I would ask a question to get her going again. (I have edited my questions out, as they don't contribute to the story.) After about an hour, Manko seemed to feel stronger and more in control of her narrative; she moved aside on the couch so that I was no longer holding her. Her story took three and a half hours to complete. By the end, when she voiced her wish that we had never come to America, she was feeling very strong and clear, and she stood tall and walked stalwartly away from the story. At that point I was in tears, but very proud of her.

In the neighborhood where we settled in New Orleans, there are only African American and Latin American children. There are no white girls the ages of Palesa and Manko anywhere near us, and in the public school Palesa and Manko attend, there are almost no whites. Therefore, Palesa and Manko, at the time of this writing, have had no dealings with white children in the United States. The African American and white adults they have met are all old friends of mine—civil rights activists, artists, and academics. These people have been very welcoming of the children and very helpful to me in re-establishing a life, but I still worry that Palesa and Manko are unprepared for racism as it occurs in mainstream USA, and I doubt even 'M'e Mpho's arrival will do much help to them in that area. My hope is that by telling their stories they may aid their own healing from a traumatic past and strengthen their self-esteem. Perhaps their stories can also contribute to discussions of racism, interracial families and relationships, and internalized racism as it occurs in their new environment. Explanations in brackets are my additions, but the stories are in the girls' own words, and I have not "corrected" their English.

PALESA'S STORY

I have lived in three countries: Lesotho, South Africa, and the USA. Going to school is different in each country. There was nothing good about school in Lesotho. I didn't enjoy the schools because teachers beat you up, and they forced you to do things you didn't want to do. Like when it's lunchtime in Lesotho, they make you eat porridge, they don't have good food, you eat *papa* [a mixture of corn meal and water] and *moroho* [wild vegetables, often called "weeds" in other countries]. In South Africa you had to bring your own lunch, and we always took sandwiches, but in America you have great school lunches, like hamburgers and pizza and fried chicken. People in America don't even know how rich they are. They just take it like it's every day, nothing, they just used to it. In Lesotho the school I went to was not a rich school. We didn't have books, and if you lost your pencil, the teacher would hit you with a thin whip, they put oil on it, and every time it goes around you it makes a sound like a loud clap. They would beat you with that whip for almost nothing or anything, just if they feel like it. And after school, there used to be this man who stood in the woods, waiting for children to come from school, so he could rape them. And he used to walk out of the woods with a knife, a basin, and a big plastic jug for water. The teachers told us that once he caught a child and he killed it. He was scared of big people. He would run away if he saw you walking with a grown person. Then there was a crazy man who lived near us, he was really crazy, he could go under cars, he wore underwear on his head with shit on them, and nobody really liked him. Children would tease him, do anything to him. After school we played skipping rope; *mantloane,* like playing house and you build it up with stones, you have pretend food, you play husband and wife. And we had a game with tins, you take as many tins as you can stack up, and you take plastic bags and put sand in them and wrap them around to make a ball. Some people make a ball with newspapers, wet them, put them in a plastic bag and wrap it, and then put another plastic bag or old pantyhose and make a ball. You stack the tins and throw the ball to knock them down, and the one who knocks down the most tins, wins.

On weekends we used to go to an old lady in the village, every time she calls us, to come and practice the songs and dances of girls. Girls and boys had different songs to sing, they didn't sing the same ones. Once I went up in the mountains and had to go sing there, and we came to a school and we had to go in a circle and do a step, and I used to go in the middle and dance, and people would throw coins and food, they'd be laughing and clapping, and shouting out my name. It made me so proud, and the more people shouted, the more I danced. I used to be good at doing that, it was nice. Every time after we finished doing our stuff, when we go home after, we used to bring peaches, money, it was great. When I came home I gave all the money to my mother. She would take some of the money to go buy *joala* [home-made beer] and drink, or buy candy for my brother. She used to work at the university, washing clothes, and on pay day she would go to the butcher after work and get meat, we would eat it and enjoy it. Sometimes she was fun, sometimes she wasn't. When I didn't want to cook, she would beat me up. She never taught me to cook, but she said I had to do it. I asked my brothers to show me how to do it, but they wouldn't show me. I used to take care of my little sister, take care of her, feed her, change her nappies, and my brothers would go and play with friends. It's hard to be a girl in Lesotho, you have to do so much work, and it's not fair, because the boys just get to play all the time, they don't have to do anything. I used to have fun with my little sister, because my little sister liked me best. If my mother wanted to carry her or feed her, she said no. She wanted my breast, but I was too little. My sister loved me best, and every time I cried, she cried with me, and wherever I went, she always knew where I was going. She would call out my name if she didn't see me, till she found me. I didn't like my brothers that much. I liked my little sister. After school me and my friends, we would go to my house and eat *papa* and water and salt.

My friend used to live in the mountains above the village, most of my friends lived there, and I used to walk there alone; especially at night when I walked back alone I was scared. The dogs scared me. And frogs. And once a scary thing happened to my little sister. At the back of my house we had a big tree with a hole where bees lived. My sister went to go and play with the bees, and a bee went in her ear, and she was screaming and jumping around, and she said there was a bee in her ear, and we took her to the hospital, and her ear was damaged. I told her to never go and play with the bees, she thought they were like flies, but she learned her lesson.

In winter it snows, and I didn't have any clothes. I used to wear some of my mother's clothes, but they wouldn't fit, they would fall down. I would take any clothes I could find, and I was so cold, I used to think, imagine what it would be to live with white people who wash themselves with milk. [A popular myth in Lesotho is that white skin color can be acquired by bathing in milk.] We said new clothes smelled like white people's farts. [Basotho children have almost no contact with whites. On the occasion that they do, the whites they meet are usually professional people—nuns, priests, researchers, university professors. Basotho children seem to experience these whites as people who smell clean and always wear new clothes, and they imagine that white people's farts smell like new clothes.] We used to say that because we were so excited when we got new clothes, we thought they smelled so good.

Now I realize that white people don't bathe in milk, and their farts smell the same as ours, but I bet if you went to Lesotho today and you bought the children new clothes, they'd tell you they smell like white people's farts.

I went to two different schools in Lesotho: Roma Primary, near the village where I lived; and then later, St. Rose Primary, the boarding school in Peka. What was good about St. Rose was I had friends, and I also liked *Nkhono* Ntetta [literally, "grandmother," a term of respect for women of a certain age; this woman was the nun who accepted both children into the school and took a special interest in them]. I also liked some teachers, and this one teacher, I used to be so good to her, and whatever she wanted I would go and get it for her. But she used to take a stick with thorns on it and she used to beat me up with it, and it felt like she didn't feel how sore it was, but I did. She was a nun. The school work was hard. I couldn't understand anything. It was a thousand times harder than Roma Primary. We just played there. But in Peka you had to work, but I didn't know what that work was about. I used to do *Litolobonea,* it's when you wear a fluffy skirt made of plastic bags, shredded, and you push your bum back and move your body a certain way to make the skirt flip up and spin around, and I was very good at that.

When we moved to Pietermaritzburg, the biggest difference was English. In Lesotho we hardly spoke any English, like we would say, "Good morning teacher," and that was all the English we ever knew. But in Pietermaritzburg, everybody spoke English all the time, except some people who spoke Zulu. The first day when I went to Class One, I had the same lunch tin as a boy named Wayne Paul, and we had the same bread and everything, so we didn't know whose lunch tin was whose, and we were fighting. He was talking English, and I was talking Sesotho, and the teacher was looking back and forth, and the teacher said to me, "I don't understand what you're saying, talk English," and I was talking in Sesotho and saying to her, "I don't know what you're saying, talk Sesotho," but she didn't know any Sesotho at all. In my head they were going blablabla it sounded like rubbish, but in their head they didn't know what I was saying. That's the way people think. Then the days went on and I tried the English words and I found English easy and nice to speak, though I wasn't perfect at all. No one's perfect in English.

The school in Pietermaritzburg was more loving, more understanding, no beating people, no forcing them to do things. There were lots of white kids there, too, and most of the teachers were white. The uniform was a flowered dress, and I liked the colors, but I hated the hat. I always lost it all the time, and when I was there I met this girl named Taryn, she was my best friend, and we used to fight sometimes but not very much. She couldn't say my name properly, she would say pa-LAY-sa, but after a while she learned how to say it right. Taryn wasn't white and she wasn't black. In South Africa her family was called "Coloured," which is the word they use there for people who have black and white ancestors. I liked the school, and I made a lot of friends, and I understood the work. The teachers explained it, so I knew what was going on. And then I had to come to America.

America is a nice place, they have big cars here and nice houses, but a lot of the children are mean. Some are okay. All the black girls in America have to have long hair and the black boys have to have short hair. My hair is short, 'cause I think I look pretty that way. In Africa most of the girls my age have short hair. Sometimes they get braids or extensions, like here, but only if it's a special occasion. Not for everyday. So these people here, they say my hair is too short, and I need to have braids to make it long. But I had braids, and braids come out. They don't stay forever.

They just ugly children here. If anybody came from South Africa, these people want them to feel shamed of themselves. They're interested in my accent, but one boy in my classroom makes fun of my accent and my country. If I have to read out loud, they laugh at the way I talk. They don't even try to call me by my name. Like today, Miss Fudge says that this boy, he must stand up and call out the quiet children, and he called out all the children except me. Every one of them, he called them out and they got to go get lunch, and he left me sitting there. Finally he said, "Africa girl, you can go to lunch." Like I don't even have a name. That's what they call me. Africa girl. My life is not easy. It's hard to live in this country, just 'cause I'm different people treat me like I'm a dog. I want to feel fine the way I am. They call me bald-headed, ugly face, fat face, and they usually say, "Oh shut up you bald-headed Africa girl." One boy called me "African monkey." Sometimes they call me and Manko "African dogs." At first I hardly had any friends in my classroom, and I'm short, and I try and buy all these high shoes, like platform tennis shoes, so I can be tall like Americans. I hope I'll improve and grow and be tall some day. I'm starting to have friends now.

The school work is a little bit hard. Because of my age, they made me skip from fourth grade to sixth. Seems like in America they don't care what you know, they just care what age you are. Sometimes I don't know anything that's going on. I just guess the answers, and sometimes I'm right and sometimes I'm wrong. The teachers don't have time to explain anything because the kids are so bad they have to yell at them all the time to shut up and you can't really learn anything. But not everything about America is bad. I have friends outside the classroom, in the neighborhood. I have two friends around the neighborhood. I love their accents. I like their clothes, like high shoes, nice skirts, long dresses. I like nail polish. Nobody in Lesotho had nail polish. If my mother in Lesotho saw me with nail polish, she would pull my ear and tell me to take that thing off, it looks gross and disgusting. If she saw me with a short skirt, high shoes, she would tell me to take them off because she would think I was looking for men. Because boys are a problem in Lesotho. When a girl gets to be twelve there she's supposed to get married. Boys try and rape girls and the girls hate that. A girl can't even get to be fourteen before some boy rapes her. Not even one girl. You have to hide from the boys there. But at night in Lesotho, at night you see glow worms. They don't have lights there. Where I lived nobody had lights or electricity, they used candles or paraffin lamps or they used torches. I would put glow worms in my hair and hold them in my hand so I could see where I was going at night. If American people could see glow worms, they would see how pretty they are. In the morning you can't see them, but at night they glow green, and they're so nice to catch.

My little sister used to have bad dreams, and they used to come true. One day she dreamed about long black bugs with lots of legs and she dreamed they were walking on her blanket, and then she used to feel itchy all over her body, and every time we opened the blanket, we would see one. Whatever she dreamed at night came true. She used to cuddle up to me and be scared, and I would tell her she must not cry, and sometimes I would sleep alone with her, and my mother would go to a bar and my brothers go out with their friends, and I would be lonely. Sometimes I would have fun with my little sister, play catch, play jumping games like you call hopscotch here. I would tickle her and make her giggle, and I used to love the way she said my name, in a cute little voice, Palesa, and I loved the way she danced. I hope I'm going to get a job after I get my education in America, I'll get a job and go see how my family is living, and if they're living bad, I'll try to bring them to America. My dream is to bring them here, but I couldn't bring all of them. I would bring my little sister. I would like them to have food, and clothes, and a place to live which is safe.

If my little sister could be in America she would think all these people are funny, the way the boys hang their pants down, she would tell them, "Your pants are falling down, boy," and she would laugh at the way they dance and move. Nobody would understand her, because she would be speaking Sesotho, but I would understand her. And if I buy her new clothes, she'd say they smell like white people's farts. It would be fun to bring my sister here and also my brothers. My brothers would think it was cool to hang out here. I would support them, and if my brothers want to wear their pants hanging down low, I'd say cool, go ahead. It would be hard for them here if they went to school, because they wouldn't understand English and they've never been in school. I would try to make a little school at my house to teach my family English, before I would bring them here. I would start with ABCs and try to teach them. The people here wouldn't respect them. They would love to hear them talk Sesotho, but they would treat them ugly like they do me. Once I took a photo of my little sister and showed my classmates in America my little sister, and this girl in my classroom said we look just alike, like we were twins, and it's true. It would be hard for her to get along with friends here, because the kids here are so mean.

I never met any white kids in America, except once, my mom's friends had some nieces they introduced to me. Just that one time. There is one white boy in my classroom, he never gave me any problems, he never even said anything to me. Nobody who is white ever said anything ugly to me here, just black people, black Americans, they think you have to have long straight hair, be skinny and tall. I think you should just feel proud the way you are. But these black Americans make my life miserable as much as they can. I think why are people so ugly to me, why do they treat me so bad. But I don't really care, because I know I'm an African girl and I feel proud of myself and nothing can change that, nothing. I think the black kids are jealous, they wish they could go to Africa and see how it is and how people are, and that African girls don't have long hair.

MANKO'S STORY

The first time we went to Pietermaritzburg, in South Africa, driving in the car from Lesotho, it was Easter holidays in 1995. Palesa and I rode together in my [adoptive] mother's car, and we brought our friend Mosa for a visit. She was a student like us, at St. Rose Primary School in Peka, in Lesotho. It was night time when we got to Pietermaritzburg after riding all day in the car, and there were lots of lights. We were on a hill, looking down at the city, and it looked like orange and yellow and red stars, but instead of being in the sky, they were below us. I was excited, because I knew it was going to be my new home, but I didn't know what it was going to be like.

My mom parked in a big garage like I had never seen before, and it was a tall block of houses called flats. We went upstairs to my mother's house, and we saw we had new dolls, a yellow ball, and a big yellow truck, books, and crayons. Next day we went outside to play, but when we were going up the stairs, we forgot to count the floors. We just kept running up and up, and Mosa couldn't keep up with us, and then we found we were lost. The floors all looked alike, and we forgot the number of our flat. We called out, "*Ausi* Mosa, *Ausi* Mosa!" *Ausi* means sister. In Lesotho we always say Sister, or Brother, or Mother, or Father, before we say a person's name. It's how we show respect. We don't just say a person's name.

Ausi Mosa said she was downstairs. We said, "Where?" and we went down and then up again, and we started to be tired. Finally we went all the way down the stairs to the ground and started to count, and we counted till we got to the third floor, where we lived, and we found home again. We knew to turn left from the stairs, so we got there. At that time we didn't speak English. My mother could speak Sesotho, even though we laughed at her because she talked like a baby and she made mistakes sometimes, still we could understand her and she could understand us. We still have jokes about the mistakes she used to make. One time she was trying to ask if we liked to eat bones. We do. Basotho like to eat the bones of chicken. But anyway she got the words mixed up, and she asked us if we like to eat shit. We still laugh at that. So at that time, that first Easter visit to South Africa, we didn't even know one word of English, so we watched the TV, but we couldn't understand what anybody was saying on it. We sometimes saw TV in Lesotho, because the nuns had a TV, but they only let us watch it when it was news in Sesotho. Otherwise they didn't let us watch. So we didn't even know that most of what was on TV was in English.

After Easter vacation we had to go back to Lesotho for a few months, before we could move to Pietermaritzburg to live with my mother. That would happen in June. So then in June, we came to stay, and Palesa and I started school at Ridge Junior Primary School in July. I didn't speak any English, but everyone was nice to me. Nobody hit anybody there. I never saw a school like that till that day. One day in school, I wasn't doing anything, just watching the other children and listening to them, trying to understand what they were saying, and I was thinking that I wanted to use their scissors. My first words of English were, "Can I borrow," and the teacher said, "Borrow what?" I pointed at the scissors, and she said "scissors" and gave it to me. That was how I started to speak English.

When we went to lunch I was sitting by myself, and then Zama came and sat by me. Zama was my first South African friend. She was a Zulu girl. Most of the black children in Pietermaritzburg were Zulu. I had white friends too. That's one thing that's different from being in New Orleans. I don't know any white kids here. They don't go to our school. I guess they go to different schools. My mom's friends know some people with white kids, but we only met them once.

Zama and me were best friends because we played with each other every single day. We would run races, and play a game called "Catches," where you run and someone tries to catch you, and if they touch you, then you're "On" and you have to try to catch them. We also played skipping rope, and another game: we would draw a circle in the dirt, and put stones in it. Then you throw one stone up in the air, and while it's in the air, you have to get five or six other stones out of the circle before the first stone falls on the ground. Then the next time you throw it up, you have to put all the stones back in, but you leave one out. This is a Zulu game, called *Makendas*. Zama and I would always eat lunch together, and soon other kids came and ate with us too. We all brought sandwiches and we would trade. When I took eggs with mayonnaise, Ntokozo always wanted my sandwich and she would trade me her burger. If one of us had fruit, we would share it with the others. What I liked best about school was always playtime.

I liked computers too. We would do art on them, and sometimes we would make cards, like Mother's Day cards, or bookmarks.

My first teacher at Ridge was Mrs. Robertson. She was my first white teacher, and she was the nicest teacher I ever had, except maybe Mrs. Dudley, who was my second-grade teacher. Mrs. Robertson never hit anyone, ever. She gave us easy stuff to do, and she would give us stars on our foreheads if we got things right. When you finished your homework, you got a star, and when you got ten stars in your book, you got a big G for Good, and she would say, "Hooray, hooray, Manko made my day!" That made me feel good. It didn't take me long to learn English. By the time I got to second grade I knew it very well. Mrs. Dudley was wonderful. She was always giving me hugs. I didn't know teachers were supposed to love you, until I got to Pietermaritzburg. I liked going to school there.

My mother's best friend in Lesotho was 'M'e Mpho Nthunya, who wrote a book with my mom, and she went to live with my mother in Pietermaritzburg before we got there, so after we got there we called her our Granny, but she wasn't really our Granny. I loved her a lot, and I still do. We are waiting for my mother to have enough money to send for 'M'e Mpho. 'M'e Mpho is waiting in Lesotho now, and I know that is hard for her, and my mother misses her a lot and cries sometimes from missing her. So one day I was walking with 'M'e Mpho, and we met a Zulu lady on the way, who was walking with her child. I thought it was a boy, but she said her child's name was Anna. Anna was going to be my very good friend at home, like Zama was my good friend at school. My mom gave Anna a ride to school every morning, even though Anna went to a different school from us, so we saw Anna first thing every day, and then when we got home from school we always went to see if Anna was home, so we could play again. We would play with our dolls, and take sheets and make like little houses in our bedroom, like our room was three little houses.

There was another girl who lived in the flats near us. Her name was Pretty, and Pretty was a Xhosa girl. She spoke Xhosa at home, and Anna spoke Zulu at home, and we spoke Sesotho at home, and none of us understood the other one's language. So we had to speak English when we all played together, and this helped all of us learn English better. Also because my mother was American, we spoke English and Sesotho at home, and my mother was always teaching us English. Sometimes Anna and Pretty fought over who would play with me, but I liked to play with both of them. Now that I'm gone, I think they probably play with each other. I wonder if they miss me. What I miss most about Pietermaritzburg is my friends.

Way before we left South Africa, for a long time, we were excited to ride in an airplane. We didn't know what it would be like. When we got on it, and it first went up, the air pressed against my chest like a heavy weight. I was afraid to look out the window, because I was afraid we would fall. The people who worked in the plane gave us gifts, like back packs and a little purse in South African flag colors, and they gave us a cap that said South African Airlines, and I still have mine. I loved the food they gave us. There was cake and everything. We were in the airplane such a long time I began to think we lived there and it would never be over. I got used to it, and I wasn't scared at all anymore. We went up and came down and changed planes several times. When we got close to New Orleans, we saw the swamp. It was all green, and it was trees and water, but it looked flat, very flat. When we got off the plane, my mom's friends met us with balloons and beads and signs that said "Welcome to New Orleans." We didn't know how hard it was going to be. I think if we knew what was coming, we wouldn't have been happy at that time.

There are two things I hate about America. I hate the questions people ask about Africa, and I hate the way people laugh at me because I'm different. People tease me about my hair because it's short. They say I should get a perm so it'll be longer. They ask me a lot of stupid questions, like "Can you speak African?" I tell them there's no such language as African. There are lot of African languages, probably more than a thousand. They ask,

"Do they have normal clothes in Africa like people here?"

"Do they have roads, and streetlights?"

"Do they have candy in South Africa?"

"Do they have TV? Have you ever heard of Michael Jackson?"

"Did you guys wash yourselves and your clothes in a river?"

I say, "No, we washed our clothes in a washing machine, but some poor people there do have to wash their clothes by hand, with water from a tap in the yard." Then they don't know what a tap is. There's no way to explain everything about Africa, because Africa is a very big place, and everybody isn't the same. There are poor people, and middle, and rich, and they all live really differently. Even I—I lived really differently in different places. Maybe I was very poor when I was little, but I didn't know I was poor, because everybody I knew was the same. But when I went to South Africa I saw the people in Lesotho were poor. The first Christmas in South Africa, Mrs. Robertson said we must say what we want most for Christmas, and I said, "I want bread for everyone," and Mrs. Robertson cried, and she told the principal, and the principal cried, and they sent for my mother when it was time for assembly, and my mother cried. They gave me some kind of award for being a nice person. I didn't know why everyone was crying. I was laughing, me. I still do want bread for everyone.

There are so many different kinds of people and languages. I can never explain it, and most of the time I don't want to, because the kids who ask the questions don't really want to hear. They just want to laugh at us. My mom says I should tell them to go read a book about Africa and leave me alone.

The hardest thing about being in America is that people laugh at me because I'm different. I come from Africa, and they call me names; sometimes I don't even know what those names mean, but I know they aren't nice. That really hurts my feelings. I think the black Americans hate people from Africa. I don't know why. I'm starting to have a few friends now, but it has been really hard. We've been here nearly four months, and I'm just starting to have some friends. It seems like a year.

I guess it isn't all bad. I do have some new friends. That would be the best thing. Thanksgiving was nice. We ate at a big hotel with a lot of my mom's friends, and they had shrimp and crawfish, but I thought they were disgusting. They had eyes, and some people said they ate the eyes, but I think they were teasing. I think they're gross. I like to eat burgers from Burger King, and Popeye's chicken. We had burgers in South Africa, and we had Kentucky Fried Chicken there, and Indian restaurants. My mother and my sister like Indian food, but I don't like it that much, so I don't miss it. And my mother has some friends who are really nice. They take me and my sister places and show us around New Orleans, like to the French Quarter, the Children's Museum, and City Park. Mardi Gras was really colorful, it was fun to see all the people marching, and the big floats, and the beads people threw, but I wasn't really fond of the beads. I threw most of them away.

Me and my friends like riding our bikes around the block. The houses here are really close together, and there are big oak trees and lots of squirrels. There's also a lot of traffic, so we ride on the sidewalk when the cars come, and sometimes squirrels get squished by the cars, and that's gross to look at. If I could go back to South Africa right now, and never see America again, it would be fine with me. I'd be glad. I'm sorry we came here.

NOTES

Update: In July 1999, Palesa, Manko, and their adoptive mom moved to Wharton, Texas, where their mother is now division head for communications and fine arts at a junior college. Palesa is repeating the sixth grade; Manko is also in the sixth grade; and both are now doing very well academically and socially. Their new school is much more racially and culturally mixed than was their school in New Orleans, and they report they have experienced no ridicule or "stupid questions" from children in their new school. Most of their friends are Mexican-American girls, who have been very accepting of them, and they have a tutor who is a college student of Jamaican ancestry born in Montreal. As they begin to meet and bond with other girls who have experienced mobility and cultural change, they are finding the transition to living in the United States less stressful. Even Manko is now happy to be in the United States.

1. For general information on Lesotho, see Ambrose (1993); Eldredge (1993); Giesen (1993); and McDonald et al. (1998).

2. For the history of theater for development in Lesotho, see Ganter and Edkins (1988).

3. Background on the status of women and children in Lesotho appears in Chadzingwa (1991); Epprecht (1993); Gill (1992); K. L. Kendall (1999); Kendall (1995); and Moshoeshoe-Chadzingwa and Mapetla (1996).

4. For a full discussion of rape and rape statistics in South Africa, see Mlangeni (1997); Morris (1997); and Pillay (1997).

5. See Gay, Gill, and Hall (1995) for an explanation of Lesotho's poverty and lack of social services.

6. 'M'e Mpho dictated her autobiography to Kendall in many sessions over two years. Kendall typed it for her, edited each chapter with her, and arranged for its publication.

WORKS CITED

Ambrose, David. 1993. *Maseru: An Illustrated History.* Morija, Lesotho: Morija Museum and Archives.

Chadzingwa, Matseliso M. 1991. *Women in Development in Southern Africa: An Annotated Bibliography. Vol. 2. Lesotho.* The Hague, Netherlands: CTA (Technical Center for Agricultural and Rural Cooperation).

Eldredge, Elizabeth A. 1993. *A South African Kingdom: The Pursuit of Security in Nineteenth-Century Lesotho.* London: Cambridge University Press.

Epprecht, Marc. 1993. "Marxism Versus the Patriarchy: Gender and Historical Materialism in Southern Africa." ISAS Wroking Papers Series Nos. 4–6, Lesotho.

Ganter, Elvira, and Don Edkins. 1988. *Marotholi: Theatre for Another De-*

velopment: A Photographic Report. Lesotho: The Village Technology Information Service.

Gay, John, Debby Gill, and David Hall, eds. 1995. *Lesotho's Long Journey: Hard Choices at the Crossroads.* Lesotho: Sechaba Consultants.

Giesen, Johanna A.M., ed. *Lesotho: Kingdom in the Sky.* 1993. The Hague, Netherlands: Afrika Museum, Berg en Dal.

Gill, Debby. 1992. *Lesotho: A Gender Analysis.* Lesotho: SIDA.

Kendall, K. Limakatso. 1999. "Women in Lesotho and the (Western) Construction of Homophobia." *Female Desires: Same-Sex Relations and Transgender Practices Across Cultures,* ed. Evelyn Blackwood and Saskia Wieringa. New York: Columbia University Press, 157–80.

Kendall, ed. 1995. *Basali! Stories by and About Women in Lesotho.* Pietermaritzburg, South Africa: University of Natal Press.

McDonald, David et al. 1998. *Challenging Xenophobia: Myths and Realities About Cross-Border Migration in Southern Africa.* Lesotho: Southern African Migration Project.

Mlangeni, Bongiwe. 1997. "Outrage as Rapists Walk Free." *Star Headlines,* 27 March. Available at <http://www.inc.co.za/online/star/headlines/1997/03/032697/rape.stats.html>.

Morris, Alan. 1997. "SA Tops the Rapist Charts." *Electronic Mail & Guardian,* 26 February. Available at <http://www.web.co.za/mg/news/97feb2/26feb-rape.html>.

Moshoeshoe-Chadzingwa, Matseliso, and Matseliso Mapetla. 1996. *Women in Lesotho: An Annotated Bibliography. Vol. 3.* Lesotho: Institute of Southern African Studies.

Nthunya, Mpho. 1997. *Singing Away the Hunger: The Autobiography of an African Woman.* Bloomington: Indiana University Press.

Pillay, Tashica. 1997. "Suspect Faces 40 Charges of Rape." *Sunday Times KZN* (Durban), 9 February, 5.

· 2 ·

From *Foutou* to French Fries

Life on the Edge of African and American Cultures

Bosson Caroline Kouassiaman and Susan Frazier-Kouassi

THE VOICE OF CAROLINE

$\mathscr{I}$was born in Boston; we lived in Boston until I was five years old. Then we moved to Cameroon—to Central Africa—in Douala and we spent six months in Douala; I attended a bilingual school there. Then we moved to Côte d'Ivoire where we spent a year and a half, and then my mother and I moved back to the United States, to Ann Arbor, Michigan, when my mother was pregnant with my little brother—that was in the winter of 1990. So, we lived in Michigan for one and a half years, then we moved to this "rinky-dinky" town called Wooster, Ohio, where the population is like twenty-eight thousand or something like that. I was the only black child in my classes from third to fifth grade, and I guess I was starting to become a small-town Wooster girl. I was getting into that whole rock-n-roll, heavy metal scene. I was going really punkish and coming up with these really weird preadolescent phrases.

After three years of living in Wooster, my mom decided that she'd had enough of having the family separated, so we moved back to Africa. My mom was in Nigeria, my brother and I were with my dad in Cameroon (once again), and he had a different position. My brother went to a private school, which was really good. He liked it a lot, except for the fact that there was this one really retarded guy who kept on beating him up. Anyway, that's beside the point. I went to this really crappy bilingual school, which I didn't like at all because, first of all, they must have had at least five thousand kids in that school. It was bilingual, half-English,

23

half-French. The reason I went to this school was that it and another school of its kind were the only schools where they spoke English in Douala. The next closest school would be in another province, which would mean that I would have had to go to boarding school, and the boarding schools there really freaked me out. I decided to stay home; anyway, we had a swimming pool too, so that was okay.

The school, the reason I didn't like it, was because people had a lot of problems with me being an American and having an American accent and not being able to speak Pidgin. In Cameroon, I experienced both racism and discrimination because the students prejudged me based on a simple thing like the diplomatic license plate of my father's car. Based on his license plate, they decided not to talk or associate with me because of whom they thought I was. In fact, they actively avoided me.

In addition, because I didn't look like a Cameroonian. Very few students wear glasses, as do I. I think I was the only person in the class who wore glasses. Half the time we couldn't understand each other because my accent was different from their accent, and I just had different ways of thinking.

The second day I went to school, I had these really long braids and a woman (I guess she was the director of the school), she came and she pulled them really tight, and she was like, "Why are you wearing these? Don't you know that this attracts teachers?" There was some crazy belief that a girl student would unnecessarily attract the attention of the male teachers if she wore her hair in a certain way, for example, styled or in long braids. It was considered distracting and disruptive in the classroom.

I guess braids make you look attractive, and you're not supposed to distract your teachers. She said that the next day when she came into class if I hadn't taken my braids out, she would cut them all herself with her scissors. I also learned that you can't wear braids and you can't have your hair relaxed. If you do have it relaxed, it has to be constantly braided. No, no, you can't even have it relaxed, you can't have it relaxed at all, and it can't be braided. It can be braided by itself, but no extensions. No extensions whatsoever. Thus, your only options are to braid it with no extensions or to cut it short. This is crazy, it's as if the teachers cannot be responsible for their own behavior, they are easily sucked in by the attractiveness of young female students. That's crazy.

I remember once I had my hair permed; I was wearing it in a ponytail (my hair wasn't that long, so it's more like a bun). The door person stopped me and [motioning with his hand for her to leave], made a turn-around signal like a U-turn. I was like, I don't get it. I still tried to get in the gate . . . He said, "Go home." Mind you, our house was like thirty minutes away from the school, it's like two different parts of the city, and that's by car, so there's no way to walk there. The driver had just gone, and the guy is like, "No, you can't come to school like that. You go home, you cut your hair, or you take those products out, you don't come back to school with your hair like that." Basically, I spent my whole day walking around the neighborhood, drinking Coke, and I guess I learned my lesson. That was that.

At school I didn't have friends. I was doing a lot of bribing to have friends. I know these incidents traumatized me pyschologically. I was perceived as rich because my father occupied a very high position and he had the status of an ambassador. We had about five or six different cars coming to pick me up at different times. This was really unusual because it was a public school, most of the students don't even have cars, a lot of them don't have TVs or anything else; they live in shacks and it's just . . . they don't understand. I remember our driver was waiting for me one day, and some kids walked by and said, "Oh, this must be a white man's kid who goes to this school." Then they were like, "There are no white kids in this school!" The driver didn't say anything. He was just laughing. When I came in, he told me what they said, and they were very, very surprised to see me get into that car. I guess I liked the attention, especially since nobody wanted to be my friend. Since they were all prejudiced against me, I just decided to play the snob. I would just go bribe them and would say, "I'll buy you a Coke, come with me, we'll go to the store," buying Coke and whatever, of course that was tempting. In some ways, I was bribing them, 'cause I just wanted some friends, and as soon as they finished drinking their Coke or whatever, they would be gone.

Basically, I didn't have any friends until two weeks before I left Cameroon. I changed schools for the next year because I told my dad that if I had to go back to that school that I would be the last in the class and I would rather sell tomatoes in the market than go back to that school. He said okay, we'll look for another school for you. I guess somebody at his office found this other school, which happened to be really near the house, called Sacred Heart College. And it was, actually I think it was a Catholic school run by nuns. It looked okay; I actually saw computers there. I was really surprised . . . computers and a lab. There were no computers at my previous school. Oh yeah, and the new school had real bathrooms too. At my old school, there were no bathrooms, the bathrooms were like this room where there are like holes in the ground. They were more like a sink kind of like in the ground. The way you used these bathrooms was to squat and then you go into the hole. I went in there once. That was my last time I went in there. I saw the holes, because I asked someone to take me to the bathroom, and I asked, "*Where's* the bathroom?" They said, "Here *is* the bathroom." I went in there and pretended to do something, and then came back out. I never did anything. I never went to those bathrooms again.

The day before I was going to cut my hair for the new school my dad told us that we were going back to Côte d'Ivoire. The first thing I thought was, "Thank God, I don't have to cut my hair." The second thing I thought about was, "Oh my God, I'm going to have to go to a French school," because the American school costs about $10,000 a year there, and it was really expensive.

The school where I went was right in our neighborhood. When I started off, I was okay. I guess people thought I was a snob, but I was really shy, especially with the language barrier. But I managed. I made one friend the first day, named Danielle. By the end of the semester in December, I wanted to have a party, and I invited a whole bunch of students from class. I was happy. I mean, when I came back in January, I had many new friends.

In December, I had a party, and my mom cooked. She cooked good food, and it was jamming. Everybody was happy because there was good food. They were happy because they could say that they were invited to the American's house.

In the beginning, there was a general impression that I was more American-like because I wouldn't take notes like everybody else. Teachers had me doing different stuff, and then, later on, I adapted quickly.

This was much more different than in Cameroon. I think the anglophone Cameroonians are just generally hostile. They're hostile to others who are not like them. There are only two English-speaking provinces in Cameroon, and there are ten altogether. The other eight provinces are where all the capitals are and where they are more prosperous. They are all French speaking. And the English-speaking Cameroonians have to be able to speak French fluently, where the French-speaking Cameroonians don't have to speak English.

In Côte d'Ivoire, I showed my classmates that I was making an effort. A lot of people wanted to be friends with me, and I was just closed.

I didn't want to associate with anybody. Yet, Edith, Danielle, Alimatu, and I sort of became this group altogether—I forgot what the French teacher used to call us because when you see one you see all of us. We were always together, eating *foutou*,[1] *alloco*,[2] *attieke*.[3] Every time you saw one of us, you saw the whole foursome. That was the way it was basically until the end of the year.

My mother is African American, and my father is Ivorian from Côte d'Ivoire. My [maternal] grandparents were originally from the South, my grandfather from South Carolina and my grandmother from Texas (originally Georgia). Their ancestors were, of course, slaves. My great-grandmother was a Choctaw Indian of the Cherokee Group, and my mother thinks there was some slaveowner-slave mixing on my grandfather's side.

My grandmother was one of my idols. She knew what she wanted in life. She was very courageous and perseverant; she had a lot of goals, and she was able to accomplish her goals. She was like the glue of the family. She held everybody together as one big family; we shared a lot of traditions with her.

My paternal grandfather was a king of the area. Our village is twelve kilometers from the border of Ghana, and we have a lot of farms. My grandfather had twelve wives and forty-something kids. My grandmother was his first wife.

Sometimes I feel that there are too many relatives . . . always wanting something. I have a very complicated family history on that side. Then again, I am complicated. I think I'm African. I think everybody's African. The origins of humanity have been traced to Africa. So many traits in people can be traced to Africa.

In America, I feel like a stranger. I think about a lot of things that other people don't think about. I observe more; I don't talk a lot. I just observe, and if people could only see in my brain and see what's happening there, they'd have a heart attack on the spot. Because I make a lot of fun of people, but they never know it. I do so much observing and listening that I think a lot of people don't do. They don't stop and they don't know how to appreciate certain things. I appreciate the teachers who take time to explain things to you and who will see you after school, before school. I appreciate the computers. I appreciate having heat and air-conditioning in our school, and electricity that works all day long. I appreciate having a locker, someplace to put my stuff, so that I don't have to lug it around and walk with a cane thirty years from now. I appreciate having edible cafeteria food. I think my appreciation of different and varied things comes from my experiences, everywhere I've been in Africa, not only just in America.

In America, I'm not like my peers. This is an old corny phrase, but they don't take the time to smell the roses. They listen to music; they don't appreciate the sound. They walk in the halls; they don't appreciate that there are tiles on the ground. They talk back to their teachers; they don't appreciate that their teachers aren't being paid well enough to come every day to teach them. I think, for a lot of these kids, the most important, exciting part of life is going to the mall. I don't get it. I want to travel, I want to see the world, and I want to eat different foods (that won't make me sick, I hope). I want to learn different languages. I want to meet new people. What do you like to do? [referring to students]. "Go to the mall, go shopping, I don't know, go to the movies, yeah, come to Pioneer dances, watch TV, watch MTV videos." Why do you want to limit your life to that? Their sight is very limited, what they hear is very limited, and they've been listening to one kind of music since middle school. That's the only kind of music they will listen to. I just don't see how you can limit yourself to that.

As a multicultural person living in Côte d'Ivoire, I didn't find it really hard because I had a lot of family, a lot, I mean, a lot. I had at least three or four cousins living with me at home, so it was easy to adapt because of them. Because I have my paternal grandmother's name, they all sort of accepted me more. They tried to make me more Ivorian, but they sort of disregarded the American side.

We moved to Burkina Faso in 1996 because of my dad's job. In Burkina Faso, it was different. Well, at first I hated it. I cried every day for the first three months, and I didn't adapt very well in the beginning because everybody thought I was a snob, so I decided to be a snob. I didn't want friends in Burkina Faso. I didn't want to be in Burkina Faso at all; I wanted to be in Côte d'Ivoire. I didn't try hard. I didn't make any efforts. A lot of people were friendly; a lot of people tried to be friends with me and everything. But after getting turned away many times, they were like, "Oh, screw you then!" Later on, I guess I had decided that it wasn't worth it. Because I was going to stay in Burkina Faso, there was nothing I could do about it, so I decided to try and gain back what I had lost and accept their friendship.

As an Ivorian American living in Burkina Faso, it was more the American side of me that appealed to them. At the beginning of the school year, I had just come back from vacation in America. I had all these American things, clothes, and candy, and I was . . . the new music, the magazines, so, I guess I was perceived as a big-time American. It was the American side that appealed to them. The African American side was accepted because they knew the music, which was what everybody was listening to, rap, R & B, so it was like, "Okay, you can fit in."

As a girl living in West Africa, I felt that all of the cultural attitudes toward women were pretty positive. In Côte d'Ivoire, girls had reigned academically in the school. All of the top five students of every class were girls. Of course, the schools that I attended were all private, so, I cannot say for the majority of girls who were not in school, still living in the village, or who were in the large public schools.

However, as a girl in Cameroon, which is in Central Africa, it was sort of hard because there were a lot of macho kids in that class, and in the school in general. They were a little bit more traditional; they were like, "You should be lucky you're at school, because normally you should be cultivating bananas in the village." I found that people had a problem with me being the first in my class. Most of the girls in my school were lower-end students or like the middle, but very few ranked at the top. I think I was the only girl among the top ten. In Cameroon, I was the top of my class in the city, Douala.

Coming back to America after being away for four years, it has been very bad . . . It still is. I find that American teenagers are ignorant, stupid, self-centered, and closed-minded. For them, the world begins and starts with the United States; Americans are the best. They also think, "Poor world, we're always saving it, what would they do without us?" When I tell them that I'm African, they're like, "Oh, my gosh, that's so cool. What kind of houses do you live in, in Africa?" And they ask me really weird stuff like, "Do you speak African?" I find that a lot of them have a problem with me being different. Of course in Africa, I was different too. But I think I'm more extravagant here. I have my own style, and I'm not afraid to have my own opinion.

They're [the Americans] all about mostly makeup, boys, clothes, shopping, partying. These are not my top five issues. What's important to me are issues dealing with violence/war, cultural clashes, political conflicts, capitalism/corruption, and sexuality. In fact, I want to be a sex therapist, as one of my occupations. I am interested in becoming a sex therapist because a lot of people struggle with their sexuality. They need a lot of help, especially teenagers. A lot of the parents don't want to talk with their kids about sexuality and about the options that they have. A lot of schools are like that too because it's always like "abstinence, abstinence" and they know that teenagers ain't stupid. It's usually when you say "abstinence" that more teenagers are going to go out and have sex; if they are going to have sex, they need to be protected. They need to know what can happen to them; they need to know the consequences; they need to be prepared.

I am also interested in anthropology, business, fashion design, and music. First, I want to be a DJ [disk jockey], because music is an international language that everybody speaks. I want to be a cultural anthropologist, because understanding culture is one of the most important things in the world.

Being multicultural, it's the best stuff in the world. *"Le metissage, c'est l'avenir"* or translated, "Mixing is the future." It was Nayanka Bell who first said this. She is a multiracial, French-Ivorian singer, a very popular singer in Côte d'Ivoire. The way I interpret that quote is, you have to mix to get somewhere. The world is nothing without mixing. So, for us to advance for the society and the world, mixing is okay. It's what made us, us.

As an Ivorian American, I feel that I can eat French fries without tiring and I can still dance *bashenga*.[4] I feel that I can draw on both worlds without being a part of one or the other. I guess people expect me to choose between one of the worlds, and I just don't feel like choosing. I like being like God, sitting down on one side and looking down on the other side. It gives me certain pleasures, certain advantages that somebody who isn't multiracial doesn't have. It also has its disadvantages, but it has more advantages than disadvantages. Some African Americans, they're like, "You're not black enough" or whatever, and some of them will get into, "Oh, my ancestors were African stuff." They see me and they're like "phfuff!" They see an African in the school and they won't even consider them. They want to be, like, "You'll never know what I've been through." The problem with a lot of them is that they still have a lot of hate in their hearts. They have hate against the white man, and they have hate against their own ancestors—the Africans that were stupid enough to exchange things with the Europeans. They have a lot of hate in them, and I think that is also why they're always trying to promote this whole African American, this black-power thing. Because they still have a lot of hate in them and they think, "Okay, well then that's the case, then let's just screw the world and let's feel good about

ourselves; let's just be ourselves." Okay, that's fine. You want to promote yourself—which is okay. But you don't have to go discriminating
against others because of that. Because you've been discriminated against
many times isn't reason to go back and discriminate against others; that
doesn't make any sense.

In terms of the African American students at my school, I think
they've given up on me. In the beginning, they were sort of looking at
me like, "I'm curious," and I guess they sort of felt I was weird. I guess
a lot of them expected me to join the BSU [Black Student Union], and
I didn't join. And you rarely see me talking with an African American.
I guess a lot of them have a problem with that because I get staredowns,
and I get comments behind my back whenever I'm walking in the halls.
I am who I am; I'm not going to change that. I'm not going to pretend
that I'm more African American than anything else. It's just not me.

REFLECTIONS ON THE VOICE

A significant number of studies addressing the complexities and ideas
surrounding multiculturalism among individuals of African heritage have
focused on those who are generally "biracial," that is, offspring of one
African American parent and one European-American parent. Thus,
these discussions have been narrowly limited to "mixed" or "biracial"
individuals who have their own set of issues and problems deeply em-
bedded in the sociocultural history of America.

Virtually no discussion has focused on those individuals who, for
reasons of physical attributes, seem to disappear in the woodwork—in
this particular case, individuals who are descendants of one African
American parent and one black African parent. For all physical purposes,
this individual can easily "pass" for an African American or a citizen of
one of the many sub-Saharan African countries. But culturally, linguisti-
cally, or stylistically, there may be a gulf of differences creating an uneasi-
ness for the person.

African Americans, although they may have a sense of identification
with Africa as the "Motherland," are *not* Africans; and, if placed within
an African context, will quickly discover that the fit is not a perfect or
harmonious one. African Americans share a racial, rather than an ethnic
identity with Africans, and the emphasis being placed on racial identity
often obscures the lack of ethnic identity (Adeleke 1998, 191). Similarly,

by 1775, the vast majority of blacks in British North America were the grandchildren of persons born in the New World. Hence, a gulf widens between modern African Americans and their blood brothers and sisters remaining in Africa. "That Black Americans subscribe to Euro-American cultural patterns, even as they retain facets of African values, underscores the complexity of the identity problem. Though of African ancestry, African Americans are also Americans and consequentially need to acknowledge and come to terms with the fact that it is impossible to turn their backs completely on the American experience and its cultural ramifications" (Adeleke 1998, 191).

Racial identity is more likely to be highly salient for African Americans who have historically had to struggle to affirm their identity in the racially hostile environment of the United States, in order to affirm a sense of pride in their blackness (Helms 1990, 10). On the other hand, for many Africans, racial identity is likely to be less salient due to their early experiences in racially homogenous settings, and, subsequently, ethnic identity tends to be more highly salient (Phinney and Onwughalu 1996, 130). Being neither completely African nor African American can be an unsettling state of mind, particularly for a young woman coming of age straddling both cultures.

Until recently, social identity theory and research have given relatively little attention to the functional possibility of multiple group identities that can be held simultaneously. Brewer's theory of optimal distinctiveness attempts to take into consideration the various possibilities of multiple group membership and its implications for social identity. This theory attempts to account for the motivation underlying group identification that simultaneously acknowledges the dynamic nature of social identity and the chronically high levels of identification with specific groups. Brewer's theory supposes that one's social identity is derived from the opposing forces of two universal human motives—that is, the need for inclusion and assimilation, as well as the need for differentiation from others (Brewer 1999, 188). In its formulation, the theory focused on resolving opposing needs for differentiation and inclusion by adopting a single social identity that could meet both needs.

In the case of Caroline, her multiple identities as an African and as an African American can perhaps be best described as being two identities that are experienced as separate aspects of the self. She may be aware of having these separate identities but does not engage them simultaneously (either because they are independent or possibly incompatible).

Furthermore, these identities can shift within a particular context. For example, identity A (the African American identity) can be relevant for self-categorization in one situation and identity B (the Ivorian identity) can serve this same function in another situation. Furthermore, each identity separately fulfills the need for both inclusion and distinctiveness within its context (Brewer 1999, 190).

Traditional sociological theorists such as Stonequist (1937, 8) held the view that "a marginal person is biologically or culturally from two or more races or cultures." Furthermore, "marginal status exists when an individual occupies a position somewhere between cultures but does not wholly belong to any. . . . This person has a marginal personality when he or she has trouble dealing with the marginal status position, is torn between cultures, and develops psychological problems" (Hall 1992, 250–51). Such a negative interpretation of bi- or multiculturalism does not necessarily hold for certain individuals, particularly those like Caroline, who can at times easily hide behind the mask of physical features and move smoothly between the two groups, deriving benefits and advantages from both group identities. On the contrary, membership in multiple racial, ethnic, or cultural groups can be perceived as a distinct advantage over individuals from a more homogeneous racial/ethnic/cultural background.

As Caroline says, *"Le metissage, c'est l'avenir"*—multiculturalism is the future. A growing tolerance and acceptance of others unlike ourselves and our ethnic group at the societal level has to take place both here at home in America, as well as the world, if we want the concept of "global village" to mean something.

NOTES

1. *Foutou* is a popular African food specialty. A somewhat heavy starch accompaniment, it is typically made from boiled yams, plantains, or cassava that are pounded in a large wooden carved mortar bowl to the consistency of firm mashed potatoes. It is then eaten using one's fingers (or fork, if you like) with an African stew or soup like groundnut soup or palm nut soup.

2. *Alloco* is the local name in Abidjan, Côte d'Ivoire, for deep-fried ripe plantains. They are usually eaten with a peppery sauce, and often accompanied by grilled beef brochettes. A local snack or "junk food," it is typically sold in one's local neighborhood by young men and women.

3. *Attieke* is another Ivorian food specialty. Made from fermented cassava, *attieke* is locally processed and sold to accompany grilled or fried fish or chicken.

4. *Bashenga* is a popular contemporary dance in West Africa, which is believed to originate from the People's Republic of Congo (formerly Zaire); it was made popular by one of Africa's beloved musicians, Koffi Olomide.

WORKS CITED

Adeleke, Tunde. 1998. "Black Americans, Africa and History: A Reassessment of the Pan-African and Identity Paradigms." *Western Journal of Black Studies* 22(3): 182–92.

Brewer, Marilynn B. 1999. "Multiple Identities and Identity Transition: Implications for Hong Kong." *International Journal of Intercultural Relations* 23(2): 187–97.

Hall, Christine C. Iijima. 1992. "Please Choose One: Ethnic Identity Choices for Biracial Individuals." *Racially Mixed People in America,* ed. Maria P. P. Root. Newbury Park, Calif.: Sage, 250–64.

Helms, Janet E., ed. 1990. *Black and White Racial Identity: Theory, Research, and Practice.* Westport, Conn.: Greenwood.

Phinney, Jean S., and Mukosolu Onwughalu. 1996. "Racial Identity and Perception of American Ideals Among African American and African Students in the United States." *International Journal of Intercultural Relations* 20(2): 127–40.

Stonequist, Everett V. 1937. *The Marginal Man: A Study in Personality and Cultural Conflict.* New York: Russell and Russell.

· 3 ·

"Mommy, I Just Want to Fit In!"

An African Girl's Story

Joy Ekema-Agbaw and Vivian Yenika-Agbaw

After reading Mary Pipher's much publicized book, *Reviving Ophelia: Saving the Selves of Adolescent Girls,* I pondered many issues. I had several questions about girlhood in the United States, in general, and black girl-hood, in particular. Like most studies about adolescent girls, the book focused predominantly on, and revealed some disturbing evidence about, white girls' experiences in the United States—the world with which the author is familiar. She claims these girls lose themselves partly because of the media. They conform to social expectations by giving up their personal dreams and aspirations in order to be pretty and desirable for their male peers. The findings affected me greatly and made me re-flect on my daughter's fate, for she is a black, immigrant female from Africa. If it is that difficult for native-born white girls to negotiate per-sonal identities in American culture, what is it like for her and other minority girls?

One of the few black adolescent females who were participants in Pipher's study seemed to have a strong sense of self. A daughter of two professionals, Evonne (the girl's name) had a clear vision of her life as a middle-class black female. Pipher's assessment of this girl's adjustment to the adolescent culture triggered my curiosity, for there's a consensus that black females are *strong*. They are black, strong, and can fight their way through any situation with or without anybody's help. Based on this logic, black girls then are little black women who are equally strong. (And, yes, many white females subscribe to this and actually fear the black woman, depriving themselves of the opportunity to understand the fate of being black and female in America.)[1] Consequently, experts

35

rarely conduct organized studies to understand how black females survive emotionally and psychologically within the United States.

In this chapter, I discuss the significance of being black, African, and an immigrant girl in an all-white rural town as I attempt to uncover ways to "save the selves" of adolescent girls on cross-cultural boundaries. Pipher postulates that "something dramatic happens to girls in early adolescence. Just as planes and ships disappear mysteriously into the Bermuda Triangle, so do the selves of girls go down in droves. They crash and burn in a social developmental Bermuda Triangle" (1994, 19). She claims that girls begin to lose their "selves" as they seek desperately to conform to sociocultural expectations of girlhood vis-à-vis boyhood. In the course of occupying the social spaces allocated to them as females in a patriarchal society, they lose their individuality.

There are consequences for those who resist conforming to sociocultural pressures. They may end up friendless, dateless, or become social outcasts among their peers. These alternatives are as bad as "losing" the self for the simple reason that girls who resist, like those who conform, can become angry or depressed from acute isolation. Preadolescent and adolescent girls, therefore, have little choice in the matter, unless they practice what Pipher describes as "intelligent resistance," the only way to "keep the true self alive" (1994, 44). My daughter, Joy, must therefore develop survival strategies that will enable her to deal with the challenges of maintaining her sense of self in a complex culture dominated by white patriarchal values.

Because it is important to me that Joy realize her potential as a human being, I have searched for possible solutions to the adolescent female problems in different places. I have watched documentaries on this issue and read self-help books. I decided to write about Joy's experience as a step toward finding a solution when Sherrie A. Inness created this forum for dialogue. Nevertheless, I approached the project with some ambivalence and caution. I had tangible reasons to be wary of such a dialogue. First, I doubted it was necessary to make my daughter's private struggle a public issue. Second, I wondered if white women could truly understand black women's struggles beyond class and gender concerns. With encouragement from Inness, however, I decided to go forward with the project. It is my hope that this chapter will shed some light on the plight of adolescent girls in general and expand the literature on gender and cultural studies.

Before sharing Joy's story, I should mention a little bit about my background. I am an African woman, a mother of three, a wife, and an English Education professor. For reasons I can never understand, some of my colleagues consider me *strong* (they say it to my face frequently). Unfortunately, as Trudier Harris has demonstrated, this is a label that is often used in America to further marginalize successful black women.[2] I must maintain a low profile in order not to bother colleagues and alienate those who would like to patronize me. I have been described as being "too angry" because I demand justice. Being aware of some of bell hooks's works that address these forms of oppression, I am prepared for this.[3] It is the fate of every black woman who tries to earn a living in a competitive white-American world. We are supposed to be silent, invisible, and thankful for everything.

In addition to being black, I was born and raised in a foreign country. I had to quickly assimilate and work ten times as hard in order to be recognized. As most people implicitly and explicitly suggest to me, whatever material gains I receive here must be much better than what Africa would ever offer me. I am thankful for the opportunities American society has offered me, but it is often frustrating to be treated as an outsider, even in professional circles. I am cognizant of the fact that when a black person demands to be treated with respect, people dismiss him or her (Hill 1997, 140). In the case of a black woman with a foreign accent, people accuse her of being too sensitive and overreacting when she points out instances of injustice and disrespect. This has been my experience as a graduate student and as a university professor.

With the understanding that blackness "has been used to rationalize and legitimate domination, subjugation, and even extermination" (Goldberg 1993, 148), I am constantly aware of my environment. As an African woman, I am all too familiar with the image of the "naked African savage" that is pervasive in both the print and nonprint media.[4] It is a stereotypical image that lurks behind the minds of most westerners, making them resistant to alternative appearances and representations of Africans. As a people who have been shown and reminded repeatedly that they are "primitive and uncivilized," African immigrants in America must deal with the challenges of a highly competitive society from a position of weakness and disempowerment. We are often treated and placed in situations that make white people feel good about themselves, while they use us as instruments to further marginalize native-born African Americans. This is our collective plight. In her struggle to negotiate space with her American friends, establish a personal identity as a girl within a dominant white patriarchal culture, and deal with the stigma of being a black African immigrant in America, Joy has also been exposed to this plight. Because life on the margin is difficult for me, a foreign-born black woman, I know it must be even tougher for this young black African girl.

My daughter is an immigrant from Cameroon. She is an eleven year old who has learnt to pay attention to issues of social justice prevalent in our society, as well as to deal with sociocultural pressures confronted by preadolescent and adolescent children in America, even though she cannot find easy solutions. She is constantly seeking ways to be happy, a concept she links with fairness and harmony. In a piece written for her father in November 1998, she notes:

> Happiness is about people having fun and enjoying themselves, . . . helping others. Confidence is what makes you happy because when you [are] confident, you feel good. I am happy, but sometimes I am mad or angry. To be mad means you are feeling hatred towards someone or something that caused you to get angry in some way. When you are sad, that means that you or somebody else could have gotten hurt or teased in some way and feel sad or sorry for them or yourself. To be neutral is to not care.

Happiness to Joy, therefore, involves socioeconomic, emotional, and psychological states of being. It is something individuals across race, class, and gender lines search for in different ways throughout their lives. It is what Joy constantly struggles to attain.

To understand how Joy Ekema-Agbaw—a sixth-grade student who has been living in the United States since 1991 and attends an all-white middle school in Bloomsburg, Pennsylvania—survives on the margin, I conducted an informal study that focused on her experiences as a preadolescent girl. I developed an informal interview protocol with open-ended questions for her and supplied her with a tape recorder to record her responses at her convenience. I also transcribed notes from a taped interview (two hours) that a white family friend made two summers ago for a class project to understand Joy's struggles as a black African girl in the United States. In addition to this, I conducted a series of informal interviews with Joy and her two older brothers on Joy's experiences as an African girl in Bloomsburg. Joy's responses varied with each subject. At certain moments during what I prefer to regard as "informal chats," she was enthusiastic and willing to talk more. At other times, she was reluctant to share her experience. The latter usually occurred when we shifted to sensitive subjects like hair, friendship, and looks.

The focus of this study is on Joy's experiences. She sat next to me by the computer on April 23, 1999, to go over the material in this chapter. We read sections of the write-up aloud (sometimes twice) for her approval before I mailed the manuscript. During this check session, she asked me to delete some information, expand other sections, and emphasize certain aspects of her story. What we have here is what Joy feels comfortable sharing with the public, for as she says, "there are more mean things," but all she wants to do is "fit in." I cannot blame her, especially since I know full well that "talking about race is quite literally dangerous" (Jacobs 1999, 1). I have used some of her own writing pieces to tell her story. I will introduce Joy as she describes herself in an autobiographic poem she had written earlier for a class:

Joy

> Smart, determined, kind, and hard working
> Daughter of Steven and Vivian, sister of
> Steven and Michael.
> Who cares deeply about the rights of all females.
> Who feels strongly about the equality between men and women.
> Who needs to learn.
> Who gives help to people in need.
> Who fears spiders and snakes.
> Who would like to see a woman president.
> Resident of 365 Hillside Drive, Bloomsburg, Pa 17815

JOY'S STORY

Joy was born on February 26, 1988, at *l'hôpital Centrale* (government hospital) annex in Yaounde, Cameroon. At the age of two years, seven month, she was enrolled at the first government, semiprivate, English-speaking preschool meant for children of anglophone civil servants. The routine was simple. Packed lunches, checkered blue uniforms, light blue aprons, lots of craft and phonic work, recitations and skits—all between the hours of 7 a.m. and 12 noon, five days per week. Joy had many friends in her class.

Joy, almost three, celebrating her first Christmas at Caisse National Preschool in Yaounde, Cameroon. She's standing between two of her peers, holding her present from the school, a white doll. (Photo by Steven Ekema-Agbaw.)

In August 1991, Joy and her two brothers accompanied us to Carlisle, Pennsylvania, where her father had a job at Dickinson College as a Visiting Scholar. Joy enrolled at the Carlisle Early Education Center. It was a different experience. No packed lunches, no uniforms, and few children of color. Hanover Street, where we were able to obtain lodgings in a two-bedroom apartment, had one other black family. This was good for Joy, since she could at least count on playing with a black girl in her neighborhood. The two girls shared a mutual desire to protect each other from danger and keep each other company, even though the African American girl was three years older. It was a short interlude in Joy's life.

The very next year, when her father's contract was renewed, we moved into a Dickinson town house on West Louther. It was much better than the previous lodging. Next door was a white girl, two years older than Joy. With no other little girls on that street, there was the mutual desire for company between Joy and her new "friend." The two gradually began playing together every now and then, and always in Kim's (not her real name) house or backyard. The rules were clear. Joy had to wait for Kim to invite her over to play before she could go out and join her "friend." Whenever Kim had her white friends around, Joy was not allowed to play with them, neither was she allowed to go over to Kim's when Kim had company. During such moments, Joy would lean on the wooden rail on our back porch and watch them play "house"; eat ice pops, candy, and cookies; and play with dolls until the friends left. Only then could she call out and ask Kim if it was all right for her to walk over. Kim never introduced her to any of her play dates, and Joy never embarrassed her in front of them. So began my daughter's struggle for equal partnership in the friendship ritual. There would be time when she would go upstairs to her room and peek through the window, sucking her thumb quietly—just watching the events outside and waiting to hear that it was her turn to come over. On such days, she would wait in vain and retire to bed, sulking.

The summer of 1993, when her father received a tenure-track position at Bloomsburg University, Joy moved again with us. At this time I had started working on my Ph.D. and was shuttling back and forth to Penn State University, where I was taking courses full-time and teaching two sections of undergraduate courses. At Bloomsburg, we took lodgings on East Third Street in town close to the university. Since there were no girls her age to play with, Joy kept to herself most of the time or played with some of the boys. Next door lived a Jewish family whose son played constantly with Joy until they moved to Philadelphia a couple of months later. Then a Caucasian family of five moved in. Their children interacted well with Joy and her brothers, even though their daughter was much younger than Joy. This experience too was brief. The following year, we bought a house and moved into a different neighborhood.

Her school and neighborhood are virtually all-white, with a few minorities dotted around, each trying hard to stay away from the others. She explains, "I don't know why. And it was only three of us, I think. Maybe more, but not many." Possibly the need to be accepted and belong in the predominantly white school unconsciously discourages the few minority children to identify with each other. In Joy's case, the goal of securing friendship drove her to act in strange ways. First, in order to be considered a friend of a particular white girl, she was asked to kick an African boy while she and this "friend" stood in the hall and mocked him. Joy kicked him hard, and he stumbled and almost fell on the floor (one of her brothers had noticed this from a distance and made sure he told us). Her "friend" cheered. It was a sad experience; Joy felt extremely bad afterward, and we made her apologize the next day. Even this act did not earn her friendship with this particular girl. Joy remained friendly but not particularly close to anybody.

While seeking friendship and acceptance in Carlisle and Bloomsburg, Joy has had to deal with her looks and her hair.[5] As a black girl with nappy hair who has been convinced by the media that straight, shoulder-length hair is the standard of beauty, she continuously seeks ways to give her hair the proper look.[6] There is constant pressure from some of her friends at school to "let down her hair" so they can see how long it actually is. At first, Joy couldn't because it was always in cornrows and braids and not long enough. Swimming at school, especially without a cap, is always hard. Her hair can never dry as quickly as her Caucasian friends'. She remarks, "It is spongy and soaks in water. Then it seems dry when it isn't." She adds, "There's not many other girls in my school with similar texture to my hair." The desire to have long hair became a reality when we used longer extensions for the braids. She was particularly pleased when some girls in eighth grade complimented her on her beautiful long braids. At her soccer camp, many said she looked like Naomi Campbell with those braids. For Joy and me, this is a comfortable compromise between maintaining her hair naturally and chemically treating it on a regular basis. Joy enjoys those compliments and says "they keep me going." She only wishes she could receive more from her peers.

Joy's brothers explain that she tries too hard to be liked. To them, she "socializes in such a way that it is obvious that she wants to be popular, and this backfires," and she also "talks weird when she's with her friends." Joy says she tries "hard because I just want friends. I just want to fit in." The boys are right. Although Joy speaks English without an African accent, her speech mannerisms are neither those of black nor white Americans. Thus, when in the company of her white friends, she tries hard to speak like them—using what she considers a white accent. Perhaps this is what her brothers refer to as "talking weird." Joy is ex-

Joy, in third grade at Bloomsburg Memorial Elementary School, 1995. (Photo by David Flores, a professional school photographer at Bloomsburg.)

tremely social, and she struggles to get friends who will consider her their "best friend."

Although Joy realizes the amount of effort she exerts in socializing with peers, she considers it a way of life for her. From every indication, she is still struggling to find a balance between her "political and personal selves" in order to survive the sociocultural pressure (Pipher 1994, 34). This concept of the two or multiple selves is also echoed by Trinh Minh-ha. In an article on postcoloniality and feminism, she refers to it as a "policy of 'separate development'" (1995, 265). At her age, Joy hasn't yet understood that as a black girl her daily experiences will involve dealing with "patriarchy, racism, and xenophobia" (hooks 1995, 24).[7] As an African, she is still grappling with the fact that certain cultural practices are not part of her heritage. She cannot tell her friends that her favorite African food is *eru* and *dodo*—"They wouldn't understand what it is."

She explains that if she were to advise an African girl in a similar situation, it would be: "To feel confident and don't let anybody push you around because you can do anything you want to do. Because there's a lot of people who may not like you and try to hurt you in some way. Just ignore those people who would do that." In spite of this, she comes to my room and says, "Mommy, I feel sorry for myself sometimes.

Joy, hanging onto her maternal grandmother (Joy Yenika) who was visiting from Cameroon, summer 1997. (Photo by Vivian Yenika-Agbaw.)

Do you think I'm pretty? Smart? Oh well." Then she lays down beside me on the bed and sucks her thumb until she falls asleep.

In an earlier interview with a family friend who teaches in Pakistan, Joy had remarked that there were times when people teased her. When this happened, she usually asked them if they liked being teased, and they always said no. Most recently, she enumerated a series of names they use to refer to her at school. They call her "big nose," "troll hair," "funky hair," "fake hair." The name-calling bothers her. Consequently, she sees little beauty in blackness and in everything connected to this racial category. She now refers to herself as a "brown girl" as opposed to a "black girl," and compares skin colors with her siblings to make sure she isn't really black as in the color black! With her new perm, she does her hair in a ponytail (not very long, though) like those of her friends, with fancy barrettes.

This new awareness of her physical appearance is a prelude to the far more challenging phase of the dating game. Joy has already heard horror stories about dating. They disturb her. One particular incident left an impression on her mind. Another black girl in the school told Joy of an experience she had when she asked a white boy out for a date. The boy had bluntly told the girl that he wasn't allowed to date black girls. This incident affected Joy deeply, but she was impressed by the way the girl had handled it. Joy says that, instead of being angry, the girl simply left the boy alone. It is an aspect of growing up in a white patriarchal society that she must come to terms with, for appearances define male-female relationships in the adolescent world—a world that mirrors its adult equivalent.

Like most of her friends, Joy is experiencing early puberty. This is something she is aware of and often anxious about. When another friend (white) said she had just had her first period, Joy was frightened. She hopes hers will delay, for she doesn't want to deal with sexual pressure. To her, menstruation is an indication to boys that one is a big girl (her friend had mentioned this to her). She winces as she says this. She has never dated, but is constantly anxious about the pressure boys put on girls. She also says she has friends who are struggling to lose weight in order to look pretty. She is afraid they will become anorexic like Barbie, a joke she shares with her siblings. She thinks she is okay and doesn't want to believe that she will be anything but a "normal" size girl.

Joy's struggles coincide with popular media images of immigrants, Africa, and gender relations. Immigrants are usually portrayed as filthy, dependent, and culturally ignorant. In movies, there are equally stereotypical images about Africans. Joy and I usually have informal discussions on race/ethnicity, class, and gender issues each time we watch television shows or movies, for instance *Family Matters, Boy Meets World, The Gods Must Be Crazy, Congo,* and *Coming to America.* It was on one such occasion that Joy suddenly burst out, "How can Topanga give up Yale to be with Corey? This sucks!" Then she shrugged her shoulders in a resigned fashion. This was the same way she had felt when Dana in *Step by Step* was paired up with a boy that Joy considered "too stupid for Dana." I began to realize that she consistently finds intelligent white American girls making sacrifices for their boyfriends or settling for boys even the audience wouldn't have expected them to date. In *Boy Meets World,* the interracial relationship between Shawn and Angela continues to drag. Although it doesn't seem to have any future, we watch on.

All these images of girlhood, blackness, "Africanness," and "immi-grantness" that she sees on television and in other media confuse her.[8] Whether she likes it or not, she must continue to explain the "back-wardness" of Africans to her peers, friends, and, at times, her teachers. She must constantly address questions such as, "Is it dirty in Africa? Do you speak African?" She says her response to the last question is always, "There is no African language." This is a burden she cannot escape from, and it continues to impact on her sense of self as she struggles to also deal with other race and gender issues. It is a responsibility Joy states emphatically that she doesn't like, for as she reminds me, "I'm only a kid, you know!" Unfortunately, most of her peers and some adults may not always realize this fact.

NOTES

1. bell hooks has discussed these issues in *Killing Rage* (1995) and *Teaching to Transgress* (1994b).

2. See Ekema Agbaw's article, "Trudier Harris Criticizes Notion of 'Strong Black Woman' " (1997).

3. See hooks's *Outlaw Culture* (1994a) and *Black Looks* (1988).

4. See hooks's *Bone Black* (1996, 31); Toni Morrison's *Playing in the Dark* (1992) also explores the connection between blackness and primitivism.

5. See Herron's *Nappy Hair* (1997) and Rogarsky's *Rapunzel* (1982). These picture books depict two specific hair types and their advantages and disadvan-tages. Herron's book has caused some commotion in a New York school district.

6. Mitchell and Reid-Walsh discuss Barbie as a doll that manifests "an impos-sible standard of beauty" (1997, 113).

7. See Jelloun's *Racism Explained to My Daughter* (1999) for more information on racism and xenophobia.

8. See Rosaldo's *Culture and Truth* (1993, 209) for information on immigrants and American dominant culture. Also see Searls (1997) on the concept of double consciousness in regard to appearance.

WORKS CITED

Agbaw, Ekema. 1997. "Trudier Harris Criticizes Notion of 'Strong Black Woman.' " *Making Connections: A Newsletter for Teachers of Culturally Diverse Literatures* (Spring): 8.

Boy Meets World. 1999. Michael Jacobs Production. ABC. WNEP, Wilkes Barre.

Coming to America. 1988. Starring Eddie Murphy. Paramount Pictures.

Congo. 1995. Paramount Pictures and Kennedy/Marshall Productions.

Family Matters. 1999. ABC. Starring Jaleel White.

The Gods Must Be Crazy. 1986. Dir. Jamie Uys. Perf. Marius Weyers, Sandra Prinsloo, and Xao. Videocassette. Playhouse Video.

Goldberg, David. 1993. *Racist Culture: Philosophy and the Politics of Meaning.* Oxford: Blackwell.

Herron, Carolivia. 1997. *Nappy Hair.* New York: Dragonfly.

Hill, Mike. 1997. "Trading Places: Majorities, Modernities, A Critique." *Education and Cultural Studies: Toward a Performative Practice,* ed. Henry Giroux and Patrick Shannon. New York: Routledge, 139–51.

hooks, bell. 1988. *Black Looks: Race and Representations.* Boston: South End.

———. 1996. *Bone Black.* New York: Owl Books.

———. 1995. *Killing Rage: Ending Racism.* New York: Owl Books.

———. 1994a. *Outlaw Culture: Resisting Representations.* New York: Routledge.

———. 1994b. *Teaching to Transgress.* New York: Routledge.

Jacobs, Bruce. 1999. *Race Manners.* New York: Arcade.

Jelloun, Tahar. 1999. *Racism Explained to My Daughter.* New York: New Press.

Minh-ha, Trinh. 1995. "Writing Postcoloniality and Feminism." *The Post-Colonial Studies Reader,* ed. Bill Ashcroft, Gareth Griffiths, and Helen Tiffin. London: Routledge, 264–68.

Mitchell, Claudia, and Jacqueline Reid-Walsh. 1997. "And I Want to Thank You Barbie: Barbie as a Site for Cultural Interrogation." *Education and Cultural Studies: Toward a Performative Practice,* ed. Henry Giroux and Patrick Shannon. New York: Routledge, 103–16.

Morrison, Toni. 1992. *Playing in the Dark: Whiteness and the Literary Imagination.* Cambridge: Harvard University Press.

Pipher, Mary. 1994. *Reviving Ophelia: Saving the Selves of Adolescent Girls.* New York: Putnam.

Rogarsky, Barbara. 1982. *Rapunzel.* New York: Holiday House.

Rosaldo, Renato. 1993. *Culture and Truth.* Boston: Beacon.

Searls, Susan. 1997. "Race Schooling and Double Conscious: The Politics of Pedagogy in Toni Morrison's Fiction." *Education and Cultural Studies: Toward a Performative Practice,* ed. Henry Giroux and Patrick Shannon. New York: Routledge, 153–76.

· 4 ·

Childhood Misconceptions

Reflections of a Biracial American (Colored) Girl

Wendy M. Thompson and Lisa B. Thompson

> I want the freedom to carve and chisel my own face, to staunch the bleeding with ashes, to fashion my own gods out of my entrails. And if going home is denied me then I will have to stand and claim my space, making new culture—*una cultura mestiza*—my own lumber, my own bricks and mortar and my own feminist architecture.
>
> —Gloria Anzuldúa, *Borderlands*

*W*hen my eldest brother, Guy, and his wife, Carmela, had their first child, I was an awkward teenager trying to figure out how to navigate life in the turbulent racial, sexual, and political landscape of the Bay Area during the early 1980s. I remember the clarity in Guy's large brown eyes as he explained how he felt witnessing Wendy's birth. I have also been in awe during the past eighteen years watching my brother dedicate his life to being a loving father of three girls. Many times he has grappled with finding ways to protect his growing daughters both from the world's ills and his own frailties. Having no children of my own, I have taken my role as aunt very seriously. My relationship with Wendy has always been special. I provide my niece with a sounding board, a tutor, and, at times, a sanctuary from the ever-present parental gaze. I babysat her during my teen years, wrote to her while I was away at college, and, when I moved back to the Bay Area for graduate school, nurtured her burgeoning interest in literature and race with books of poetry, short stories, and essays from Toni Morrison, Sandra Cisneros, and Maxine Hong Kingston. Wendy reminded me of myself—too much energy and too many questions.

How does one experience disenfranchisement in a middle-class family living in the most powerful nation in the late twentieth century? Wendy has the benefits of life in the center, her own room, plenty of clothes, and, now, her own car. However, as a biracial child she also resides in borderlands of the African- and Chinese-American communities. Working as a community activist while living in a comfortable middle-class home provides Wendy with a unique perspective.[1] As a young girl trying to make sense out of her different cultures and encounters, she survives many tumultuous experiences. What she reveals in her narrative suggests that scholars studying girls' culture, race theory, feminism, and sexuality must constantly complicate their notions of identity, oppression, and community.

Hip hop, now an intricate form of popular culture, influenced American youth during the 1990s and helped shape racial and gender dynamics in many ways.[2] I love hip-hop music and many things about the culture; coming of age when rap music was in its infancy, I understood it as part of the broad African American culture and community. For Wendy, the only unmediated interaction with African Americans who were not family members came through stolen images from television and magazines. Although her parents refused to allow their daughters to watch music videos (or *The Simpsons,* for that matter) or to read popular periodicals such as *The Source* or *Vibe,* Wendy found a way to see the images either with friends or when she visited me for the weekend. I suspect that, as with most teens, her parents forbidding the material made it more enticing. Without an adult presence that could help her process what she read and saw consistently, Wendy made her own opinions about what it meant to be a black girl. Moreover, Wendy often witnessed black people and black culture through a skewed medium and through negative messages she received from her immigrant mother about blacks. Carmela did not fully understand how race operates in American culture, and her experiences living in a working-class neighborhood in Oakland only provided her a limited view of black people.

Unfortunately, dominant representations of the African American community focus on one segment—urban instead of rural, working class instead of middle class. Moreover, the black middle class is often constructed as a problematic force within the community.[3] Considered elitist and disengaged with the struggles of blacks in general, the black middle class until recently has been largely omitted from popular culture. Racial performance and racial authenticity are part of America's cultural landscape, and, subsequently, Wendy's exposure to blackness has been filtered through a lens that depicts the "ghetto" almost exclusively as a place where blackness is "real" instead of depicting the African American community in all its contradictions and diversity.[4] Thus, the day-to-day accomplishments of black family members pale in comparison to the exciting images of blacks on television and in movies or the raging, seductive voices on the radio.

Raising biracial children in northern California brought unique challenges to my brother and his wife. My sister-in-law confessed that they simply never considered how race would factor into their daughters' lives—it had never occurred to either of them. Unfortunately, they had very little guidance to help them to understand the importance of race or how to explain race to their children. My brother and his wife are not alone in ignoring how race will affect their daughters, as psychologist Marguerite A. Wright explains: "But until recently, race has been a taboo subject in the child-rearing literature. Even today, of the hundreds of books about parenting now available, few advise parents on how to teach their children about race. This oversight is lamentable because, along with gender and social class, race shapes a child's life more than anything else" (1988, 4). Wright also acknowledges the influence of familial and community views of race on the child's self-esteem. In their study of biracial children in the United Kingdom, Barbara Tizard and Ann Phoenix concede that "communicating about race within the family can be seen as an important, if indirect, strategy on the part of parents for helping their children deal with racism. In only half of the families was there any overt communication about race and racism, according to the young people" (1993, 123). Moreover, Anne Wilson's research on black-white children in Britain indicates:

> The children with the most positive and secure identities had mothers who were open and secure about their own racial identity (whether black or white), who encouraged their children to think of themselves as black *and* mixed race and represented racism realistically to their children, as a force which would affect them personally. Children who were more prone to identity conflict tended to have mothers who were in conflict about their own identity, who saw the children as 'coloured' or 'almost white' and underplayed racism as a factor in the children's lives. (1987, viii)

However, most studies of the phenomenon acknowledge that there is much to be learned from children of mixed-race heritage about how they see the world. It is no longer acceptable to claim biracial people will suffer tragic lives simply because of their racial identity, and it seems apparent that they benefit from the opportunity to process and come to terms with their mixed heritage.[5]

The notion of race is often synonymous with blackness in U.S. culture. Black-white liaisons have been discussed since the beginning of racial dynamics in colonial America. However, Wendy's story goes beyond black and white to show another side of interracial unions. In Wendy's essay and consciousness, her Asian identity is often diminished. She does not discuss her worries about "acting" Asian or being accepted as Chinese. I can only speculate about how being rejected by segments of the Asian community has hurt her and her mother. It is particularly significant given that my brother and his wife have raised their children in a household that predominantly embraces Chinese culture. However, Wendy's sense of her Asian identity is overshadowed by her love/hate relationship with her blackness. In U.S. popular culture, Asian stereotypes are less frequently depicted; their image muted, Asians are regarded as the invisible "model" minority.[6] I suspect Wendy's view of her Asian heritage will change over time, especially as America alters its relationship with the Asian American community both politically and socially.

In addition to race, sexual experimentation, sexual violation, and sexual celebration also help to shape Wendy's sense of self. In *Stolen Women: Reclaiming Our Sexuality, Taking Back Our Lives,* Gail Wyatt explains the difficulty black women have becoming healthy, respected sexual beings:

> Black girls tend to have less than adequate knowledge about how their bodies are changing, the consequences of those changes, and the possibility that people known to them might attempt to abuse or exploit them. Further, they have little appreciation of how the stereotypes about black females threaten their health and self-image, even with the support of mothers or mother figures who are trying to guide and help them. (1997, 117)

In her struggle to find solace, Wendy often made decisions that put her in danger. It is not surprising that she would suffer from confusion. Confronting negative sexual stereotypes about both Asian and African American women made finding a healthy self-image quite difficult. However, Wendy's difficulty with her sexual agency did not hinder her develop-

Wendy at seventeen. (Photo by Alison Fong.)

ment; instead, it fueled her determination to become a full and complete person.

Wendy's story is not unique, but it demonstrates how one's self-esteem is influenced and in some ways determined by one's racial identity. When I received the call for papers for an international anthology examining girls' lives, I knew Wendy's experience as a young biracial teen would be interesting to other girls who imagine the United States as a place of wealth or perfection. The diminished spirits of teens in crisis illustrate that location is only part of the difficulty of becoming an adult. Years ago I realized that, of all my brother's children, his oldest daughter would have the most trouble. I recall watching Wendy's confused face when an African American cousin admired her soft, straight dark hair and unblemished, creamy tan skin. I also remember the absence of her mother's Asian-American family during holidays and birthdays. These conflicting messages forced Wendy to determine for herself how to define her self-worth. She is still struggling with that process, but, as she continues on her path as a young adult, she accepts that both her inner and outer beauty are worthy of celebration and love no matter what others think or do. What follows are the words of a young girl trying to find her way in the margins and borderlands by using language to help understand herself and redefine the world.

WENDY'S STORY

My scars rim deeper than the life of an ordinary seventeen-year-old girl. My scars stemming from my emptiness, my own lonely world. I am everything from extremely exotic to the confused silent question coming from lips of passers-by when they ask, "What is she?" My scars twist wickedly across my small brown war-torn body. A reminder of my hatred, my shame, and my strength in survival. I am liable to transform, to blend and push on limits until I destroy them. I have found my home, although it is still evolving; I am still evolving. No community is "mine." I am the outcast—envied, excluded, shunned by both my races, yet admired and coveted by those who dare to know me. I am my own secret, my own wild blend. One who looks back into her shadows but never surrenders to memories.

I was born in Oakland, California, in the early eighties at a time when drugs had already infested the ghettos, and crime and violence were an accepted part of normal living. I was born to two people whose worlds were very much apart. My father, a San Francisco native, was a young African American man who came from a shattered family. Like many blacks in the 1940s, his parents migrated from Louisiana to California to work in the shipyards, building machinery and such to serve overseas as artillery and ammunition. At an early age, my father was introduced to pain. His father would often stumble into the house intoxicated, drinking brandy (that badass chose his liquors with taste) and smelling of lies. My father would lie in his bed listening to his mother venting in the other room about her husband's womanizing and drunkenness. In turn, his father would respond to her criticism with closed fists, beating her sometimes in front of their wide-eyed children.

My dad grew up, followed the Black Panthers for a little while in high school, and eventually became the first one in his family to attend and graduate from college. He used his experiences—the abuse, the racism, and the tormented boyhood in San Francisco—to pave an independent life for himself, all the while never letting go of his beautiful Afro-American heritage. He met my mother while he was working at a part-time job in San Francisco's Main Library and pursued her with a persistency that was somewhat frightening to her at the time.

She had just emigrated from Taiwan at the time and had come to San Francisco to be reunited with her mother and siblings. They had previously fled communist rule in Burma and were slowly conforming to "American ways." Life in San Francisco was difficult for my mother, who spoke no English and shared a house with her nine brothers and sisters. Her mother was always working, trying to support the family since Carmela's father had been killed in a suspicious surgery that caused him to bleed to death. His portrait still stands on the mantel in my uncle's house. I see his round, unsmiling face every time I go to visit on Chinese New Year; with a red stick of incense I am told to bow, preferably three times, to show respect to a man I never knew.

My mother won't tell me the truth now. She won't tell me how it really was back then, when she was younger and nobody used to love her. She won't tell me the reasons why she thinks Mexican boys are dirty or why she submits herself to my father whom she serves with little complaint. I assume it is because many things happened to her for which she could find no reason or were too painful to reformulate. The one thing I do know is that my mother finally let down her guard and moved in with my father upon completing high school. My father had already graduated from San Francisco State University and was working in Woolworth's as a store manager. They were very young but very much in need of love, as are people who have been neglected and abused since birth. Their love was not uncommon during those days when everybody was still fucked up from all the drugs they'd consumed in the sixties, and well-known neighborhood girls carried the bastards of long-haired flower children from Woodstock summers.

My parents' relationship was controversial, since it was already preconceived that the only Asian women who got with black men were prostitutes. Her mother called her a whore and tried to discontinue the

relationship by sending her away to different relatives, but the love letters did not stop. My mother suffered beatings, a black eye from a high-
heeled shoe thrown at her the night before her prom, and was eventually
disowned: a discontinued daughter. But she was in love with a man who
carried as much grief and sympathy as her dead father. Who would have
known?

I was conceived from their fateful union; a quick signing of papers
at the courthouse downtown and she was Ms. Chi-Hwee Thompson. If
only my parents knew of the torture and pain I would face, would they
have thought twice of bringing me into this world? I lived with a mother
who carried a bruise in her heart, ostracism for marrying a black man.
For this, she abhorred the "ghetto" black because, after all, it was all
interrelated—"Asian girl love black man. Black man love Asian girl.
Asian family throw Asian girl into street to live with black man. Asian
girl not happy no more." Even after I was born, her mother never got
around to forgiving her. After I was delivered, the doctor diagnosed me
with a case of jaundice that distressed my mother to the point of crying.
Her disgusted mother, my "po-po," replied sourly, "Why you crying?
If she die, you can always have another one." The reconstruction of
their mother-daughter relationship still remains incomplete.

I was very small when race entered my life. Living in Oakland, my
parents chose not to push my ethnicity and therefore allowed me to
grow up colorless. I never realized how my family tended to lean culturally to the Asian side—we ate almost every meal with rice and soy sauce,
our living room furniture set was specially ordered from China, and ever
since I was born I've been attending a Chinese Independent Baptist
Church. The overabundance of my Asian culture was constantly ob-
scured by my focus on "blackness" and where on that spectrum I belonged. I would hang my head in shame or turn away when my mother
or a significant (nonblack) person pointed out as "those black people."
Those slight remarks hit me between the eyes. Was I part of "those black
people," or should I hate them as well? I surely knew it wasn't me—
roughneck boys fighting over a nickel-sack of wine, loud pregnant girl
screaming at some drunk man, little kids yelling, "Fuck you, nigga!"
What was it all supposed to mean? I felt too many generations removed,
like a white-washed relative with lighter skin, better hair, and no way of
understanding Ebonics.

My struggle with education has been no different. I moved from
private to public school and back again. I hated school because I could

never fit in. In elementary school I was very shy and wore big pink glasses. I was a weak nerd who all the other little kids would beat up, calling me names like "bitch" and "skank." I often would sit alone on the bench in the schoolyard because I felt inferior—too "black" for the white kids, and not "black enough" for the black kids. I was like an unwelcome shadow that spoke a foreign tongue and dressed like an alien. My classmates excluded me from four-square at recess; I was one of the last ones chosen when they picked soccer teams for PE. The boys in my class made me feel ugly, and that was one thing that never changed over the years. I was an ugly, four-eyed, puffy-haired geek, and they never let me forget it.

I chose to deal with it the easy way, shut myself off from every aspect of life. I was already a nobody, taunted at school for being a half-breed Oreo, coming home from school crying to parents frustrated within themselves. My father used to say, "Shut your mouth or I'll give you a reason to cry." I withdrew, not wanting to be affected by the girl who punched me in the chest at school or the boy who told me I looked like a dog. My life at home was no better. Nobody knew of the torment that was lashed upon my body in the form of my father's belt blows or an occasional shoe. In all the times my father hit me, I cannot recall even one time when my mother intervened, but it wasn't her fault, she was only playing her role as the dutiful wife, which was more like an obedient Chinese maid-servant. It was just like her to be exploited and yell at me about traits she herself carried. This and all other pain I transferred onto blank sheets of white paper my father brought home from his clerical job at the marine terminals by the Oakland estuary. I converted the rage and hideousness into little childish drawings of people and cities and landscapes. My art transformed me, gave me time to reflect and develop, although I was already beyond disfigurement. Inside I was crying, scribbling out the hidden pieces of my emotionally damaged soul. But the more my father hit me, the more I hated him and being like him; I ended up hating black people as well, since he symbolized the race. My mother, on the other hand, was the first person I loved; I literally fell in love with my mother. She gave me everything in life, in effort to subdue her little girl's traumatized spirit. Her money could correct the wrongs done to me for an hour or so before my interest wore off and I heard their shouting voices through the whitewashed bedroom wall.

I grew up, a broken little girl, searching for someone to love me, for a hand of acceptance. My parents viewed this as a sign of a troubled

Wendy in art class. (Photo by Wayne Meeks.)

child and put me into a private Christian school, hoping I would be reformed into a modest, godly young woman. I saw this move as the last step they had in controlling my life, so I began to rebel. I was tired of being quiet, tired of being subdued, tired of being mistaken for something else. I wanted to stand up; I didn't want the other kids to laugh at me anymore.

Finding my voice was a process of devouring book after book about troubled, rejected teens, in the library. I would read about some alcoholic girl who would run away from her abusive father and get fucked over by her boyfriend. My obsession with these books was a cry for help; I needed a way out of my life and fast. My morphine was *Crosses,* a book by Shelly Stoehr. It was a harmless venture, the distorted cover boasting a story of two girls who became friends and dealt with their pain by cutting. Actually it was self-mutilation, and after reading halfway through the book, I decided to give it a try. I didn't mean to, but ended up carving a crooked cross into my left shoulder, which I still remember. Funny thing was, it all began with a book, with someone else's life, someone else's mind in that small black print. I read it over and over until it was my life and those tiny words began to drip devastated drops of blood into my mind.

I destroyed myself, cutting little jagged lines into my arms with pieces of shattered porcelain. I did this, not because I was stupid, but because it was the only way I could get back at the world for being incapable of realizing my existence. I mutilated myself from adolescence to my early teenage years until, out of my frustration and anger with the negative results of cutting, I attempted suicide. I was crying from an earlier fight with my mother and had retreated to the bathroom. My whole face was swollen as I looked at myself in the mirror before swallowing a handful of pills. I wasn't rushed to the hospital or taken seriously. Instead, my attempt only proved to my parents that I was truly deranged. They forced me into therapy shortly after this incident, wanting me to change. I hated them even more for doing this, making me talk to some stupid person who was probably the reject of his family. All I wanted was for the fighting to stop, to be understood and taken seriously, but the blame would be pushed on me, and family dysfunction was written off as "my fault."

I continued to read those books before stumbling onto stories of gangs and how, by banding together, the members were feared and nobody could fuck with them. I fantasized this ideal, of finally having friends who would have my back and be down for me no matter what. I closed the book covers and searched for "troubled kids" at school who I thought would provide a hopeful path in my desire to become a gang banger.

It was common around eighth grade for girls, regardless of skin color, to wear dark lipstick and tie bandannas around ponytails set high on their heads. Most of the boys donned creased Dickies or jeans in size XXL with accompanying flannel jackets that reminded me of *mojados* who had just crossed the border. The gangster image was in. To me, it was more than just a fashion statement, it was a way of life. I saw this way exemplified by most of the Mexican-American kids my age, boys wearing hairnets and tattoos seated on lowrider bikes, girls with pencil-thin eyebrows (almost always drawn in) and mousy hair watching them. Their hard-core, "I don't give a fuck" attitude attracted me, and I decided to hunt down a tight crew of *vato locos* who would embrace me with hard, battle-scarred arms. I followed these kids and impersonated their wicked ways, seeing them as allies who'd be less likely to hurt me on the basis of color. I adopted the attitude, a hard front and a bad mouth, drawing my face dark like the homegirls. I talked with a classmate named TJ who boasted allegiance to XIV and showed me old cut-out tattoos given to him by homeboys. I took the name Trippy, because my paranoid behavior always made me worry, scared-like. TJ called himself Dough Boy AKA Lucky, but to others' eyes he was just an overweight white boy with Mexican friends. He wrote me notes about getting jumped in and getting high, things my childhood mind had yet to experience. One day my mother found those letters and showed them to my father. It was the last offense to my parents—a wannabe gangster daughter, a little girl who thought she was brave enough to walk the streets at night. They saw the opposite effect therapy had in my life, how I still cut my body, how I longed to fit in, and they believed that the evilness of the ghetto was rubbing off on me. They felt threatened, as if their parental purpose was at stake, as if they were losing me. Which was true, they had lost me; I was secretly formulating my own identity for all the times my mother or father never sat me down and explained, "Wendy, this is who you are." As I transformed, they had their own subtle mutations, growing more like tyrants, controlling and insane, just as their parents had been.

My rebellion became my standing, my voice. In the past I had only taken small sips of vodka, lit a cigarette on a kitchen stove before taking a hit and putting it out, and remained a virgin with an unviolated snatch. I wanted to be bad but was too much afraid to go beyond my parents' limit of tolerance. I was still a good girl, so naturally I was perplexed when my parents hit me one day with the proposition of moving to the suburbs. My first reaction was, how dare they? I had lived on 3635 Lyon Avenue all of my life. Foul-mouthed neighborhood boys terrorized stray cats with bee-bee guns while girls with perms and weaves and four-inch nails dug the sweet ghetto thugs that stood on street corners in front of liquor stores with their pants at their knees. It was my Oakland, and I loved the constant commotion of the city. The noisy brawls in the streets, the dirty shrieking wino, the dazed white hookers, they were so very much a part of me that I wanted to express. It was my world and I cursed my parents' every motive in forcing me to live in a new one.

They finally decided to let me take summer school at an Oakland public high school, believing it would scare the ignorance out of me, but the experience only made me want to anchor myself deeper. Wanting to identify with what I perceived as my African-American roots, wanting to run with the "bad kids," I took advantage of those few weeks only to be faced one day with the news that my family had found a new home in Fremont. My only thought was, "Are there any black folks there?" It was a time of desperate confusion, in which I had lost myself, clinging to changing identities and trying to fit into a world that was moving too fast.

I went through a slight culture shock and a deeper disappointment when I first moved to the suburbs. The uniform surroundings gave me a homesickness I could never really describe. Everything was clean, all those perfect little green lawns spread fittingly in front of tight little houses, complete with flower beds and cypress trees dripping crisp green leaves onto the driveway. Where did this dark/half-breed child belong? A few weeks before school started, my fear began to eat at my heart; would these kids accept me or would it be a rerun of my preteen years? I would lie on the edge of my bed, looking at the sky that was so severely blocked by the peachy stucco wall of our neighbor's house, wishing I would one day turn into a bird and fly far away. This was my hell, and, in time, it would only get worse.

I don't know why I didn't trust myself, maybe it was because I was too afraid to exist on my own, to open my mouth and let people have a piece of me. I was afraid to live, afraid to love, and afraid to let go. My desperation caused me to latch onto the first thing that came to my rescue while wandering the hollow halls of my high school. It was a black girl who first came up to me, promising friendship with an enticing buck-toothed smile, so I grasped her hand while she led me to the group. They were hoes, the girls who sauntered around too loose like a pack of wild tramps, devouring anything in their path with their curses and hatred. And I fell for it, thinking they would receive me wholeheartedly, spilling my gut-wrenching stories while they bore holes in my back with their treacherous claws. They used me as their way of having fun, my "friends," calling me names behind my back, cutting me down. They used me and left me more busted up than they had found me, entrapping me in lies. Those were my friends, my people, who robbed me of my dignity and self-esteem, yet in all my naiveté, I still went back for more. I became just like them, a vulture who fed on the helplessness of others, tearing limb from body until only the carcass remained. My desire to be accepted, to be loved, drove me so blind that I did not see myself shattering within. I did not think about what I was doing or had done until I had lost my soul to the devil.

The reason I do not address him is not because I want to protect his identity. The last thing I want to do is to protect the motherfucker; it is because I do not want him to take (or be given) any recognition for what he has done to me. This part of my life will be reconstructed as much as possible from memory even though I have fought so hard to forget. I was fifteen at the time.

He was a poor kid with crooked teeth who always tried to impress everyone with his fake layers of gold chains encircling his scrawny throat. He reminded me of those dirty loud boys who wrote graffiti on the back window of buses and dreamed of being rap stars—the little skinny bad kids who wore their pants too low and screwed little girls in their asses to show their unrefined masculinity. He was my Lucifer, infatuated with my innocence, and my little girl pussy was all that he desired. I thought that getting with him would help me finally achieve the status of being a "real" black girl, and so I stupidly gave in. He moved way too fast, leaving uneven blood marks on my neck and breasts, clutching my wrists until they bruised, but I never told him to stop. Maybe I did, but what good was it to me, a girl who had no previous experience, especially with a black boy? My defenseless body caused him to push even harder, for he saw the little girl who wanted to grow up too fast, a little girl searching for love. It was an offer that could not be refused, so he threw me a line. Like a starving dog, I was hooked.

What happened to me wasn't like some other girl's story, in which the boy held her down while she screamed and kicked, repeatedly raping her with his dick. I went through a more psychologically traumatizing experience, a literal mind fuck. I had followed him into his bedroom thinking we were going to make out again when he threw me the proposal of wanting to "hit it." It was a matter of kisses and heavy breathing that led me to the decision, "No, Wendy, this shit isn't right," so I got up and began to move toward the door. He must not have liked my answer because he shoved me hard enough to cause me to stumble. I became angry, my voice rising from my body, to which he only smirked, feigned apology, and proceeded to pop my cherry without even the vaguest feeling of emotion or sympathy. To anyone else, it sounds more like a mistake than rape, but when a man takes your body against your will, it is rape.

It was painful to me, having to live in a bruised, ripped-up shell. My mother tells me I should have fought back. I should have screamed for surely someone would hear me; anything would have been better than to just lie there obediently while someone else's son/cousin/ brother/uncle/father takes your life. But I was too quiet, too weak, too ugly to speak up for my own good. My mother told me that I had "asked for it," that it was my fault, that what I went through was not rape. The entity of the rapist has since become a small shadow in my life (although his occasional phone calls still haunt me to this day), occupying a small unsewn bullet hole inside my heart. I may survive, but I will never forget.

Every day after that, my feelings became a little weaker. I continued to hang around kids who struggled—accepting their marijuana and offers of crank although my flight with drugs never got off the ground. I was chasing shadows, trying to repair the remains of what the devil had left me with. I was a whore, and my sex was the cross I had to bear. When I looked in mirrors, I could not see myself; I was too ugly, too fucked-up. I picked at my face and practically removed my eyebrows because it was much easier to destroy. I continued to die, over and over again, my struggles becoming less meaningful. I cursed and became intolerable, self-destructive. It wasn't me who bled or cried or suffered, it was someone else. And although I felt sorry for her, she could never be me.

I decided to dump the whole "black experience" concept and, along with it, I dumped half of myself. I hated black men. I felt that they had little more than their illegitimate children to give to society, and I would never again fall victim to their godforsaken lies. I struggled with my inner demons, writhing uncontrollably like a moth caught by its wings in a spider's web. My confusion worried my father's mother, who grew concerned with me not having enough "good black people" in my life, but the damage had already been done. I was not like them; I was not black.

My identity became reinvented, from myself being darker skinned than my two light-complexioned sisters, to me exclusively avoiding any contact with blacks outside of my family. It was as if I was removing the negativity from myself by rejecting my African-American heritage, by becoming an outsider looking in: the one who viewed the black race in disgust, crossing the street every time a black person walked by. At times, when Latino boys would poke fun at black girls, I would lightly tell them that I was an African American, leaving them in shock while I turned away with pride. Sometimes the tables were turned, and it was I who became defensive and angry when people accused me of being a "typical" black girl.

This charade became my game. Finally, I was in control. It was a bitter, angry secret; my life a half-truth, turned out like a spinster in the street. I was frantic, unleashing my grief that I mistook for power. I made everyone hate me, walking the earth like a solitary angel with dismembered wings. I was the shadow of a long-dead experience, a void in the sky, until one day I met El Chingon.

That wasn't his real name, and for the longest time he had no name. He was just a boy who stood in the darkness, with a cap pulled low over his cola-brown eyes, a mystery that always stood under a tree in the park, waiting for a bus, watching me. He was a gang member, although he never professed his allegiance to any particular gang. He hardly ever spoke, but it was without words that he spoke—the way he swaggered down the hall, the way he glared at everyone, the way he held himself together as if on the brink of destruction—that said he was a marked man, running away from the barrio, holding his life like a fine sand inside his clenched fist. He was the first man I made love to and the only man I ever loved. (I was seventeen; he was eighteen.) I was almost complete with him in my life. Him, holding my heart in his skin-split palm. He resented the fact that I wanted to join a gang. Speaking to me in broken English, he made me desire him, and I wanted to save his life.

Our promiscuity originally stemmed from our lack of love. I needed someone to heal me; he needed someone who would make him feel important. I was still insecure with myself and my identity, my degraded status, and thus leaned on him, expecting him to change my life. I felt someone who performs such a deed should be given something in return, so I gave my body to him, sacrificing myself like Jesus. At first, the sexual escapades were harmless, our innocence running across the TV screen in the form of a cartoon or hiding under dirty sheets; our bodies twisted together, two wounded people who thought they were in love. A love or perhaps a fantasy that began to slip away after we discovered flaws in our relationship that only continued to become crazier as time went on. I had a tendency to fuck around with any guy who gave me the time of day; I wouldn't literally sleep with them, but steal curious kisses around dark corners and behind closed doors. He swore his commitment to me, but grew more and more controlling as his jealousy welled from his suspecting gut. To suppress the anger, he started punching walls; I resumed slicing my arms. The frustration we both had, being confused and unable to carry each other's worlds on our own shoulders, led us to violent rampages in which I would lash out at him and he would hit me back.

The first time he hit me, I accepted it. After all, it was my fault, and that's what I deserved for hitting a man. Yet the physical abuse was deeper than that. I overglamorized his Chicano ways, his machismo, which was entirely about muscles, lowriders, fighting, and sex. He had little use for respect and manners, and would often engage in fistfights, something he learned while growing up on the streets. It made me feel like somebody to walk with him, side by side. Me in the hard crook of his arm, an accessory to this crazy *cholo*. It made me feel important, like those tough girls who fought for their man and had the power to inflict just as much pain. So the bitter day El Chingon called me a bitch, I accepted it as who I was and made sure I walked the earth as the biggest bitch there ever was.

We broke up many times after that, and no longer did it matter anymore. My involvement with him had destroyed any remaining sense of independence and self-esteem I had left. I was a renegade with a vengeance, and it was me against the world. I was through with letting people screw with me, letting them tear me apart and leaving me unstable. I vowed never to love again, only to hate and be surrounded by so much anger that no one would be able to penetrate me. It was my step forward in regaining my strength. I became inspired with artists, deranged people who expressed themselves in warped forms on paper. I understood their desire to bring forth hallucinogenic images regardless of pain or suffering, their ability to accept themselves no matter how fucked-up the situation was. I looked at that, and was reborn.

I still fought with my parents, only now the altercations occurred more frequently. What started off as simple threats and semiviolent gestures intensified into explosive battles and blatant streaks of my surfacing self. They punished me for not being the way they wanted me to be. My poetry was garbage to my father, who told me he "didn't want to hear it." My mother still replies sourly when I bring up the idea of a family friend (who is Chinese) attending a black Baptist church. It's not so much the stupidity that angers me; it is their outright stubborn mentality, the fact that my parents refuse to accept me because they have not yet learned to accept themselves. But I cannot hate them. They are like an unspoken history, the intentional evil of human nature, which repeats itself. All this shit was never my fault.

These were the things that set me apart and proved that I was nothing like the other girls. I didn't want to conform. I was an individual, the queer daughter of straight-laced neurotic hypocrites who worshiped their religion rather than their God. The psychotic girl who went through walls and swallowed fire with a passion. Whore. Punk. Freak. Bitch. I was unrestricted, kicking down age-old stereotypes, making my own. I cursed like a man, sat with my legs spread, and voiced my opinions out loud. I hit boys, carved tattoos into my arms, and hardly ever cared if somebody saw me crying in public. I cheated on tests, burned things, and drove like a maniac. I was insane. I screamed when there was no more room for holes in my door. Screamed my pain, screamed my happiness. It was like consuming the poisonous insides of battery acid, burning through my organs.

I was an "all-American girl," complete with an attempt to run away, and dealings with police who ignored the fact that my father had just wrapped his ugly hands around my throat and strangled me, ignoring the large collar of bloody-red bruises, and threatening me that if I ran away, I would be picked up and taken to juvenile hall. However, my pain was nothing compared to the mental anguish I went through when I first noticed that I had developed what I thought to be symptoms of STDs. It was nothing like the nights I stayed up worrying about what I'd do if I was pregnant. This time, I thought I was going to die.

In the past, I had always wanted to take my own life with the blunt edge of a kitchen knife or the length of a rope, but suddenly when I was faced with the psychological side of actually wasting away on a hospital bed, I was terrified. Every time I went to the hospital, they insisted on taking tests, tests that felt more like genital mutilation than a cure or hand of healing. I felt cursed, knowing that my sickness was a direct result of the drastic predicaments I had experienced in my life.

I felt alone, a black sheep who finally got nipped in the ass. A little cloud fallen too far behind the rest in a broken sky of azure blue. I was nobody until she entered my life deeper than she had before. Her warm hands, tones like rich polish-soaked wood, passing over my wild billows of hair. Her comforting smile, a laugh that broke to sobbing, her low voice rolling down my window-pane eyes like rain. My father's youngest sister, Lisa. She was the one who taught me how it is to be a woman in this universe that falls to its knees for a man. She was my mentor, a "bad girl" pioneer, the only woman who I could truly, proudly look up to and say, "I want to be just like her." And she came at no better time. Her long dreads smelling of dark lipstick, satin sheets, and Billie Holiday. She embodied who I was, where I was going, and what I was going to do when I got there. She told me to tell her, tell her what it was that I was tired of. And I said, "I'm tired of hurting, tired of pretending, tired of being ashamed," and she looked up at me and said with her mouth closed, "It's okay."

And it was okay, because I no longer wanted to go on living incomplete, or telling my life story in painfully fragmented sentences. I was supposed to be proud like all the other half-breed kids, the ones that couldn't care less what color they were and where they'd fit in. Race wasn't supposed to matter, and besides, people already labeled me as crazy, what difference would it make if I was anything else? It was just another story about an inner-city kid whose parents relocated her to the surburbs in a last-ditch effort to save her screwed-up soul. The little girl who was supposed to stay innocent forever, but died somewhere in the process. The small growing woman who destroyed herself by allowing a man to silence her mind with the back of his hand. Transformations into a slut once her virginity was wrenched from her, to a mediocre black girl when she talked too loud. I looked at the person my mother was and vowed never to be like her. Because, in fact, I never had a mother. She never comforted me after my painful experience of being raped of my mind, body, and soul; she didn't know how to love me. It was difficult for me, developing into womanhood without a mother or an adequate role model. She was physically there but she could never connect with me on an emotional level. Our cultural differences never permitted us to cross, only to push and cry and fight—a daughter who refused to surrender, a mother who fought to forget. I knew why I did not love myself and broke mirrors with my reflection. I knew why. It was all the times my father mocked the natural kinkiness of my hair and my mother's struggle to correct it. My unhappiness arose from the lack of an early positive self-image throughout childhood. I was a torn person, ripping at the seams.

It took much breaking and scarring in order for me to see myself. Like pulling the petals off a rose that is still budding, only to see the painful, bleeding center, I was stripped of my hard ugly outside, standing face-to-face with my soul. Being able to see myself barefaced and naked without cringing, without denying, only made me stronger. The familiarity of the voices of strangers, telling me to accept myself, never sounded so raw. I became a new person, pushing forward—an individual who respected her mind like a revolutionary soldier, a woman who was more than just somebody's tits and ass. No longer did I want to succumb to the waste of my young rising life. I remember food stamps and bad baby-sitters just as clearly as the abuse and racial intolerance I went through. For once in my life, I recognized what it was to look at the big picture, the conspiracy that nobody tends to talk about anymore. The suicide that I believed would fix my life became an old notion as I transcended to a new level. All things once important to me began to fade away—my dependency on the psycho boyfriend, the sex, my old self. Even now as I stand on the brink of adulthood, I sometimes get so overwhelmed with how much I've sacrificed that I just want to run and keep on running, as fast and as far away from this place, as fast and as far as I can from myself. Because from life, there is no escape. Sometimes in order to move forward, we must abandon all things that have held us back. Sometimes in order to survive, we must disregard the voices calling us into the streets. Nobody ever said life was simple.

Now and then, as the remains of the day slowly dip into night, I hear their voices, calling me. And somehow, a part of me will never walk away.

NOTES

We wish to thank Valisa Dougherty and Darwin E. Farrar, whose comments and suggestions greatly helped the development of this chapter.

1. Gloria Anzuldúa argues for a space where "two worlds merge to form a third country—a border culture. Borders are set up to define the places that are safe and unsafe, to distinguish us from them. A border is a dividing line, a narrow strip along a steep edge. A borderland is a vague and undetermined place created by the emotional residue of an unnatural boundary. It is in a constant state of transition. The prohibited and forbidden are its inhabitants" (1987, 3).

2. For instance, in many hip-hop videos, females are sexual accessories to males who act out their sexual and violent aggressions. For a discussion of sexual politics in rap music, see Niesel (1997) and Rose (1994).

3. For critiques of the African American middle class, see E. Franklin Frazier (1962) or Hare (1970). bell hooks's essay, "Spending Culture: Marketing the Black Underclass" (1994), also criticizes the middle class for being too focused on their own interests.

4. The plethora of black middle-class autobiography as well as novels that focus on middle-class life, attempt to balance the representation of African Americans without diminishing the lives of blacks from other backgrounds. See Andrew Lee, *Sarah Phillips* (New York: Random House, 1984); Gwendolyn M. Parker, *Trespassing: My Life in the Halls of Privilege* (Boston: Houghton Mifflin, 1997); Jill Nelson, *Volunteer Slavery: My Authentic Negro Experience* (Chicago:

Noble Press, 1993); and Lorene Cary, *Black Ice* (New York: Vintage, 1992) for a diverse literary representation of black middle-class women's lives.

5. See Lise Funderburg's anthology, *Black, White, Other* (1994), which attempts to complicate representations of biracial people. In addition, Kathleen Odell Korgen's sociological study *From Black to Biracial* (1998) and Danzy Senna's novel *Caucasia* (1998) make similar interventions.

6. For discussion of the model minority myth, see Gotanda (1995) and Kao (1995).

WORKS CITED

Anzaldúa, Gloria. 1987. *Borderlands/La Frontera: The New Mestiza.* San Francisco: Spinsters/Aunt Lute.

Frazier, E. Franklin. 1962. *Black Bourgeoisie.* New York: Collier Books.

Funderburg, Lise. 1994. *Black, White, Other: Biracial Americans Talk About Race and Identity.* New York: William Morrow.

Gotanda, Neil. 1995. "Re-Producing the Model Minority Stereotype: Judge Joyce Karlin's Sentencing Colloquy in *People v. Soon Ja Du.*" *Reviewing Asian America: Locating Diversity,* ed. Soo-Young Chin et al. Pullman, Wash.: Washington State University Press, 87–106.

Hare, Nathan. 1970. *The Black Anglo Saxons.* London: Collier-Macmillan.

hooks, bell. 1994. *Outlaw Culture.* New York: Routledge.

Kao, Grace. 1995. "Asian Americans as Model Minorities? A Look at Their Academic Performance." *American Journal of Education* 103 (2): 121–60.

Korgen, Kathleen Odell. 1998. *From Black to Biracial: Transforming Racial Indentity Among Americans.* Westport, Conn.: Praeger.

Niesel, Jeff. 1987. "Hip-Hop Matters: Rewriting the Sexual Politics of Rap Music." *Third Wave Agenda: Being Feminist, Doing Feminism,* ed. Leslie Heywood and Jennifer Drake. Minneapolis: University of Minnesota Press.

Rose, Tricia. 1994. *Black Noise: Rap Music and Black Culture in Contemporary America.* Middletown, Conn.: Wesleyan University Press.

Senna, Danzy. 1998. *Causacia.* New York: Riverhead Books.

Tizard, Barbara, and Ann Phoenix, eds. 1993. *Black, White or Mixed Race? Race and Racism in the Lives of Young People of Mixed Parentage.* New York: Routledge.

Wilson, Anne. 1987. *Mixed Race Children: A Study of Identity.* London: Allen and Unwin.

Wright, Marguerite A. 1988. *I'm Chocolate, You're Vanilla: Raising Healthy Black and Biracial Children in a Race-Conscious World.* San Francisco: Jossey-Bass.

Wyatt, Gail. 1997. *Stolen Women: Reclaiming Our Sexuality, Taking Back Our Lives.* New York: Wiley.

· 5 ·

Mah-Rukh Ali

Profile of a Norwegian

Mah-Rukh Ali and Elisabeth Sandberg

$\mathcal{M}$ah-Rukh Ali is unique. She is among the few thousand girls born in Norway to parents who are originally from Pakistan. She is a Norwegian whose native language is Norwegian, whose skin is brown, and whose religion is Muslim, living in a country with a Lutheran state church. People around the world and in Norway, for that matter, think of Norwegians as being blond haired and blue eyed. She does not fit that description. Mah-Rukh is among a pioneering generation of distinctively different looking, multicultural Norwegians. At the millennium, she is going through the pain of being the first generation of marginalized citizens in one of the quietest, most homogenous, western European nations. Mah-Rukh Ali is a fascinating young woman in herself, and her first book, published when she was sixteen—*Den sure virkeligheten* [*The Bitter Reality* 1997]—provides fertile ground for scholars and general readers interested in feminism, ethnicity, and postcolonialism.

Norway is a country that prides itself on its policies and general ethos of gender equality. bell hooks states that "at its most visionary, it [feminist theory] will emerge from individuals who have knowledge of both margin and center" (1984). Mah-Rukh is an insider outsider. She is at the center in Norwegian society by virtue of class. Her parents bought a beautiful house in a privileged neighborhood on the west side of Oslo in part to avoid racist slurs, possible violence, and poor education. Since there are no brown-skinned children in the new area, there are no Norwegian-as-a-second-language classes. Mah-Rukh has always been at the top of her Norwegian class, and she has honed her language skills since she was twelve, when she started to write a regular column

Mah-Rukh Ali

for *Samora,* a magazine dedicated to eradicating racism in Norway.[1] In terms of class and education, Mah-Rukh is at the center.

The focus for her book is on how Norwegians stereotype "typical Pakistani" girls. Few studies have yet been done on Asian Muslim immigrant girls in Europe, but two, written in English, have focused on Pakistani schoolgirls—one study in Norway and one in England. Both address the commonly accepted notion that children of Muslim immigrants are torn between two cultures:

> The Pakistani girls/boys in Norwegian schools are exposed to Norwegian influence. . . . Pakistani parents have fears and doubts about this social pattern of life. The majority of Pakistani parents do not allow their daughters to participate in different types of activities after school, therefore they spend most of their times after school inside their homes. Parents want to see their daughters stick to their own values more rigidly than the boys as girls are considered the transmitters of cultural heritage to the next generation. But if they transgress and break Islamic norms of sexual behavior, they bring dishonor and

shame on the family and this may cause intergenerational conflicts. (Riaz 1994, 43)

The description that seems to apply to Mah-Rukh Ali more closely is found in Tehmina N. Basit's analysis of Muslim schoolgirls in England: "[M]embers of the rising generation are extremely mobile in linguistic, religious, and cultural terms, draw eclectically on every tradition available to them, and are strongly committed to ordering their own lives on their own terms" (1999, 17). Mah-Rukh's parents also fit the description of British immigrant parents, probably not least because of their own high level of education: "The main objective of the parents seems to be to enculture the girls to become effective members of British society, without losing their Islamic religion" (Basit 1999, 16).

The Bitter Reality is a gem for scholars who read Norwegian because of its broad treatment of the young author's public and private life. For example, Mah-Rukh fulminates against Norwegians' obsession with the Pakistani custom of arranged marriages, which flies in the face of Norwegian modernity and perceived individualism. Most Norwegians refer to it as *tvangsekteskap* (forced marriage). Mah-Rukh deals directly with the issue in *The Bitter Reality* by criticizing the media and Norwegian "experts" of white cultural supremacy for not listening to the Pakistanis themselves. That is a trend that is changing slightly, and Mah-Rukh is currently invited across the country to speak about her book and her experiences.

Norwegians also force racial heritage on Mah-Rukh as her primary identity. *The Souls of Black Folk,* written in 1903 by W. E. B. DuBois, captures the dual identity that Mah-Rukh depicts: "It is a peculiar sensation, this double-consciousness, this sense of always looking at one's self through the eyes of others, of measuring one's soul by the tape of a world that looks on in amused contempt and pity. One forever feels his two-ness—an American, a Negro; two souls, two thoughts, two unreconciled strivings, two warring ideals in one dark body, whose dogged strength alone keeps it from being torn asunder" (1997, 615).

Mah-Rukh tells her story of belonging to one nation but identifying with two. She is a Norwegian with strong family, language, and religious ties to Pakistan. In her book, she states that she cannot choose between the two extremely different countries to which she belongs. She is a Norwegian of Pakistani descent, a heritage to which she consents. Her self-perception falls in line with the pluralist theory of minority integration, which argues that "minorities can maintain their distinctive subcultures and simultaneously interact with relative equality in the larger society" (Parrillo 1994, 61), which was the focus of DuBois's reflections, too.

Norway has a very short and finite history of immigration. In the early 1970s, Norway needed cheap labor. The laborers came from around the world until 1975, when Norway shut its borders to immigrants who did not come from northern Europe. That year is to Norway more significant than 1924, with its restrictions on immigration, is to the United States. Today, the two ways to settle in Norway are either to be granted political asylum or to seek family reunification. Pakistanis, the largest and oldest immigrant group in Norway, tend to arrange marriages so that there is a constant flow of new Pakistanis, primarily to Oslo, and only to certain, primarily eastern, regions of Oslo. Although the numbers are small, Norwegians feel that there has been an invasion of Pakistanis, a response that reflects the homogeneity and insularity of the people.[2]

Since Norway has effectively stopped immigration, I would argue that Mah-Rukh is a postethnic Norwegian in a country that never gave itself a chance to become multicultural *(flerkulturell),* which is the most commonly used word in Norwegian debate about immigrants.[3] In *Postethnic America: Beyond Multiculturalism,* David A. Hollinger argues that multiculturalism has outgrown itself because it is primarily an anxious defense to maintain a fixed cultural identity in a hostile or merely different environment (1995, 2). Mah-Rukh writes that she is continually emotionally on guard (Ali 1997, 109), but her wariness stems from the cruel and unintentional slurs she encounters regularly. Her defensiveness, however, is not grounded in ascertaining a fixed cultural identity. Her parents lovingly support her and her brothers as they negotiate different cultures to create an identity that works for them as a new kind of Norwegian. Hollinger claims that postethnicism "defends certain elements of multiculturalism" (1995, 3) and grows out of its cosmopolitan element, which "promotes multiple identities, emphasizes the dynamic and changing character of many groups, and is responsive to the potential for creating new cultural combinations" (3–4). Yes, Mah-Rukh Ali is multicultural in that she is both Pakistani by heritage and Norwegian by birth. But I see her more as postethnic because she claims both identities and sees herself as creating a new cultural combination. She and I have never met, but we have corresponded intensely, and my sense is that she cherishes the social order and *de jure* egalitarianism that predominate in Norway. Still, while remaining devoted to family, she seems much more individualistic and aggressively articulate than most Norwegian teens.

Even though Norway is a modern country with an emphasis on the Romantic idea of self in private matters and a lingering sense of the communitarian values of the Englightenment in public issues, it is still a very conformist country. In a 1933 novel, Aksel Sandemose captured the national ethos when he coined the term "Janteloven." This "rule of Jante" is a code of conformity that Norwegians internalize from infancy. Jante is the name of Sandemose's small fictitious town where the people must not feel superior to other townspeople or that they are smarter or more capable: "Creative and inventive talents are seen as a threat to overall equality" (Avant and Knutsen 1993, 5). The solidarity and caring that such an ethos fosters help create an orderly society. Norway is orderly, and Norwegians are complacent. It is this complacency and self-congratulatory attitude that I believe Mah-Rukh refers to when she describes Norwegians as perfect. When I first read her descriptions of "perfect" Norwegians, I thought she was venting adolescent anger. But the conformity and concomitant complacency can make Norwegian chauvinism sound as if the country is perfect.

Postcolonialists may be interested in Mah-Rukh Ali's text for its depiction of one girl's experiences and its implicit description of Norwegians. For example, the media was not thrilled with Mah-Rukh's description of *hadj,* the pilgrimage to Mecca, which she made when she was twelve. In particular, one journalist was incensed by her naïve idealization of Mecca and her religion. Didn't she know, for example, how *shari'a,* the law of the Koran, suppresses women? I think her critics missed the point. First, I sense that her most important experience there was feeling completely accepted. She could let down her defensiveness, which is her constant mode in Norway. Malcolm X similarly describes being flabbergasted at the sense of equality he experienced in Mecca. Second, all the world's major religions are patriarchal while they simultaneously profess equality between the genders in the private and spiritual arenas. Finally, a pilgrimage encourages a limpid state of mind that is free from the clutter of everyday life, including politics. So, I read her account of *hadj* as an accurate description of her experiences and respond to its rather clear message of how liberating, euphoric even, it feels to be accepted, since Norwegians are not renowned for being accepting of difference.

Patrick Williams and Laura Chrisman claim:

"Colonial discourse analysis" . . . still tends to position colonial/impe-
rial subjectivity as having epistemological and ontological primacy. . . .
What has been less explored is the extent to which the subaltern may
have played a constitutive rather than a reflective role in colonial and
domestic imperial discourse and subjectivity. Rather than being that
other onto which the coloniser projects a previously constituted subjectivity and knowledge, native presences, locations, and political resistance need to be further theorised as having a determining or primary role in colonial discourses. (1994, 16)

There are only two generations of immigrants in Norway, and Norwegian studies might benefit from looking at the presence of the "Other"
in the dominant culture.[4] *The Bitter Reality* is a serious contribution by a
young woman regarded as the "Other" in her homeland. In the following translation of her work, I have incorporated, in bold, chapter titles
where I have translated continously from one chapter's end through the
beginning of the next chapter. Throughout, I have indicated the page
numbers in parentheses of the original book. I have selected passages that
show Mah-Rukh's sense of self as she depicts her family, school, the
larger Norway, and, finally, religion. Prejudice marginalizes her, yet she
is extremely centered in herself, in her supportive family, in her religion,
in her writing, and, currently, in her politics. Despite the title of her
book, she is optimistic that Norwegians will become more tolerant and
inclusive.

Unlike Hillary Carlip's *Girl Power* (1995), touted on television by
Oprah Winfrey to help give voice to American girls, *The Bitter Reality* is
written by a girl who uses her voice to introduce the vantage point of
the very people who are the subject of so much public debate in Norway. She challenges traditional Norwegians to recognize the variety
within their own borders: "A world of multiple cultures requires not
just that people tolerate differences. They must, like it or not, tolerate in
the sense of enduring the effect of those differences. This may seem a
slight difference, but it turns out to require an extraordinarily difficult
change of attitude, especially for those accustomed to the assumption
that their world is all that matters" (Lemert 1999, 666).

Mah-Rukh stands out because of her physical appearance. Yet she
is a Norwegian, and she is a significant person who can help Norway

redefine itself to fit its self-image as a progressive and altruistic nation. Mah-Rukh Ali emphasizes that integration is a two-way process, challenging immigrants and Norwegians alike to take responsibility in creating equality and harmony.

THE BITTER REALITY

When I started school, the teachers asked with great interest where I came from. I always started my long story: "I was born in Norway, but my parents were born in Pakistan . . . then they moved here . . . and then one day I was born." I clearly remember their angry and stern looks when they replied, "Well, then, you are a Pakistani." "Oh, well," I thought. "I guess I am a Pakistani since my teacher says so, because I have been taught that the teachers are right. Everybody says so, at school and at home." Even though I did not understand much of this as a six or seven year old, I accepted what the teacher had decided about me. It felt wrong, and I often thought that it would be much simpler to be either Pakistani or a "real" Norwegian. As I got older, I saw that there was not much difference between the other "totally" Norwegian kids in my class and me. The only difference was that my name was Mah-Rukh and my skin was dark and not Maria with light skin. When I started to cut out the story and say that I was a Norwegian girl, people were skeptical; "But you're dark-skinned!" A teacher (!) made this observation. I was not being accepted as Norwegian because of my dark skin. Did my skin color decide my identity? (9)

Who am I? Yes, who am I? . . .

Am I two persons in one body? One according to society and one as I want to be and actually am? Lots of people experience this split, and it is the situation of many immigrant children in Norway. Their search for identity collides with society's view of them. The prejudice around them is too much. Who am I?

If I plan to use a Norwegian yardstick to answer this question, I have two answers, each terribly extreme.

Either I have to be a "typical" Pakistani girl who goes to Koran school every day after school, wears baggy pants and long shirts down to her knees, munches raw garlic, and doesn't speak a word of Norwegian, (10) much less understand anything Norwegian. Yes, then people say that I am a Pakistani girl because it is this image that Norwegians probably conjure up when you mention Pakistani girls. But, on the other hand, if I want to be a Norwegian girl, then I have to be totally ignorant about Pakistan. I must not say that I have a Pakistani background and am proud of it; instead, I am supposed to trample on Pakistani culture. And, most important, I have to tell Norwegians how beautiful Norway is with its stunning natural surroundings. If I want to brownnose even more to make them happy, I can brag a little about them and tell them how clever and pretty they are. Then I have to smile and nod to everything they tell me. I must not disagree or discuss anything with them because they consider that degrading. . . .

But what about me who wants to find a place in the middle? I, who was born here but have a Pakistani background. I want to be accepted as any Norwegian girl without having to give up the cultural background I was born into since my parents were born in Pakistan and later came to Norway, the country where my brothers and I were born. The country with inhabitants who prevent me from discovering my multicultural identity.

I cannot deny that I have roots in Pakistan, nor do I want to because I have no desire to believe that I am someone that I am not or let others think so. (11) But why should that keep me from being accepted as a Norwegian girl? But often Norwegians want to hear that I am Pakistani.

I do not want to be an immigrant child split between two cultures and used as a shuttlecock between different countries. I love both countries and appreciate the positive in each, and I am very proud of my foothold and background in both nations.

Hence, my situation is impossible—I cannot choose.

In my search for identity, I have learned a lot from my parents, of whom, incidentally, I am extremely proud. They have given me tremendous stability—as intellectuals—and helped me to become who I am and always will be. But shall I grant society at large the right to label me? It cannot accept that I am Norwegian. It does not seem as if Norway wants its immigrant children. Does that mean we are not Norwegian?

A very important question arises: what is it to be Norwegian? Am I Norwegian only if my family is Norwegian? Do I have to have blond hair, blue eyes? Am I Norwegian if I am a Norwegian citizen and belong here? Or don't nationality and belonging count, just personality, looks, and opinions? (12) . . .

Really, is a good Norwegian one who eats only porridge, fish balls, and other typically Norwegian foods at home, wears the national costume every holiday, and who hikes in the woods and fields every week-end? Somebody who cultivates typically Norwegian, old traditions? (13) . . . The reality is that you are considered a Norwegian as long as you do not stick out because of clothes, skin color, food habits, or other distinctive characteristics. It is still not possible to have a different skin color and a different faith and simultaneously be Norwegian. Otherwise, there are many such unwritten rules for being Norwegian, rules nobody admits to but that many immigrant children experience. For example, I am Norwegian if I do something well, but if I mess up, then all of a sudden I am an immigrant. Can we thereby deduce that everything im-migrants do is wrong and that what Norwegians do is totally perfect?

Because Norwegians *are* perfect; their thoughts and actions are per-fect. They have a solution for everything, like how to get rid of immi-grant garbage. Norway is a perfect country with a perfect population, white and pure, with only happy carefree people. They don't need im-migrant rowdies who are just criminals that will soil this clean white population with colorful faces and traditions. Those people who pollute the air with their strong and spicy foods. Of course, you have to stay away from those immigrants. Immigrants ruin the safe conditions of Norway, it is touted, because they are terribly criminal. This peaceful country is not used to such criminality. There would be no thieves in Norway if there were no immigrants here. A lot of Norwegians actually believe this (14) . . .

When I was six and a half, my parents applied to have me enrolled in school since I was born at the beginning of 1982—just a few days after my classmates who were born in 1981. This application to start school early was denied by a director of education. Norwegian was my first language and I had no problems with it. Still, I had to take several tests to see if I was fit to attend school. When I passed these tests, my kindergarten teacher wrote a secret letter to the people who were decid-ing my case. They wrote that I did not speak Norwegian sufficiently well! After many more tests, they were shown to be completely wrong. (19) . . .

The drama at school continued, where it took a different turn. Nor-wegian 2, that is, Norwegian for non-native speakers—or dark-skinned pupils—was offered into the higher grade levels. Even I, born and raised here, had to take these classes for a long time before my Norwegian lan-guage skills were tested. I never had problems with Norwegian; still, it was a tacit rule that children with parents from a different language background could not participate in the regular classes. (21) . . .

Because I protested against this instruction, my abilities in Norwegian were finally tested in a reasonable and professional manner. (22) . . .

Almost everywhere in Norway, I am regarded as an immigrant; even my closest Norwegian friends have asked, "What's it like being an immigrant?" How on earth am I supposed to know? I have never in my life immigrated to any country. I was born as a Norwegian girl, and that is what I have always been.

So what is the problem? Yes, I have dark skin, claim an "unknown" religion, and bear an unusual name in Norway. I am a mysterious being from afar, used as an exotic doll. . . . I want to be multicultural; and I want to belong to the dominant culture. When is it going to be my turn to say who I am and what I stand for? When will I have that "right"? (26) . . . I am a completely new kind of Norwegian girl, and there will be many of us in the future, which just has to be accepted.

Since Norwegian society increasingly consists of different cultures, everybody must be allowed to remain who he or she is. And, since people from so many cultures are becoming Norwegian, Christian values can no longer be the sole foundation for Norwegian ethics. Then, Muslims could not become Norwegian. People used the word "integration," but if it is going to be used in the future, its real meaning cannot be misused. Integration is a two-way process, where both parties have to contribute and sacrifice something to achieve desired social goals. It has to be a two-way street, and therefore, people cannot simply exclaim that immigrants must adapt themselves. People must stop looking at something from one side only. Everybody must develop and move toward a more open position where it is not just immigrants who labor at becoming integrated but where Norwegians also (27) can expand their understanding of their new compatriots and understand their cultural heritage. (28) . . .

"Next, Ali . . . Maru . . . crap! The dentist is waiting," said the dental hygienist with a laugh before she followed me to an X-ray room. "Sit down," she practically commanded and crammed some hard plastic bits into my mouth. I opened up and the bits hurt, so I tried to shuffle them into a comfortable position with my fingertips. "No . . . You've got to stop touching that thing in your mouth!" she said with a decidedly angry look then asked if I had been doing gymnastics, since I was carrying a sports bag.

"I came from PE," I mumbled with the piece in my mouth.

She pursed her lips and said, "Physical education is the same as gym in Norwegian!" and threw in that I needed to learn the language. I was shocked by her vehemence but had no chance to answer before she closed the door and went behind it to x-ray my teeth. When she returned, she quickly walked back and forth to adjust the X-ray machine. After a while, she removed the pieces in my mouth, and I moved my jaw after I sensed it was okay. "Where do you come from? Obviously not Norway," (29) she said with a smile that seemed both cruel and contemptuous.

"Yes, I come from Norway," I said firmly and quickly got out of the chair, grabbed my bag, and was on my way out of the room when I heard her say, "Jeez, these immigrants," as if she were calming herself.

This is an example of my interfaces with the surrounding world. I have gotten used to it because I constantly stand out. This is just one example of what I encounter daily in the most unbelievable places. Who would have anticipated such an experience at the dentist's? Every time I meet nasty people, the first question that pops to mind is, "Was this person mean to me because I am a 'Pakistani,' or are there other reasons?" But, after a while, I discover what kind of person it was because a xenophobe never manages to hide prejudice for long. Still, it is not the case if a person disparages me that I call the individual a racist because I do not do that at all.

What I and many other so-called immigrant children in Norway suffer from is the same kind of hatred, a hatred that cannot be explained in words because it has to be understood physically. I have to be twice as strong, twice as brave to survive the day without anxiety or fear because there is no place where I might not hear degrading comments or experience prejudice. (30) . . .

When I was in the fourth grade, a school friend said, "Pakkis [the derogatory Norwegian term for a Pakistani] stink! Can you believe all the garlic and curry they eat? It's gross. Their food sucks. When I walk by someone's house, I can tell if Norwegians or Pakkis live there." I turned around shocked when I heard her say this stuff to another kid in class. She looked down and actually looked kind of innocent.

"What are you saying?" I asked, dazed and dumbfounded.

"Well," she tried to calm me, "of course, I'm not talking about you. I've been to your house lots of times and you guys are Norwegian, so your house doesn't stink at all. But I'm talking about Pakkis; you know, the kid in 4B . . ."; she continued and launched into another story about a so-called Pakkis girl. Totally stunned, I returned to my desk and felt some unwanted tears in my eyes, which I quickly dried, and ran out of the room as soon as the bell rang.

When I got home, the house was quiet, as usual. Mom and Dad were at work, and just one of my brothers sat watching Cartoon Network. I could hear him giggle, but he didn't notice that I had come home. "Hi, Awais, I'm home!" I said somewhat sadly, closed the door, walked into the living room, and sat down next to him.

"Oh, hi Mah-Rukh. Did you have a good day at school?" he asked as he continued to watch the funny Tom and Jerry cartoon. (52)

"No, school is never *good*," I answered jokingly, as anybody else might have said. Later that evening, when we had chicken and rice in curry sauce, I looked skeptically at the food. "Am I a Pakkis if I eat this stuff?" I thought aloud.

"What are you saying?" my mother asked with surprise as she dished out some food for my little brother, Sohaib. Finally, she got the whole story out of me. She immediately contacted my homeroom teacher, who promised that she would do something about the situation the next day. In the morning, I didn't want to go to school and made up lots of excuses not to have to go.

"But, Mom, I really do have a headache." But no way. Mom had decided that I was going to school that day, and Dad agreed completely. At school, everything went as usual, but when the bell rang, the other girl, Anita, and I were taken into the hall. After a long talk with the teacher, Anita started crying and also apologized. Suddenly, I was struck by the question of whether it was she or I who should be crying.

After that day, I never heard her say anything similar, at least not when I was around. But that doesn't mean that everybody has stopped because, to this day, I hear myself being called "Pakkis" but only as fooling around. Otherwise, I have also heard that I am the exception to certain things, as Anita had indicated. If people talked about what was wrong with immigrants, they always said, "But you're not like that." Lots of people I know have heard similar things. Are all people exceptions to the stereotype? After all, if I am acceptable in certain situations, then aren't also the thousands of children who are almost like me? (53)

When I was little, the world seemed peaceful. With time, I learned from my surroundings that I had to wish for peace on earth. It became natural for me to say, "I want peace on earth . . . and a new doll with a pink dress and a little candy and . . ." But peace on earth became the answer I consistently thought of as the right answer when somebody asked me what I wished for. I didn't know the meaning of the word, but I said it because I had learned it was the right thing to say. In kindergarten, books and songs became interesting. I believed everything I heard and saved it as knowledge. One day I saw the sentence: The children—the black children in Africa—we must feel sorry for them. I had to thank God for everything I had. The children in Africa didn't have what we did in Norway, and they never experienced happiness. Through stories and songs about Hottentots, I learned how wild and warlike and poor they were, which gave us the feeling of being the best. But I also discovered that I was not among the best . . . my friends were the best—my white friends. I was brown. And that's when it started . . . when my real interests awoke and I discovered that nobody was perfect . . . and that the children in Africa were lucky, too, because they also had a childhood like everybody else. I discovered that all children around the world are equally innocent, sweet, and sensitive and that we all need love and that African children also are happy; they had something I was missing, and I had something they were missing. We were equal. I can still regard children as innocent. They learn; they are open to opinions and are easily influenced. They should be the last to be victimized and used as guinea pigs in public debates where extremists want their views made public. Children are lives, genuinely valuable lives that are being exposed to actions that benefit no one. (54) . . .

The Attitudes of Norwegians

In May 1995, a survey was taken of Norwegians' attitudes toward immigrants. Everyone was anxious to read the results, which were a tremendous disappointment, especially for immigrants, because one in four Norwegians was opposed to immigrants. This fact was hard, painful, and difficult for thousands of people to swallow, including me.

I was a very small, virtually invisible, girl in a big disappointed mass of people who finally could show the world their despair. A girl's feelings had become part of a game in which the large "perfect" Norwegian population had thrown the first die. There I was, brokenhearted. I smiled, pretending everything was okay; but, inside me, I wept.

It was raining outside, it thundered—the heavens were crying. A tear rolled down my cheek and the newspaper looked mean as if it were making faces at me.

Of what importance were these small feelings among those of all the others? Nobody was in the least interested to hear what I, a person of feelings, thought about these issues. I simply played a big role in the research. No, all I could do was look up at the gray sky, imagining where all the politicians sat in a row and held their hour-long speeches— because it was, after all, the turn of the high and mighty to respond. Now, they had the opportunity to score (55) in another game, earning vote after vote before the elections. Maybe it wasn't such a bad idea to have these immigrants in the country, after all. "Now they can be useful" was a thought that crossed the mind as a satisfied look crossed the face of one of our most "clever" politicians. But there I sat, tired of looking up.

I wanted to rise, to express my views up there in the sky. Then, I sat down again and looked up, but this time the heavens were clear blue. This time, there were no politicians. On the contrary, everything was clearer than ever before. I sat there anyway with a small handkerchief, a pen, and a piece of paper. Would I write on this sheeet, or would I draw my feelings?

Soon a morning came when the sun was shining and the sky was clear, much clearer than ever before. I fetched the paper, and that day it actually smiled at me. I looked at it and saw a small feeling on a large piece of paper. But it was real! On the front page there was a bold head-line, "Hurt by the Nation" and a picture of this invisible girl who now could be heard by all. For I had lifted my voice and it could be heard in every corner of the land. I reached those who liked and who didn't like what I was saying. And, the reactions? Oh, yes; they responded in droves. Letters, flowers, calls, and visits—there were many responses. But, as the saying goes, "all good things come to an end," a truth I came to learn rather quickly.

Many of the letters I received were so encouraging that I scarcely could believe the survey. Surprisingly, real Norwegians met me with sympathy. Many said that I was brave and that I had to persevere. But I also received letters stating that I was nothing but a Pakkis who should return to (56) "where the pepper grows" [a Norwegian idiom for "go to hell"]. They called me a sewer rat and other things not fit for print, which didn't bother me too much on the day after all the encouragement. Still, there were people who wanted to hurt me.

On a rainy autumn morning, I got up and plodded to the bathroom. As I was brushing my teeth, I suddenly noticed the brick wall outside our house and was stunned when I read the tagging, the thick fat writing in huge letters: "Keep Norway pure. Send blacks home. White power." A few swastikas were also sprayed on the sides. The toothpaste started to burn in my mouth, but I continued to stand there totally stunned. I thought about what to do, because I absolutely could not tolerate such a trashed wall outside my house. It was raining and everything seemed sad and gray. I went outside to get the newspaper but was again surprised by "White Power" and another swastika on our mailbox! And, when I re-entered the house, I saw our living room wall had been tagged with "Go home, Pakkis!" The newspaper slipped out of my hand and tears welled in my eys. They fell on the newspaper like raindrops. They were but two drops among the thousand falling from the sad sky. "Oh, my God," I thought out loud. The large, gray house wall seemed so empty, so empty of emotion. The roses outside had withered and seemed to bow to the rain. My hair was drenched and water streaked my face. I was so shocked that I just stood there, incredulous, with my mouth wide open. The newspaper was lying on the ground, while I felt my whole life had crumbled. Were there really people who felt this way about me? I still remember the exact day, the exact hour, the exact minute, the exact second. Everything stopped that moment; everything around me became insignificant (57). I wasan't scared; on the contrary, I felt something very strange—anxiety and hatred for the person who had done this to me. I wanted to say something bad, something intended to hurt, throw things on the floor, destroy everything within reach just to release my emotions. I felt I could see straight into a hard and insensitive heart, and it was awful. (58) . . .

First the whole family discussed the matter, and then my brothers and I went to our room to talk about what we wanted to do. My brothers [aged eleven, eight, and three at the time (61); Mah-Rukh was thirteen (62)] asked the most innocent questions while we were sitting in the room: "Why did they do this to us? Don't they like us? I thought we were Norwegian. That's what you have told us. Aren't we, after all?" I could answer only two of these questions. We had not done anything wrong because it couldn't have been wrong to express yourself when one-fourth of the country's population had expressed their hatred for you. And the second thing I could answer was that we are Norwegians regardless of what the Nazis think about us. This is our country; this is the country we have given our hearts to, but still . . .

The four of us sat there trying to figure out how to get rid of the graffiti. Should we just wait for a sunny day and paint over the swastikas ourselves, thereby pretending nothing had happened? Or should we try to make something positive out of this?

After a long discussion, we decided to invite two party leaders from opposite political poles, one for immigration policies and the other against them. We made this decision because we wanted to see two different opinions work side-by-side for something positive for once. I felt good and sensed that the long corridor I was running in was coming to an end where there was a door, a colorful door, behind which the politicians were sitting. (60) I dreamed that this time they were sitting there as humans who later would paint over the swastika, saying that the racists who had done this to us would be punished thoroughly. "It's terrible what you, Norwegians like us, have to experience," they said sympathetically as they painted and discussed how to solve this problem. However, the reality was completely different. Both of the politicians showed up, but only one would paint over the swastika. Only one of the politicians would accept that the culprits had to be racists?! The other told me what a burden I was to Norway and left my brothers and me with the swastika on the wall. (61) . . .

Here in Norway, "the immigrant issue" is extremely popular; there are constant debates about immigrants on TV, on the radio, and in the papers. Everybody is invited as a guest or expert in this field, whether the person is a racist or antiracist, but the immigrants themselves are rarely represented. The point is not to inform; the point is to show the picture of immigrants that Norwegians want to see—kind, stupid, uninformed, poor at Norwegian. Or, to phrase it in good Norwegian, they are genuine fools. This is the image perpetuated in TV debates and in the media. An immigrant is supposed to nod and smile at everything Norwegians say and do. (65) . . .

Today, only 2 percent of Norway's population is so-called multicultural. If you talk to some of these immigrants you will find that a large number are engaged with social issues and want to be heard but are denied. (66) . . .

Girls, immigrant girls, is the hottest topic of them all. Is the fate of girls the weak point of immigrants? Is it the weakest point among the thousands of other problems that we hear they have? What is life like for these girls? What is their fate? How much education are they entitled to? Or are they entitled to any at all? Why are they married off at such a young age? Why are their parents so horrible to them? Is there something wrong with Pakistani girls? Do immigrant parents really not feel for their children? Is it really true that they can kill their own children just to obtain dignity? And what kind of dignity is it?

There are many questions all at once, big and heavy for some people, easy and light for others, and repetitive and boring for still others. Some immigrant girls have been married off and suffer, but most immigrant girls—including me—have almost felt like these girls because we get so many questions due to the color of our skin. Quite frankly, I'm—mildly put—tired of all the skeptical and victimizing comments people make to me. It all just seems like a stereotype—an empty stereotype. It's an image that is painted without color or feelings, because the person it concerns does not paint it. This is (75) the bitter reality, a reality that becomes a part of everyday life, making everything so much more complicated. (76) . . .

Obviously there are immigrant women who struggle with the kinds of problems that the media present, but they are a very small minority. What sometimes irritates me and usually hurts me is that most people anticipate that I am like those women—I and the thousands of girls like me. Journalists who have known me many years have asked my parents if they have any wedding plans for me. That is the barrier I want to smash. I do not want to be victimized, and I do not want to be met with sympathy because of my color or my background. I am proud of both, and I do not fit a mold. (83) . . .

Marriage, sweethearts, love are the most interesting topics for the stereotype tabloids. What girl with an immigrant background can say truthfully that she has never been asked about these things? From my own experience, I can say that not once but hundreds of times I have been asked, "Have you been in love?" "Do you have a boyfriend?" "Are your parents planning your wedding?" "Are you going to marry a Pakistani or a Norwegian?" I have even heard journalists ask "experts" on Pakistanis when it can be expected that Pakistani girls will start having Norwegian boyfriends.

The question arises: Is that what acceptance requires? Is this the question that is the big hurdle? *When* a girl with a different background gets a Norwegian boyfriend?! The media make this the big issue and instigate the debate. Why play up the issue and create more problems than the already existing ones?

Then they turn to religion: equality and Islam. Who doesn't get excited about this issue?

People cry out that there is no equality in Islam, without exploring (84) the issue. Islam is actually the religion with the strongest and clearest guidelines about equality. Still, people blame Islam. Obviously, underdeveloped countries that struggle with much more than social problems will postpone and not prioritize such human issues. Still, people cannot blame their culture or their religion. Women in Pakistan, for example, struggle and have struggled for years. Have they achieved anything? Yes, they had a woman prime minister. (85) . . .

People disregard who I am because it is my skin that tells them the most about me. When they learn that I am a Muslim, myths are also set in motion, because then all kinds of images about my everyday life as a Muslim girl crop up in their heads. Then, they start victimizing me because I am a Muslim. This happens in my everyday life when I am not allowed to tell about myself and when I am not allowed to tell what and who I am without being prejudged. (96) On to the second problem: not only am I a Muslim, but I am also a Muslim *girl*. Then, people start imagining all of the daily obstacles I must face simply to survive. People have decided in advance how I must be treated at home, how I think, and how my private life must be . . . society has already decided everything about me. They want me to fall . . . fall into their preconceived belief in how I am and what my home life is like. "That's how things are, just admit it!" they say. And, again, they lay the whole blame on Islam, on the kind of religion it is. They play with people's emotions and what is most important to them. Why do people act that way? (97) . . .

I have also had a period when I was asking myself who I was, why I was a Muslim. . . . We talked openly about this issue at home, where I could ask all my questions, regardless of whether they were stupid or not. It was an environment that encouraged me to talk and that made me feel that my identity was at home. But that was not enough. I had been on innumerable vacations to Pakistan, where I gained a different perspective about the country than I did in Norway. I saw people like me, of the same faith; I met my grandparents, as my friends did in Norway; I had my relatives here in Pakistan. A big part of me, of my identity, belonged to this country—Pakistan; on the other hand, a large part of me was also in Norway.

My parents succeeded in clarifying this split for me. They outlined for me where I belonged, a sketch that I compared to the drawing in my heart. Over time, I realized that the outline was right. Parents must look at their children not as they want them to be but as they are, in my case as a Norwegian. If parents make that mistake, they set up their own children to fail by confusing the children, who start to withdraw into themselves, compare themselves to others, and doubt their own parents.

Pakistan is my country, but so is Norway! That is why I have, over time, become able to stand on my own feet and talk about Pakistan based on my own experiences. It is an open country with friendly people. That is why I am dying to (101) speak my mind when people talk about their concepts of Pakistan. Those who have not been to the land of their foreparents have no chance to make up their own minds, because then it is society at large that expounds grandly about what they think is information about, for example, Pakistan. But I have been there and found my identity. That is why I have managed to survive the media, the press, society, and all my surroundings. I have managed to look up to the heavens and have not needed to look down because I know my identity.

I did not find my identity just in Pakistan but also in Saudi Arabia when I went on a *hadj*—a pilgrimage to Mecca. What did I find there? I found much of myself there. I was not part of a minority as in Norway but in the majority, part of the community. This experience is among the most fantastic ones in my life. (102) . . .

The trip was filled with excitement and expectations of Mecca. Even while on the trip, I noticed something magical between people. First, everybody was dressed the same way. Everybody on the plane wore the same white clothing. Men wrapped a white cloth around themselves and most had shaved their heads. Women wore long white garments and white shawls on their heads. You couldn't tell the difference between rich and poor or any difference between the sexes. Sometimes men fed children in their laps, other times Muslim women did the same. Deep inside me, I thought, "These are genuine Muslims, real Muslim families."

It's called *hadj*. It is a special time when Muslims try to visit Mecca. It is the dream of every Muslim to do it once a lifetime. Here I sat, on my way to this enchanted place. . . .

Nobody quarreled at the airport; people helped each other. Nobody shoved each other by the baggage claim. Everybody was kind and helpful to other people (104).

When we were on the bus and had to register, everything was different from what I had experienced in England and Norway. Here we were offered seats. Mostly women and elderly people were sitting, while men and boys stood.

If there were problems, people helped even if they didn't know the circumstances. That is how it was: everybody helped everybody. It seemed as if everybody knew each other from before. More than one million people were on a *hadj,* and the only thing they did was be kind to each other. If people went to get a drink of water, they asked the person next over if he or she also wanted some, if they could help satisfy the person's thirst.

The whole trip was like this. What I experienced was truly awesome. People were angelically kind and didn't want to hurt anybody. They thought only of doing good. They shared with everyone. This was so different from what I was accustomed to. Equality—they should have seen the equality, all those people so preoccupied with it. This is the country they should see to appreciate what equality implies. What glory these women lived in, which was their right no matter how they had been treated. This right they had in the kingdom of the Muslims. This is how they wanted to live—without blood, conflict, or hate. A peaceful world with peaceful, involved, alive people who carried the voices of those who are never heard.

Everything was harmonious, everything was peaceful, and everything was fellowship.

Harmony was their religion, peace was their religion, and fellowship was also their religion. Everything that was most dear and most important to them, there (105) was their religion. They had an intimate and personal relationship to their religion. The religion that had become the new nemesis of the western world, that was their religion. The religion that had become a threat to the whole world. Theirs was the religion that was debated and written about by pundits and laypeople who didn't know a thing about the subject except for a few personal experiences.

In such a world, this religion lives. Here people could live out their faith open-heartedly without fear of attack from the outside world. . . .

For the first time in my life, I experienced a tremendous sense of community, not just among three to four people, but among many thousands, millions of people who (106) shared an identity, namely a religion, a way of life. Here were all kinds of people, men and women, white and black. People from all over the world were gathered here; nobody was cruel to another; all wore the same clothes; boys and men were alike; and girls and women were alike. Nobody stood out, and everyone was part of the community. I have never experienced such unity. . . . Everybody was kind and everybody shared. Most importantly, everybody shared the same connection to Mecca. Religion gave people fellowship. No sorrows were visible, only joy, a joy that everyone shared. This was a completely different world, a world of joy, a world where Islam was manifest, where Muslims could be seen in their wholeness and as they were meant to be. (107) . . .

It was wonderful to let go of my feelings instead of thinking about the opinions of other people. Here I could be myself and practice Islam as I wanted to, and that was liberating.

For me, and for those like me, life in Norway is like a game of chess. I have to think a thousand times before I make a move not to be attacked by somebody. I constantly get caught in uncomfortable situations and am labeled "on the defensive." I always have to be on the defensive and can never speak out freely on an issue. I get jostled here and there and people use me and my words as they will. Sometimes it has been so extreme that the meaning of a sentence is the opposite of my intention. (109) . . .

The whole trip was characterized by happiness and surprise, which gave meaning to life. I discovered and was happy to learn that here were people from around the world and that there were more of us. Even though I was the only Muslim girl in my class at school, I was not the only Muslim girl here. Of course I had heard the statistics, but I never anticipated so many "like" people, in the sense that they had the same goal in life. This was a comfort because now I didn't just hear it but experienced it as well. And I saw with my own eyes. This was one of the greatest moments in my life because so many of my questions were answered. I experienced so many revelations on otherwise closed areas. Most importantly, I discovered the commonality between me and others. I saw that I was not alone. I was not abnormal, and I was an important, very important, person for everybody else. This was an important experience for me because, so often, I felt alone. I felt that I was the only one in the whole wide world who thought and felt as I—the only one called "pig" and other curses because I was a Muslim and could not eat the same meat as Norwegians. Here, in Mecca, it was not like that. Here, nobody was called "swine": here everybody shared the same eating habits and the same way of dressing. It was important for me to feel that I belonged.

In Norway, I was an immigrant, a Muslim immigrant; I was not one of them. Nor did I belong in Pakistan, the homeland of my parents. It was not my country in all ways even though the people here spoke the same language that I could speak and ate the same food that I could eat. Still, I did not belong, not deep in my heart. (110) These were not the streets where I had played children's games. This was not the school where I made my first friends. This was not the home of my childhood.

But, in Mecca, I belonged to everything. Here were people from around the world, white and black, old and young, female and male, rich and poor. But all were Muslims and all felt at home. I had an unforgettable journey. It transformed me and shaped me into the person I am today. It gave me courage, morals, and independence. It is a trip that has characterized my life. It is a trip that showed me my rights as a Muslim girl. It is a trip that gave me true answers to true questions. It is a trip that helped me discover myself. (111) . . .

There is so much to think about. Everything sort of hangs together, all the problems. But a problem has a solution; otherwise, it wouldn't be a problem! And if there is a solution to every problem, that means . . . that means that everything is possible, nothing is impossible. It is the light in people, the faith in their goodness that must not die. There is always hope, always; therefore, people must see and believe in goodness. As long as people do not give up, there is hope; but as soon as they lose their faith, hope is also extinguished and there will be no more hope. You always have to work your way through problems. With hope on your side, to make it through and achieve your dreams. (150) . . .

The problem is not dissension; the problem is too little ability to understand. The key is understanding, mutual understanding and respect. Respect for each other's opinions, vantage points, and personalities.

I sigh deeply; it has been a heavy day with many heavy thoughts running through my mind. "Yes," I sigh softly, plod on, look at the snow, close the zipper of my jacket some more, and tuck my mittens under the cuffs. "Well, well," I sigh again.

It is not cold anymore; I don't quite know why except the candle in me, the real warmth, is lit, and I know that for a fact.

My black hair is flowing freely in the air. I walk on and soon disappear in the streets of Oslo. But my thoughts remain; they do not disappear. I think and think. I am thinking about the spring . . . (160)

NOTES

Mah-Rukh wants to thank Professor Elisabeth Sandberg for all her help with the translation of her book, *The Bitter Reality,* and for taking the initiative of joining this anthology project. Mah-Rukh also wants to thank her parents, Syed and Yasmin Mujahid, for being role models and for giving her the love and encouragement only parents can give.

Elisabeth wants to thank Woodbury University for granting her a sabbatical in the fall of 1997 to return to her homeland to interview Pakistani women immigrants; the Center for Feminist Research at the University of Oslo for the beautiful office and all the technical and practical support during the sabbatical; and her husband, Franklin Donnell, for his company during her first major visit to her home town, Oslo, eighteen years after she emigrated to the United States.

1. When I read her book the first time, I was envious of her fluency in Norwegian because it has always felt as a second language to me. Norwegian is her native language as English has become mine. (Because my father was a Norwegian career diplomat, I had lived in Norway for less than two years before I returned at the age of sixteen.)

2. Approximately 230,000 people, or 5.3 percent of the total population of 4.4 million, have two foreign-born parents and are considered immigrants. These numbers include immigrants who have Norwegian passports. Pakistanis, numbering 19,500, constitute the largest group (Høyre 1999).

3. I have difficulty regarding Norway as a multicultural society because so few residents come from abroad, and those few are segregated primarily in finite regions of Oslo. Mah-Rukh Ali cites 2 percent of Norway's population as being "distantly cultured" *(fjernkulturell)* (66). She also writes that she does not quite understand the words *fjernkulturell* or *fremmedkulturell* (foreignly cultured). Although she does explain that the latter concept is a racist euphemism, the word mystifies her (135). I was shocked when I read particularly the former word in a Norwegian newspaper, because it seemed nonsensical yet hurtful.

4. The following are some central books written by Norwegians on the issue of immigration, which might be useful in theorizing about Norway: Eriksen (1995); Frogner (1997); Johnson (1996); Lie (1986); Lien (1997); Storhaug (1996); and Wikan (1995).

WORKS CITED

Ali, Mah-Rukh. 1997. *Den sure virkeligheten* [*The Bitter Reality*]. Oslo: Tiden.

Avant, Gayle, and Karen Patrick Knutsen. 1993. "Understanding Cultural Differences: Janteloven and Social Conformity in Norway." *Språk & Marked* [*Language and Market*]. Halden: Østfold distriktshøgskole, 3–11.

Basit, Tehmina N. 1997. "I Want More Freedom, but Not Too Much: British Girls and the Dynamism of Family Values." *Gender and Education*. December. [UMI—ProQuest Direct *tsupport@umi.com* 1 April 1999.] 1–22.

Carlip, Hillary, ed. 1995. *Girl Power: Young Women Speak Out*. New York: Warner.

DuBois, W. E .B. 1997. *The Souls of Black Folk*. [1903.] in *The Norton Anthology of African American Literature,* ed. Henry Louis Gates Jr. and Nellie Y. McKay. New York: Norton, 613–740.

Eriksen, Thomas Hylland. 1995. *Det nye fiendebildet* [The new picture of the enemy]. Oslo: Cappelen.

Frogner, Karoline. 1997. *Portrett av en nabo* [Portrait of a neighbor]. Oslo: Cappelen.

Hollinger, David A. 1995. *Postethnic America: Beyond Multiculturalism*. New York: Basic Books.

hooks, bell. 1984. *Feminist Theory: From Center to Margin*. Boston: South End Press.

Høyre—HIT-redaksjonen. 1999. "Demografi."

<http://www.hovre.no/1999/notatutred/innvandrere/innvandrere-1 html>, [accessed 22 May].

Johnson, Øyvind. 1996. *Gode nordmenn* [Good Norwegians]. Oslo: Cappelen.

Lemert, Charles, ed. 1999. *Social Theory: The Multicultural and Classic Readings*. 2nd ed. Boulder: Westview.

Lie, Suzanne Stiver, ed. 1986. *Mellom to kulturer: Kvinnelige innvandrere i Norge* [Between two cultures: Female immigrants in Norway]. Oslo: Universitetsforlaget.

Lien, Inger-Lise. 1997. *Ordet som stempler djevlene: Holdninger blant pakistanere og nordmenn* [The word that identifies the devils: Attitudes among Pakistanis and Norwegians]. Oslo: Aventura.

Parrillo, Vincent N. 1994. *Strangers to These Shores: Race and Ethnic Relations in the United States*. 4th ed. Boston: Allyn and Bacon.

Riaz, Nasim. 1994. *A Comparative Study of Pakistani High School Girls' Education in Oslo*. Oslo: University of Oslo, Educational Research Institute.

Storhaug, Hege. 1996. *Mashallah: En reise blant kvinner i Pakistan* [Mashallah: A journey among women in Pakistan]. Oslo: Aschehoug.

Wikan, Unni. 1995. *Mot en ny norsk underklasse: Innvandrere, kultur og integrasjon* [Toward a new lower class: Immigrants, culture and integration]. Oslo: Gyldendal.

Williams, Patrick, and Laura Chrisman, eds. 1994. *Colonial Discourse and Post-Colonial Theory: A Reader*. New York: Columbia University Press.

· 6 ·

Fighting Shame

A Somali Single Teen Mother in Canada

Ayanna Anamoor and Merlinda Weinberg

Pregnancy and motherhood when coupled with the terms "single" and "teen" shift connotations from positive to negative. Adolescent pregnancy is viewed by many as "highly undesirable" (Orton and Rosenblatt 1993, v), necessitating prevention and intervention. Concomitantly, parenting by single teen mothers has been identified as "children having children" (Pearce 1993, 46), inappropriately engaging in adult behavior, neither developmentally ready for the tasks of parenthood nor economically prepared to meet their responsibilities to the society at large (MacIntyre and Cunningham-Burley 1993, 62). Such characterizations can lead to an individual feeling shamed. Unlike guilt, which pertains more to individual acts than to the person as a whole, shame is the ongoing premise that one is fundamentally bad, inadequate, unworthy, or defective (Fossum and Mason 1986, 5). When the youth in question is also a Somali refugee, racism enters the mix of factors that contribute to feeling ashamed. "Black mothers under 20 . . . provide an example of the intersection of three negative social constructions (black people, teenage mothers, and female-headed households)" (Phoenix 1993, 86). One should add lone mothering to the list of taboos. An adolescent's decision to be a sole mother, like pregnancy, serves "as a condensed symbol for social upheaval associated with gender roles, the role of sex and pleasure, and the inequities of race and socioeconomic class. . . . [It] serves as a stand-in, a convenient displacement of complicated social problems" (Irvine 1994, 7). In this intersection, single teenage mothering is demonized, rather than the poverty and racism that give rise to this experience.

To a large extent, what has been missing from the dominant discourses is the voice of the young women themselves. Both the marginalization and omission in cultural studies of young single mothers are consequences of the interlinked oppressions of race, class, age, and gender. How do single teenage mothers see

97

themselves? Do these young women accept the dominant interpretations of their identity, or do they fight them? What aspects of their experience lead them to feel shame? How do they wage the battle against notions of immorality and inferiority?

Like the anthology as a whole, this chapter attempts to redress the silence of young women and to begin to answer some of these questions. It is an interview with Ayanna,[1] age seventeen, a Somali refugee in Canada. The interview explores her unique development as a shamed but resisting young woman. As a result of extreme persecution as a minority in her country of origin, the ongoing racism in Canada toward black refugees, and the victimization that occurred both in her family and in society at large due to her decision to become a single teenage mother, she felt blamed—and indeed was blamed—for that victimization. Violence had been perpetrated against her in the form of loss of her father and ancestral home, in the circumcision of her genitals, and in banishment from her own family, all issues that Ayanna addresses in this chapter.

This interview took place at a critical juncture for Ayanna. She was about to be spirited away to another city as protection from her own family. It was feared that her brothers might harm her for having had a baby as a single young woman without a partner. No one but the social service staff who arranged her move was to know where she was going. Her identity was hidden, to shield her. Consequently, this snap-shot provides an important window into understanding the development of shame.

As Ayanna came into conflict with the dominant societal themes that framed her as immature and irresponsible, as an individual unable to make sound choices for herself, she fought to view herself in a more positive light. Ayanna's goals were to "make something of herself" that would prove others wrong and to provide a different future for her daughter than was her experience. In this way, she resisted the imposition by others of interpretations about her identity.

While wishing Ayanna to speak for herself, in this chapter, I, too, make interpretations about her identity. It could be said that to write this chapter from the vantage point of a white, liberal, middle-class academic, someone who could never fully understand Ayanna, is a colonizing act, which translates into liberal humanism notions that are not interpretable by another culture (Niranjana 1992, 65, 70). The difficulty of writing such a piece is that it comes to represent Ayanna's experience or thoughts through the lens of another. Being aware also of the immense power differentials between Ayanna and myself, I know that the asymmetry of our relationship might have clouded that which was represented or emphasized. Additionally, this chapter represents one frozen moment in time. For example, the move toward rapprochement between Ayanna and her mother that

she speaks about in this chapter had evaporated by the time of a follow-up conver-
sation that took place a month later. Describing the "truth" of Ayanna's life is
probably not possible.

At the same time that an academic trespasses in attempting to represent an-
other individual, silence about the lives of young single black mothers is one of the
most powerful ways that young women continue to be victimized. The story of a
life in the margins attempts to be counterhegemonic by providing the possibility of
alternate ways of understanding women like Ayanna and by revealing things
about the world that people "ought to know" (Razack 1998, 38). The telling
of her story is a political and a feminist act, designed to serve the interests of an
exploited group and to act as an antidote to the dominant views of western society.
Like the Cree hunter who came to Montreal to testify about the James Bay hydro-
electric scheme and stated, "I'm not sure I can tell the truth. . . . I can only tell
what I know" (quoted in Clifford 1986, 8), I will try to do the same.

RACISM AS A DEFINING INFLUENCE

We were going to be killed. The North wanted to separate, and the
South didn't want that, so they were going around trying to kill everybody because they thought [we] were acting with the other government.
That's why we had to leave immediately or else we would have all been
dead. All of us [left]—my mom, my brothers. My father tried, but we
haven't seen him. He was in the war. He'd gone underground. Before
there was a rumor that they thought he was a spy. We don't know what
happened to him. I haven't seen my dad since I was three. [I'm] not sure
if mother had contact, but if she did have contact, she didn't tell us 'cause
we were little kids. We might say something to someone else. We
haven't heard; we're not sure if he's dead or alive.

We went to Kenya to the refugee camp and stayed there for a while.
We came through Niagara Falls, and then they said we had to stay in
Buffalo a month in a shelter. We came in as refugees. . . . We went to
the trials [refugee hearings] to see if we could stay in Canada. . . . They
approved. They gave us the landing [as political refugees].

All the stuff that we've been through made me angry. I faced a lot of
racism against Somalis. How people look at Somalis, they think [we're]
nothing, and that really hurts me because they don't know us. People
talk about how we sit there and collect welfare, but look how many
white people are on welfare. I used to hate being Somali, 'cause every-

where I went, Somalis this and Somalis that. I just hated it. My friend, this girl that I knew from grade seven, her mom didn't like Somalis, so [my friend] used to take me over to her house when her mom was at work. One day her mom came home from work and . . . called me a nigger. I didn't know what to do and she told me to get out of her house.

When I was in school in grades six [through] eight; [if] I'd get mad at home, or someone would make me mad, I used to take my anger out on other kids or else I would go off on the teachers. I fought a lot. They'd [the school personnel] try and help me. They gave me a counselor. They gave me a basketball program and they paid for it. It helped 'cause I wasn't home as much, and I wasn't around trouble because I was always practicing basketball. . . . I fought in the first semester of grade nine, and, since then, I haven't fought. I used to fight a lot of white kids, and I learned that not all white people [were] like that. I learned that not everybody was racist toward Somalis, and, when I noticed that, I kinda calmed down. I started having white friends.

I feel like I face [racism] everywhere. You experience racism in Somalia because you're a different [minority] tribe and [the dominant tribe doesn't] like you 'cause you're a different tribe. They look down on you and talk about you. Wherever you go, there's racism. People make comments about the way black people look. When we first didn't speak English, [people made] black jokes and we didn't understand. I learned that we're not bad, and, if the war hadn't happened, we wouldn't be here. The only reason we're here is for the safety of our lives, and if we could get a job we'd get a job. It's not easy to get a job, and I just think of that when they say "nigger." It's not just a black person. A nigger could be anybody, an ignorant person that can't really write. A white person could be a nigger. When they call me that, it hurts, you know, but I'm not an ignorant person.

The racism made me a stronger person for sure. I lived through it, so it didn't kill me. I didn't kill myself because of it. It just made me a stronger person. Every time somebody said something mean, it gave me a reason to live [but also] a reason not to live, because I knew, the way they talked about Somalis I knew I had to keep going, so I could be something in life and show them not all Somalis sit there and collect welfare. . . . There are Somalis that want to have a future— something—to finish college and become something, and that's the reason I want to keep on going. I want to prove to people, everyone that looks down on me, that I [am] going to be something. She [the baby] hasn't faced it, and I hope she doesn't face it.

THE INFLUENCE OF ISLAM IN AYANNA'S FAMILY: SEX AND SEXUALITY

Muslim women are accorded a high status in Islam, but with prescribed roles and expectations of behavior. Islam is not a monolithic faith and is diversely applied depending on country, community, and the interpretation that is accorded to the norms established by the Koran and the other holy writings. The interpretation, as it is practiced in Ayanna's family, seems to be fundamentalist (Hjärpe 1983, 14). In such an ultraconservative family, not being a virgin at marriage sullies the honor of the father. In some communities, a young woman can be put to death for this shame on the family name (Minai 1981, 147). Concern about maintaining patriarchal privilege is a stronger force than family ties. "Female sexuality in adolescence represents an assertion of adult status . . . [and] violates not only the hierarchy of generations but of genders as well. In patriarchal systems of gender stratification, sexual autonomy is the prerogative not simply of adults but of males. Young women are expected to preserve their sexuality to be bargained in exchange for a man's social protection and economic support" (Nathanson 1991, 208). Thus, Ayanna feared her brothers' reaction to her upsetting of the social order. In such a situation, the women in Ayanna's family may have empathized with Ayanna. It was only her mother and sister who provided even minimal support by visiting her in the hospital and speaking to her on the phone while safeguarding her by not revealing her whereabouts to her brothers.

Muslim feminists have an alternate interpretation of the custom of women covering their head and body when in public from that of western feminist scholars. This counterfiguration is that being covered allows Muslim women to walk unimpeded in public, without fear of being treated like sexual objects (Nazlee 1996, 25). But for Ayanna, the expectation that nice women are covered head to toe came directly into conflict with a cultural divide that North American women wear short skirts and go to bars. Like many first-generation Canadians, Ayanna was pulled between these opposing norms, leaving her in a quandary about her behavior. Additionally, she was aware of and fought the double standard that was applied to the girls and boys in her family.

Islam has been an influence. I believe in God, and I was always raised up to believe there is one God and that there were the prophets . . . Mohammed and Jesus. We do not believe that Jesus is God's son; he's just a prophet. We believe in prayers five times a day to the East. I don't do that, but I want to start doing that. [The Muslim rules] . . . are strict, and I believe in them. I know [the Koran] was the last book that was brought down from God. That's what we believe and [Islam is] the last religion. It says that Mohammed was the last prophet. . . . All my life that's what I've been around and that's what I believe in my heart. . . . I don't know much about the Muslim religion. I know bits and pieces, but I can't really tell you that much.

I know that God doesn't want guys to see girls' bodies. When a girl looks good, a guy sees them. [Guys] try and talk to [girls]. For you not to get that attention, that's why [the religion] want[s] [girls] covered up. . . . Cover your body up, head to toe, my mom does that. Guys won't be going up to them.

My grandfather (on my father's side) married a lot of women for wives, and they wanted my father to do that. My father was against that, 'cause he wanted to be married to my mom. [The relatives] didn't like that, so they didn't like her and they didn't help her out in any way. I remember one thing that she just told us recently, that my uncle on my dad's side said to her, "When you go to North America, don't start wearing short skirts and going to bars." My mom would never do that. [The implication that she would dress in North American garb] really hurt her.

All of our lives we [Ayanna's sisters] weren't allowed out and we had to do everything around the house. When we had to go to school, [my mom] didn't make us do anything. She wanted us to do our home-work and go to bed early. But on the weekend or the summer time, we [the girls] had to do everything around the house: cook, clean. [Ayanna's life consisted of]: sleep, eat, go to school, go play basketball, come back home. There were many different expectations [for the boys in the family]. And my brothers were [allowed out]. My brothers have girlfriends and it's okay 'cause they're boys. They can't get pregnant, that's what my mom says. I don't think it's fair. I know . . . in our religion it says not to have sex, even if you're a man or a woman. It's a sin. . . . My mom [didn't] want them to [have sex], but she can't do anything 'cause they're boys. She knows that they can't get pregnant. She says, "What's the worst thing that can happen?" I know for a fact that my little brother has sex because I know the girl he's going out with. And my older brother, he has a lot of girlfriends. My brothers always told us, we're guys and we know how guys think. We don't want [any] guys hurting you . . . and playing with your minds. So they never want[ed] us to go out with anybody or talk to anybody.

NEGOTIATING THE LABYRINTH OF PREGNANCY, MARRIAGE, AND RAISING A CHILD AS A SINGLE WOMAN

Ayanna was in a no-win situation. Islam discourages free mixing of the sexes (Nazlee 1996, 22). The importance of remaining chaste by her family's culture was supported by restricted access to information about sexuality, compounded by not being permitted to experience heterosexual relationships for herself. The restrictions of her home life had chafed on Ayanna once she was living in North America, restrictions that she suspected were compounded by the losses that her mother had experienced as a refugee. In the realm of sexuality, the penalties for making a "mistake" were huge, and Ayanna was held individually and person- ally responsible for her actions. The broader structural barriers that impeded Ay- anna from making an informed choice were not seen as contributing to her situa- tion. Indeed, Ayanna took personal responsibility for her decision, stating that in some way her agreement to have sexual relations might have been her unconscious ticket to leave a confining family environment.

Having made that "mistake," Ayanna found herself on the horns of an- other dilemma: she perceived abortion as killing, but from her perspective, only bad girls had babies before they married. Multiple factors, including religion and her family's own racism, played a part in Ayanna's decision to raise a child as a single woman. Pregnancy had become a means of escape, but at the price of pov- erty, banishment, and shame.

On my father's side [marriages were] arranged. My mom never told us that we had to do that [arranged marriages]. My mom told us we could always pick [our own husbands], but we could never pick 'cause we're never allowed to go out with anybody or talk to anybody. How are we supposed to do that?

My mom always said, "Whenever you find somebody," but I don't know when she wanted us to get married. I think my mom . . . all her life, she just had us, and, in a way, I don't think she wants to let us go because she keeps on telling me, "I lost you, I lost you, I lost you, you left me." I know that she must want to hold on to us. Even my brothers, they're going. She doesn't want them to leave home. They're going to college in Toronto. She's down 'cause of that too. In a way I wanted to leave home 'cause it was so strict, and I never was allowed to do anything. . . . I wanted my way out, to tell you the truth. The way I did it was wrong. Just like my older sister got married without my mom knowing 'cause she was just tired of all the rules.

[The pregnancy] wasn't planned. I didn't know I was going to get pregnant. My mom never talked about sex to us. It was like a big oops; we can't say nothing about that. I took some health classes, but, you know, I didn't think I was going to get pregnant having sex the first time. I thought you have to do it a long time. It was the first time.

I was in Toronto for the summer. I met [the baby's father] in Toronto. My aunt lives there, and my aunt is not very controlling. She's a Muslim, but she's young and she understands. She says, "How are you supposed to get married if you don't talk to [anybody]? Is a man supposed to come walking to you?"

My friends were down there, so my friends and I were at Caribbana and we met him. When we met, we started talking. We talked the first day, me and my cousins and my friends. We talked to him and his friends, and he wanted to get my phone number. I said no, 'cause my aunt didn't want guys calling. She's not really my aunt, she's my uncle's wife, and she [doesn't] mind if I talk to guys 'cause she knows, she's not that old, she's young too, but . . . she didn't want my uncle to pick up the phone. I said no . . . I couldn't give him the number. But he gave me the number of the motel that he was in . . . I didn't call him that night.

The next day we [saw] him again. . . . Then we talked, and he asked how come I didn't call. I said I was busy, and I couldn't call him. He asked me if I wanted to go out to a movie or something. . . . I said I don't want to go with him, and then I told him that I was going to go back to Windsor. The third day, he said he was going to go to Windsor. And he came to Windsor, and one of my friends, my cousin's friends, she gave him her number in Windsor and told him, call her, and he called her and we met up again. We went to the motel, and we stayed there and then it happened. The first time in my life.

I found out that I was pregnant at six weeks. I was scared. I didn't know what to do. I was thinking about having an abortion, but I don't believe in killing, so I didn't do it. At first, I said I'm just going to hide it and give the baby up for adoption. But I didn't know what to do. When I got further along in the pregnancy, I thought more. Then her [the baby's] dad and I got into a fight before he left for the States and I told him I had an abortion. I lied to him. See, he had said some stuff to me that had hurt me. So he didn't know I was pregnant since he thought I'd had an abortion.

[Later] he was happy when he found out that I was pregnant. I told him, "Now that I'm pregnant, my family is going to give me a hard time and they're going to say I'm not married." He said, "Don't worry, we'll get married." I said, "No." I didn't know what I was going to do. I wasn't ready, and I wasn't ready for a baby too. I had the baby.

I believe that the person I marry has to be my religion, Muslim, and he's not. . . . He's saying that he wants to become Muslim, but you can't be unless you feel it in your heart; you can't just do it 'cause I'm Muslim. I told him that if you don't have it in your heart to be a Muslim, you can't do it. His mind has to be ready and it's not ready. He wants to go out every night of the week, go be with his friends, hang around with this person and that person. You can't have a family if you're gone every night of the week.

My mother would have been happy [if Ayanna had married him], but she wouldn't have been happy. . . . It wouldn't have been a shame for me to have a baby 'cause then I would have been married, but she would have been unhappy 'cause he's black American and she [doesn't] like black Americans. She sees them as drug dealers and they kill each other. That's what she hears, and it's what she just thinks of all of them, like gang bangers. . . . They're bad and stuff.

I had so [many] things going through my mind at once. I knew that if I married him it would still be a problem; if I didn't marry him, it would be another problem. Either way I wouldn't make my mom happy, 'cause my mom said even if I married him and I had the baby she wouldn't talk to me 'cause he's black. So both ways I would have lost her.

I just want to have a future. I just don't want to get married . . . and have no school or [anything] behind me.

[If I could do things again] I would have waited and not got pregnant. I would have waited until I got married. I blame myself a lot 'cause I was the one who opened my legs. If I would have known better . . .

AYANNA'S FAMILY

There is a paradox in Ayanna's mother both being a model for her and at the same time shunning Ayanna. Her mother is seen as a woman who does not judge people, but this same person has ostracized Ayanna and told her own daughter "not to come to her grave." Yet as a source of identification, her mother's strength, perseverance, and ability to continue to look forward are attributes that Ayanna aspires to and feels she has accomplished herself. One explanation of the discrepancy might be that, having accepted the thinking that being single and pregnant is a "disgrace," Ayanna sees her mother's action as justifiable and appropriate for the situation. It seems that the rejection of her family and the banishment from her mother are the most painful of all the losses that Ayanna has sustained in her life.

[My mother] went through so much. She never shows it. She's a strong person. She had seven kids and basically raised all of us by herself. She didn't have [anybody]. When she was really young, she was sent down to live with her sister, and her father died. She never got to see him again. She [doesn't] even look like she's been through [anything].

She's a nice person. She [doesn't] look at a person and judge them for what they are. She's been there for us. Her strength is in the way my mom deals with stuff. She just [doesn't] ever look back. She just always looks forward. And I've become like that. I can see my mom in me, some parts. All that's happened to me now. . . . I just look forward.

They didn't know I was pregnant. I hid my pregnancy. I wore a lot of big clothes. My mom found out after I had the baby. She came to see me in the hospital. My sister, the one I'm closest to, called her and told her to come to the hospital. She came. She walked in the room. She had tears in her eyes. She looked at me and . . . shook her head and she said that I had a bastard baby. She didn't want to have [anything] to do with me. She told me not to come back home and that I could go to hell. She left for the night. She took my sister.

I only have one more sister. She's twenty-two and married. She supports me, too. She's got a kid, a little girl. She's three. The only people I got behind me are my sister and my older sister.

I'm scared of my brothers. They think that [I] hurt my mom and I'm a disgrace to the family, so I don't know what they would do to me if they see me. . . . I don't want them to do something to me. . . . They might have to go to jail, and I'm just leaving so they won't do something. They might kick and hit me or something. They haven't threatened me, but I know my brothers and what I did is a very big thing. If they got a chance, they would hurt me. I don't think they'd kill me.

Only my little sister and my mom know where I'm going. My mom knows where I am right now. She didn't tell my brothers where I went.

I miss . . . my brothers and sisters. One is in Kingston; the rest are in Windsor. I'm not close to them [any] more. 'Cause after I had the baby, they didn't want to have anything to do with me. It's a shame [having a baby] without being married. They all think that. They don't say it. That's something that [I] grew up to believe. My mom feels that way too. (Crying) She says she [won't] have [anything] to do with me and if she died, "don't come to her grave" and she won't come to my grave.

I talk to [my mother] now. I talk to her on the phone. She's getting better. Still she [doesn't] have as much love as she used to have for me. She tells me that. I hurt her a lot by what I did.

I feel what I did is shameful because of the way I was brought up. The way they make me feel. If people keep telling you over and over, you start believing [it]. At first I told myself, no . . . it's not a shame, but when you hear it over and over it's in [your] head.

Ayanna had been genitally cut in Somalia.[2] This tradition made the process of her labor and recovery from the labor more complicated. Additionally it added to her sense of shame as being markedly different from other young women in Canada. A problem in labor is discussed by Ayanna. If women are cut, the area that normally is elastic around the cervix becomes scarred, resulting in tearing, the requirement of large episiotomies, and prolonged and difficult labors.

When I was having the baby, I had a lot of difficulty. It was really hard for me to have the baby 'cause I'm really tight, and they had to cut me up all the way to where you go to the bathroom and now it's coming undone and . . . it really hurts. I have sharp pains down there and I think it's related to the circumcision. I was telling one of the girls and they were [saying] you should go to the doctor, 'cause I was having a lot of pains and I'm still having lots of pain but I haven't gone to the doctor.

We got circumcised. I remember it very clearly. I was six. We went over to a lady's house, my aunt's friend, me and my cousin. Me and my mom, my cousin and her mom. My uncle drove us and he dropped us off at a lady's house and we didn't know where we were going. My mom told me, "You're going to get circumcised." My cousin went first and my cousin cried. My aunt slapped her 'cause she was crying. She's nine months older than me, so she was maybe seven. . . . I was wearing a little brown dress and . . . I was thinking I can't cry, I can't cry 'cause if I cry I'm going to get hit. And then it was my turn to go up and I just held everything, I just held, no anesthetic. They cut your clit . . . clitoris, and they sew you up so you only have a little hole so you can pee. The first time it hurts. They clean you out. They clean[ed] us out with hot alcohol that burns and you just, I cr[ied]. I wished that I was dead 'cause there was so much pain. For the first two months, we lay on our backs with our legs . . . up and our legs were tied together. When we have to go to the bathroom, it really hurt 'cause you're so sewed up down there. When you push and when you pee, it burns really bad.

My little sister is not circumcised. We moved to Canada and me and my sister were older and we told my mom not to do it to her and she said okay. It's not my mom's fault. . . . God, in our religion . . . in the Koran it says just to cut a little, little, little, little, just the tip of the clitoris, to cut that little bit off the clitoris, but the Somalis they have this tradition. It's not just the Somalis but the Arab people do that too. They were supposed to cut all of my clitoris but they didn't and my mom got upset, not my mom actually, but my aunt because I wasn't supposed to have none whatsoever [left], but my cousin had all of it cut off. But me, she left. . . . I still got some; she [the aunt] got mad and wanted to take me back and my mom said no. If you didn't have that done, everybody, every family, they'd talk about your daughter and say oh, their daughter, they still got that thing hanging from them and blah, blah, blah, that's how they'd talk and my mom didn't want to be a . . . and she didn't want people sitting around talking about her.

MOTHERHOOD: DEPRESSION, ISOLATION, AND RESISTANCE

Despite the difficulties that the genital cutting created for Ayanna, she was able to give birth to a healthy little girl. Motherhood brought its own challenges and struggles. Motherhood is transformational for many women who are first-time mothers, and Ayanna believed that mothering made her a better woman, one who had settled down to take on the responsibilities of raising a child. Even more significantly, having Jasmine quite literally gave Ayanna a reason to live. At the same time, however, having a child as a single woman led to depression, isolation, and, at times, despair. Depression emerges from the isolation, high demands, and low control that come from mothering (Rosenberg 1993, 251). Poverty has fur-

ther exacerbated her depression. This depression is compounded exponentially by the lack of social support that has come with the ostracism and expulsion from Ayanna's family and community.

My baby gave me the strength to keep going. She's mine. She smiles, and that makes me happy, even when I'm down. The best part of my life is having her. 'Cause I wanted to kill myself at one point, even though she's the only thing that keeps me going. I have someone else to live for. I thought about taking pills. I try not to think about it. It comes back. There are just some days when I could be anywhere and I'll just start thinking, and cry and cry and cry and cry.

I used to have a lot of anger. I hold in my anger now. I've become a nicer person just knowing that I was going to have a kid and knowing that I was going to be a mom. I knew that I was going to have to change, that I couldn't be running. I used to [fight]. If someone looked at me wrong, I would just yell at them and tell them off and when I got pregnant, everything changed. I'm a lot nicer now, I am. I've matured.

It's hard, so hard [to have a baby and be a single mom]. There's nobody I can say, "Watch my baby." It's just me. If I had my mom, it would be nice, but I don't have her. When you're not feeling good, when you're stressed out and you have to give her [the baby] attention, that's hard. Some days you're really bummed out, and you don't feel like doing anything. . . . You have to keep on going because you have a baby. I talk to the staff [of the maternity home] sometimes, sit down and talk. And I cry. Sometimes crying helps me. I stay in my room and put her beside me and cuddle her. One of the girls, I know her. She's pregnant. I've known her ever since I moved to Canada, so she helps me out with Jasmine. And whenever I'm stressed out she takes her and takes care of her.

[The] thing we haven't talked about is not having enough money for her. It's hard not being able to buy her nice stuff. [There is] so much money that I have to spend. Welfare. It's not a lot. It's really hard trying to manage it: diapers, to buy formula. . . . She needs clothes; she needs toys and stuff. I don't have enough money to buy all of that. The lady is nice [at the welfare office]. I wish I was ready to have [my baby], but I wasn't.

I just heard that there was a place like this [a supported living environment for single teen mothers after the maternity home]. We called down there and they put me on a waiting list for housing and I got one.

It's about ten minutes away. I don't know anybody there. It's going to be hard. I asked the lady if there's day care so I can go back to school. She said there is. She was going to help me look.

Tracy [the clinical director in the maternity home] [has] been there [the] whole . . . time, since day one, and she's still there. [It] made a difference. I lost my family, but there are other people who care and don't look down on me that I had a baby and I'm not married.

AYANNA'S MESSAGE TO OTHER YOUNG WOMEN AND HER GOALS FOR THE FUTURE

If they're [other young women] going to have sex, protect themselves. The best thing is abstinence. You go without sex. You wait until you're ready. Sex is a sin because you're not supposed to have sex before you get married. Wait and protect [yourselves]. A baby is a lot of responsibility. It's not just—have one. Think. There are a lot of things that come with babies: sleepless nights, changing diapers, bottles. So it's just not, a baby is going to come and do everything by itself. You're going to need to know that a baby needs a lot of attention and a lot of loving. So if you're not ready to have one, don't, if you don't have the strength to care for one. I have the strength to care for one.

I'd like to finish school, go to college. Finishing school, going to college, having a job, then I'd have money and I'[d be] working. I did half of grade eleven. I did the first semester and I dropped out the second semester. I have a year and a half to go. . . . I want to do nursing, the one-year intensive program. My sister-in-law took a nurse's course, and she told me about it and said she thought I'd be good at it. I've seen so much in life, and I think I could do it.

[I would like to] work things out with my baby's father and get married, and have my mom back in my life and my brothers.

[The baby]'s going to be the one [for whom Ayanna has goals]. I want to do it for myself and I want to do it for her so that I can have something for her. She [won't] have to have any worries in life like I did. To have money to go to college. [Hopefully] I'll get a good job and put away some money for her.

EPILOGUE

In my last conversation with Ayanna after she had been moved to the new city, she said that it had been a hard time in her life. She was depressed, and unable to go to school. Her mother had totally rejected her at that point, and Ayanna was not having contact with any family member. After that, she "disappeared" with no forwarding address. Even the staff of the supportive housing unit did not know where Ayanna had gone, nor whether she had begun to turn her life around.

NOTES

1. My heartfelt thanks go to Ayanna, for without her this chapter could not have been written. I also would like to thank the staff of the maternity home who were responsible for introducing me to Ayanna.

Pseudonyms were used in this chapter, and identifying information was altered to protect Ayanna.

2. According to the United Nations, it is estimated that 130 million women worldwide have been genitally cut (Kassamali 1998, 39). There has been much dissension between western and African women about how the topic of female genital cutting should be addressed. Kassamali, as one source, has written an informative article on these issues. There is a risk that my editorializing will be seen as a colonizing act, an attempt to eradicate a tradition from a culture that is not mine. However, many African feminists believe this custom should be phased out. Some believe that this tradition must be dealt with only by people within the culture itself, rather than by western scholars. While giving weight to these concerns, Ayanna did not want this procedure done to her own sister, and due to the brutality and medical dangers of this procedure, I have addressed this issue.

In Ayanna's community, girls who did not have this done were mocked, humiliated, and shunned. They were led to believe that they would be unable to find husbands. Consequently shame would have haunted Ayanna in Somalia for not being genitally cut, as it did in Canada for having had this procedure.

WORKS CITED

Clifford, James, and George E. Marcus, eds. 1986. *Writing Culture: The Poetics and Politics of Ethnography.* Berkeley: University of California Press.

Fossum, Merle A., and Marilyn J. Mason. 1986. *Facing Shame: Families in Recovery.* New York: Norton.

Hjärpe, Jan. 1983. "The Attitude of Islamic Fundamentalism Towards the Question of Women in Islam." In *Women in Islamic Societies: Social Attitudes and Historical Perspectives,* ed. Bo Utas. London: Curzon, 12–25.

Irvine, Janice. 1994. *Sexual Cultures and the Construction of Adolescent Identities.* Philadelphia: Temple University Press.

Kassamali, Noor J. 1998. "When Modernity Confronts Traditional Practices: Female Genital Cutting in Northeast Africa." In *Women in Muslim Societies: Diversity Within Unity,* ed. Herbert L. Bodman and Nayereh Tohidi. Boulder, Colo.: Lynne Rienner, 39–61.

MacIntyre, Sally, and Sarah Cunningham-Burley. 1993. "Teenage Pregnancy as a Social Problem: A Perspective From the United Kingdom." *The Politics of Pregnancy: Adolescent Sexuality and Public Policy,* ed. Annette Lawson and Deborah L. Rhode. New Haven: Yale University Press, 59–73.

Minai, Naila. 1981. *Women in Islam: Tradition and Transition in the Middle East.* New York: Seaview Books.

Nathanson, Constance A. 1991. *Dangerous Passage: The Social Control of Sexuality in Women's Adolescence.* Philadelphia: Temple University Press.

Nazlee, Sajda. 1996. *Feminism and Muslim Women.* London: Ta-Ha Publishers.

Niranjana, Tejaswini. 1992. *Siting Translation: History, Post-Structuralism, and the Colonial Context.* Berkeley: University of California Press.

Orton, Maureen Jessop, and Ellen Rosenblatt. 1993. *Sexual Health for Youth: Creating a Three-Sector Network in Ontario. Report 4.* Toronto: University of Toronto, Faculty of Social Work.

Pearce, Diana M. 1993. " 'Children Having Children': Teenage Pregnancy and Public Policy From the Woman's Perspective." In *The Politics of Pregnancy: Adolescent Sexuality and Public Policy,* ed. Annette Lawson and Deborah L. Rhode. New Haven: Yale University Press. 46–58.

Phoenix, Ann. 1993. "The Social Construction of Teenage Motherhood: A Black and White Issue?" In *The Politics of Pregnancy: Adolescent Sexuality and Public Policy,* ed. Annette Lawson and Deborah L. Rhode. New Haven: Yale University Press, 74–97.

Razack, Sherene H. 1998. *Looking White People in the Eye: Gender, Race, and Culture in Courtrooms and Classrooms.* Toronto: University of Toronto Press.

Rosenberg, Harriet. 1993. "Motherhood, Stress and Depression: The Costs of Privatized Social Reproduction." *Family Patterns, Gender Relations,* ed. Bonnie J. Fox. Toronto: Oxford University Press, 245–56.

· Part II ·

Don't Look Down:
Girls Living on the Edge

· *7* ·

A Tightrope Made of Sari Silk
The Delicate, Perilous World of Girlhood in India

Preeti, Priya, Pratibha, Kamala, Lalitha,
and Ariana-Sophia Kartsonis

𝒯he stories of five girls living in Bangalore, India, in the winter of
1999 run through this chapter. Their conversations were collected during January and February of 1999. Their story begins much earlier, however, in 1993, when Prabhakar Kudva and I met in a women's studies
course at the University of Utah and started a conversation that is still
taking place six years (and numerous collaborations) later.

The words that follow were transmitted from India to New York to
Alabama by telephone, mail, and e-mail. From the girls to Prabhakar
Kudva, my translator and photographer in New York, and from Prabha-
kar to me here in Tuscaloosa, Alabama. Miles away, in every sense.

The information they share was obtained with the understanding
that the name of the orphanage where Priya, Preeti, and Pratibha are
living be never mentioned and that their real names not be used in this
chapter. "Their lives have been dramatic enough; they need not be souvenirs or symbols," said their teacher who, despite a fair portion of trepi-
dation, allowed the interview. I took the liberty of changing the names
of the other two girls at my own discretion, for similar reasons. I've tried
to do what was necessary to honor my vow to Prabhakar, who made the
original promise to the girls' teacher that names and certain biographical
facts be altered. I do mention another orphanage: the Indira Gandhi International Academy, which also deals with a good many orphans of refugees. The term "orphan" is problematic, in that it refers to children
who have lost their parents to death. Some of these children are simply
separated from their parents—indefinitely, with no certainty the parents

115

are still living, and no assurance that they will be reunited. But it is an important distinction to make when considering the terms "orphan" and "orphanage," because these children are sometimes more like orphans in limbo, with lives on hold while they wait for an answer or a visit that may never arrive.

Prabhakar has always wanted to do some type of community work for his contradictory, native country. Our talks over the years have continued to circle the conditions of Indian life, the misconceptions and the undeniable richness of a country that is simultaneously lovely and troubled. Inevitably, the conversation turns to wishes: I wish I could open an artist's co-op in Bangalore, so that those selling their earthen lamps, their batik tapestries, their carved sandalwood incense holders, their artwork could be organized, and they might be fairly compensated for their time, talent, and need. I wish I could adopt an Indian child. I wish I could send money, food, and clothes to India with the assurance that they would arrive and be distributed to the right people. Indians living in the United States never send packages or money through the mail to their families back home. The one time that Prabhakar, at my urging, sent his mother a package containing two scarves and some perfume, she never received it. In the face of abject poverty, theft is expected. Later, other Indian friends told me that sending anything more than a letter by way of the postal service into India is tantamount to throwing the package off a bridge. The means to help from here to there are complicated by many factors, most of which are aggravated by distance.

I was told, too, that people working with those in need in countries such as India learned to set small, realistic goals and view the smallest improvement, even if it simply serves to raise the level of awareness, as a victory. I remember a National Public Radio report on Mother Teresa in which she spoke of the satisfaction she received in cleaning the weeping wounds of the terminally ill, even though it was only a temporary comfort or, rather, a temporary stay from more severe discomfort. It is this philosophy that I remember in relaying this story, a hope to help, in some modest way, these girls and the girls who remain unheard. The future of all children in Third World countries is grim, but what is bad for children in general often, sadly, proves to be worse for the female members of a society. Making sure these girls' voices are heard is what I can contribute now.

When Prabhakar planned a trip to visit his family, he was armed with a questionnaire I had written, a camera, and the hope that he would return with some stories of what it means to be an Indian girl with her future poised and teetering on the edge of a new century.

The difficulty in writing about India is that there is no one India and, therefore, no real meaning behind phrases such as "Indian standards." This may seem obvious; consider the way that the United States varies in its regions enough to conjure a very different mental picture from the word "Alabama" to the word "California." The difference is that in India the variables are multiplied not just by the variety of religious beliefs—Hindus living alongside Muslims, Buddhists, Christians, Zoroastrians—but also by class and caste distinctions and by the large number of languages spoken throughout India, which are multiplied further by the dialects within those languages. Blanket statements are difficult, if not thoroughly inaccurate, when dealing with such a rich, living culture.

Consider the collage—the fragmented, pieced-together, borrowed elements, juxtaposed and seamed together by tension and euphony that comprise the whole. Both essayist and collage artist were needed in the process of this piece: the acquisition of the interview; the layout of the work; whose words appear where; which orphanages are cited and featured; the scrambling, veiling, and changing of some biographical elements, which might jeopardize anonymity. There is that hope, after all, that someday these "orphans" will be grown, educated, healthy women with good lives. The odds are against them, true, but I'd like to imagine them growing into a better life and this chapter to be a time, "back there," when their lives were more precarious.

Five Indian girls, a South Indian city, a translator, twenty-one e-mails, three packages, two dozen naive questions, numerous phone conversations to clarify and expand what I saw in the photographs and what Prabhakar saw and heard when he spoke with the girls—a beginning. In the end, I had several articles, a cassette tape full of voices speaking in Kannada—a language I don't understand a word of—and three photographs of faces I try my best to read through their expressions, the way they dress, the way they stand, the descriptions Prabhakar gives when I ask: How did she look when she answered that? How did they stand in relation to one another? What was her body language like? How far did they travel alone until someone from the orphanage found them? How much were they able to carry, to keep?

Because I can't begin to imagine what they've had to relinquish.

Preeti, Priya, and Pratibha. (Photo by N. Prabhakar Kudva.)

AT THE ORPHANAGE: PREETI, PRIYA, AND PRATIBHA'S STORY

Preeti is the oldest of the three. Two glass bangles ornament her right wrist. A third is on her sister Pratibha's little hand. The girls say that the bracelets are the small offering from the girls' mother for a someday dowry. The bamboo-thin wrists of Priya, the youngest, remain unadorned.

Gold as a raw material is a heirloom among Indian families. The ring Prabhakar inherited from his grandfather has been melted down and fashioned into a ring containing his grandson's birthstone. (Birthstones, like the exact time and date of birth and astrology, in general, are taken as very serious factors in the consideration of a child's future.) Mothers have their jewelry melted down and refashioned into adornments for their daughters, who will, in turn, melt their gold into baubles for their girls. For these three girls, it's likely there would have been more jewelry, gold possibly, centuries old, passed down then passed on. Something new, something old, something borrowed, all at once.

When Priya's old enough to marry, Preeti says her sister can have one of her bangles for dowry. She says, "We have nothing else." She adds with a gesture that flings the words away and seems to leave the air ringing—"nothing else." Except a glass bangle amounts to little or no monetary value—no dowry. A matter of little concern since orphaned girls with no family name, no background, no credentials, have no need to worry about a proper dowry; they're infinitely unmarriageable by Indian standards. Marriage, in most of the various cultures that India comprises, is heavily reliant upon the notion of family standing. Divorce is a virtually taboo concept. The child of separated parents or a single mother is considered flawed, a judgment that is doubly harsh on orphaned girls, with no family present to vouch for their quality. Within a social structure that still views women as commodities, questionable or damaged goods are hard to move.

I was surprised to learn that two of the girls had a little jewelry—a pair of post earrings, some bangle bracelets; somehow my definition of orphans didn't allow for residual trinkets. One of the problems with the vocabulary—for example, "poor" as a term for "poverty" as well as a synonym for "pitiful"—is that words are reductive; they keep the girls—and their country, for that matter—misunderstood. "Orphan" is another problematic term, colored by limited and largely western connotations of what being parentless means. Somewhere within the label lingers a Dickensian character in shadowy rags with swipes of coal dust across the brow. Three little Orphan Annies suspended in time.

Each girl wears a red skirt and a white cotton blouse, the orphanage uniform. Their hair, unlike the thick black sheen of hair I've seen plaited into heavy cables swinging down other Indian girls' backs, is shorn neatly clean. Even with the small shine from the bracelets, there is something spare, ascetic to their small persons, something almost military-strict that shakes away the nonessential. They stand without shoes in the stone courtyard outside their rooms.

As the eldest, Preeti is now the fill-in mother by default, and, at nine years old, her worries have become the worries of a grown woman; her face bears the strain. She looks far off when asked a question—thoughtfully considering her response in a manner that indicates maturity but also the gravity of consequence—the weight of which she has already felt bearing down upon her.

It is February, Bangalore, India. The streets are a blend of tan dust and stone. The landscape holds a strange beauty that combines the stark and unrelenting with the embroidered crowd in brilliant silks and cottons, the air a mix of seasoned bodies, spices, and noise—cacophonous and unmelodic but strongly human. Nothing is withheld here. Bangalore's streets are quiet compared to, say, Bombay or Calcutta, but the tapestry of the vivid and the dying is here, too.

Bangalore is the capital city nestled in the state of Karnataka, located in the southern part of India. It is considered one of the more beautiful cities in the country: pleasant and temperate in climate. Fifty-six percent of the population is literate, compared to 27 percent in the state of Jammu, whose capital is Srinigar (Kishwar and Vanita 1984, 43).

Bangalore's special characteristics—as a southern city having a heterogeneous population, as a former seat of the British, as an educational center, and as a city to which industrialization came later than to other major cities—affect its rate of change. Bangalore women tend to be more conservative than those in Bombay, yet are more subject to change than those in smaller cities in India. Like many women of a larger, more urban city, Bangalore women differ in many ways from the village women.[1]

That tells you something of the city, although it's important to understand the way that statistical data serve to distance the reader from India. It's our defense mechanism as humans to turn troubling material into facts that, though useful, don't stay with us the way stories do. I want these words to stain the reader like *mendhi*—that henna paste painted in elaborate designs on the hands and feet that doesn't wash away for weeks.

I took many breaks from those cassettes and those hours spent staring intently at the photographs. It was too hard to think about sometimes, the very minute I was gazing at them two-dimensionally, these miniature women were working through another minute in their hard, tenuous, all-too-three-dimensional lives.

Here is all the stuff of tragedy: three sisters, a buff-colored backdrop of stone, an orphanage, a stage littered with the dead. Only there is no stage. The carnage is part of the scenery. Bodies, sick and still, punctuate the roadsides. It is impossible to protect even the most privileged of Indian children from the knowledge that theirs is a lush life when they watch other children drop away from the school attendance roster each year because they can't afford to attend any longer or because disease or malnourishment has ravaged their bodies. Most simply can't afford to deprive their families of their work at home, on the farm, or out in the world. Children in India grow up with the notion of consequence almost before the fact. All roads but the narrow back alley to schooling lead to a life on the streets, and a life on the streets is what the children see in their peripheral vision when they're moving as swiftly and as steadily as their hungry minds will propel them. For girls, the path is even more treacherous. A girl without a decent family name, the proper language, caste, or dowry, has little chance of finding a suitable husband and securing a "proper" life. That amounts to a variety of dangerous options. Preeti's far-reaching gaze is valid; what she sees out there for her and her siblings is stark and vicious and nearly impossible to prevent. It's a heavy burden to be carrying at an age when it's hard to imagine being a guardian.

"They're always together, the sisters," says the teacher who agreed to allow an interview with the girls.

"Please," she says, "I chose these girls because they're strong, talkative. Other girls don't talk at all, wake up screaming each night. These three are adapting. Don't ask anything too sad. Someday things may be different for them. You can take photographs, but please don't use their names."

The teacher weighs the advantages of sharing their stories and protecting the girls from a lifetime defined as orphans. She hopes the girls can transcend this portion of their lives; so do the girls.

"I want to be a lawyer," Preeti says, "so I can get people out of jail." Preeti's parents were killed in a street riot.

"She knows," the teacher explains, "but sometimes she doesn't want to."

Those times Preeti believes her parents are in jail and will be coming back for them. She carries herself with the grace of a miniature mother. While the middle girl, Pratibha, sometimes smiles when describing her running ability or telling a story, Preeti's face stays serious. Her gaze is contemplative.

Preeti is nine. She and her sisters have been living at the orphanage for two months now. She is studying her native language, Kannada, English, and math. Preeti's life is centered on her studies. Studies and the diligent vigilance over the education of her sisters.

Of the 250 children staying in the orphanage, thirty are orphans. Many here are Sri Lankan refugees. Around fifty of those children have at least one parent living in a refugee camp. More than a hundred children have been reunited with parents. Preeti's friend is one of those.

"Her parents were in jail, I think. Then they came back. She went to live with them again."

Kerala, a state in the southwestern part of India, has a per capita income lower than that of Cambodia or Sudan (Kapur). In Kerala, a neighboring state to Bangalore's Karnataka, children are likely to beg for pens, not money. In a country where homeless and abandoned children beg for writing implements as well as for food, the message is lucid: the only way out is an education. It's not that these children, like those in Bangalore, aren't hungry; it's that they have registered the notion that food only eases the stomach pangs temporarily. They're aware that if there is a long-term cure, it lies in the pursuit of education. Preeti is betting everything on that theory. She has little choice; there is "nothing else."

Because poverty is so prevalent, even the agencies such as the academy where the three sisters stay have insufficient funds to feed the children. Institutions such as this are often bankrupt and rely on the good graces of well-wishers and other donations. Many times the institutions are running on such contingent, precarious funds that the children eat only based on the daily or weekly contributions; thus children *within* these institutions often starve.

"Whenever I am hungry, I open my book and begin studying," one child of the Sri Lankan refugee orphanage says (Seethalakshmi 1999, 7D). At noon each day, the children of the Indira Gandhi International Academy look into the kitchen to see if lunch is in the works. If they see no cooking activity, they realize that there will be no food and silently return to their classes (7D).

"Here is a little better," the girls' teacher says. "The children are clean, not too sick, have food to eat, and they are learning." Like Pratibha, her face shows a kind of optimism, an openness that seems to truly expect things to shift back into a better light. Pratibha's older and younger siblings hold a more somber expression throughout the interview. They cluster together guardedly and answer questions using few words.

When asked what she'd like to be when she grows up, Pratibha smiles and answers, "I want to be a policewoman, because I can run fast." She says she likes to play "running race" in the evenings after study time ends. The Indira Gandhi Academy, whose power supply has been cut off for the last six months, has the children study from morning until dusk each day. Playtime runs from seven p.m. until bedtime. At the orphanage that houses Pratibha and her sisters, there is power and running water for now, but no money for recreational equipment, so "catch" consists of tossing stones, and running games are marked with twigs. Still, those are the creative adjustments children are best at making anywhere and not always due to necessity but rather to the adaptability and resilience of play. Throwing a rock, running through twilight to a stick marking a destination could be the actions of any child, anywhere, and from the obvious pride in her voice when telling of her "running game" prowess it's clear that Pratibha, like any six year old, doesn't mind being resourceful.

"I'm best at catch," Pratibha says, "also at running race. I got a few prizes." It took a while to get going, but in time she was telling her story about her best day.

"My father was telling me the laughing fish story. My mother and my aunts were in the kitchen making chapatis—I love chapatis—and Priya was laughing about the laughing fish. Have you ever heard a fish laugh? I can tell you the story." And she does: a folktale about a queen, a farmer's wife whose basket held a laughing fish, and a clever young woman who untangles the story. Pratibha's eyes shine with delight at the telling. She most loves the part where the girl speaks in code to a servant delivering a gift to a handsome young man. Tell him, says the girl, that the moon is full, there are twelve months in a year, and the sea is overflowing with water. She meant that the basket should have included twelve chapatis, a bowl of porridge, and a jug of milk, but the peasant fed his young son along the way so the gift was depleted. The handsome young man speaks back in code: "Tell your mistress that the moon is new, I can only find eleven months of the year, and the sea is by no means full."

"You see," said Pratibha, "they are speaking in secret. They are smart." "They read books, I think," Preeti adds in a voice geared more toward her sisters, in a tone that suggests that's the lesson of the story.[2]

I consider the variety of languages spoken in any moment in the girls' country; not simply dialects, but whole tongues—Kashmiri, Konkani, Hindi, Urdu—and the stories I've heard translated and retold of "The Clever Daughter-in-Law," "The Night-Blind Son-in-Law." These stories focus on how well the bridegroom or the bride fit the ideal of a mate. Or others like "The Dead Prince and the Talking Doll"—about a young woman who must be entombed behind twelve locked doors with a dead prince. The young woman must massage the prince's still body and keep his quarters clean for twelve years while waiting for him to wake. After sipping the leaf nectar made for him by the young woman, the prince finally wakes to the vision of the loyal young woman. She then becomes his wife, successfully securing a large wedding and the blessings of her grief-stricken and now old and dying parents. The woman's parents knew all along that their daughter's fate was to marry a (formerly) dead man, as it had been predicted by the astrologers. Though the story says they were pained to see a dozen years of suffering before the fact, they allowed their daughter to live out her fate. The wedding illustrates how quiet acceptance pays off when the young woman's twelve years of despair end happily with an acceptable marriage. This is the way it is, the stories say. Here is the message: Ours is a culture built upon people keeping their places, their stations, their lots. The first priority is a suitable marriage, a reward for those who work hard and have sharp, reasonable minds. The characters of the tales are often humble, long suffering, and undemanding. In that landscape of the fable where the good, silent soldier pays off in a day or in twelve years or later still, Pratibha can make sense of her newly rearranged, disarranged world. It's what she keeps and carries from the past, an afternoon when she had a whole family, when bread was frying in the kitchen, when her father had stories for his daughters and all the time in the world for the telling. This part, the tale within the main tale, is what Pratibha holds onto.

Everything else is too much to contemplate. Family status, "a good name," a mother's training on how to become a wife, all are characteristics that orphaned girls lack. The acknowledgment of those missing, irreplaceable elements and what their absence means is overwhelming. Being a child in India is difficult enough, being a girl is even harder. Young Indian women know what they're struggling against under the best of circumstances, and they know from a very young age.

In a country with a pervasive preference for sons and one of the highest levels of child mortality for girls in the world—one that exceeds that for boys by 43 percent—the following facts about the treatment of women aren't surprising. Women in India face a lower life expectancy, minimal education, poorly paid jobs, poor working conditions, greater work burdens, and very few rewards relative to men in comparable situations (Goldstein 1972, 34). For Indian women, both success and failure can be attributed to femaleness (Arnold, Choe, and Roy 1998, 68).

No wonder, then, that the word *"sati"* (the practice by widows of proving their devotion to their husbands by jumping into the funeral pyre) means, simultaneously, a good and faithful wife and the custom of widow immolation.

While reading an Indian feminist magazine called *Manushi,* I came across an image that I still recall, weeks after the last time I viewed it.[3] It was the photograph of a young woman suspended from a flush pipe by the six-foot length of her silk sari. The photograph was submitted to the magazine by the confused and grieved mother of the hanging girl. The mother hoped that the photograph would raise others to question the case, which was being labeled a suicide but had all the indications of a murder at the hands of her young daughter's husband. Sadly, in spite of her mother's best efforts and much evidence to the contrary, the young woman's homicide was ultimately recorded as a suicide. Unfortunately, there are enough young women caught in the seine of a remarkably unhappy marriage, marked by unchecked physical and emotional brutality, who are unable to leave because of the shame that they would bring upon their families, who opt instead to take their own lives, often by hanging themselves or dowsing their saris in kerosene and setting themselves aflame. Consequently, it's easy to assume that a young bride's death is by her own hand.

When it's time for Priya—tiny and only four—to speak, she holds tightly to Pratibha's hand.

"What do you remember as your best day?"

She shakes her head.

Try again.

"What do you study?"

Her voice begins chirping softly but proudly, a, aa, e, ee, u, uu, the first few letters of the Kannadan alphabet.

"What would you like to become?" A question I less than half expect to hear a four year old have an answer for, but the answer is there—swift and certain.

"I want to be a doctor," Priya says in a steady voice.

Then she clings tightly to Pratibha and whispers something to her in Kannada, which Pratibha translates.

"No more questions, please." Just like that, by a diminutive sage, the interviewer is dismissed.

The academy offers a pause prior to an adulthood that will be entirely predetermined by one's family name, caste, and status. What Preeti must hope for is the chance that she and her sisters can read and write

Kamala and Lalitha selling their homemade lamps on a Bangalore street.
(Photos by N. Prabhakar Kudva.)

their lives away from the capricious mercy of others, maybe even out of India entirely one day. It's hard to avoid "sad questions" when "what do you want to be?" yields answers that seem as pie in the sky as if they'd replied "movie star" or "president" or "God." More stunning still is the fact that they don't answer anything fantastic or make-believe but instead give professions so simultaneously hopeful and practical that it's hard not to wince a bit. In hearing the girls, I thought that half the questions I'd prepared seemed foolish, unintentionally cruel or in some way inappropriate. The obvious ones: Tell me about a bad day. What do your parents do? But many of the other "foolproof" questions took on strange tones, worried me with their potential to baffle or wound: What's your favorite food? What do you want to become? If you could be anything besides a person, what would you be?

The saddest question was, What now?

BY THE WAYSIDE, KAMALA AND LALITHA'S STORY

Kamala and Lalitha's family live not far from the academy in what might best be described as a mix between a tent and a hut. These sisters, too, had been separated from their parents for a time, during which they lived in an orphanage. Since being reunited with their parents, Kamala and Lalitha make and sell small earthen lamps to tourists for a very few rupees. As in many impoverished Indian families, the children are integral components of the family income. Without their small contributions, the family would likely starve. Consequently, the girls' education must often go by the wayside. For a time, after returning to their family, Kamala and her sister were attending day classes to keep up their studies. They were attending school for half a day and then helping the family in the afternoons. Little by little, their attendance grew spottier, until finally they were needed at home full-time. Understanding the interdependence of manual labor and survival means understanding the vicious cycle it promotes: parents need the added income of children. The birth of more children brings about more mouths to feed, which requires more hands at work, and so on. One typical portion of food served at most American restaurants would be an adequate serving for an Indian family of five for an entire day. In light of such poverty, some Indian families are undernourished to the degree that eye and brain development in their young children are stunted beyond repair.

Without education, little to no hope exists of the girls ever doing much more than barely surviving like desert plants in the face of unbearable conditions: little water, hot dusty air, little nourishment, and roots clinging desperately to the difficult ground.

Still, their situation seems livable in comparison to the four-year-old girl who rises at dawn after people living outdoors have completed their morning ablutions. The girl then gathers the day's human excrement and deposits it in a pit for burial. She's paid less than the equivalent of three cents for her efforts, but it's enough to buy a small bit of food to eat. Weekly.[4]

There are also the flower children, flower girls, phrases that ring of hippies and weddings, but refer to something else entirely here: young (usually four- to ten-year-old) girls and boys are sent out with cloth bags nearly the length of their bodies and asked to pick flowers to be sold by a flower vendor; they receive little more than a pinch of rice for wages. Often they are beaten. The laws that should be in place to protect such children are hard to enforce. The employees are also too young to know to whom to complain and too desperate to even want to try for fear of losing the bit of food or few *paises*—an Indian coin with a value even less than the rupee—and facing certain famine. It's odd to imagine being five and worrying that you may be fired because your fingers are just learning the physics of flower stem to tug. Perhaps you've gathered too few blossoms an hour or picked them too close to the bud or too far down the stem. In any case, you're five and you imagine your parents working in other fields or factories, perhaps long gone for one reason or other, and your siblings relying on your wages to sustain them.

It's an almost unfathomable childhood. When I consider the three orphaned girls I've just left and then other children, pulled from school into the dismal class of the desperate, underpaid, and abused employed, it's hard to determine which of the lives are more difficult.

Kamala, seven, and Lalitha, eight, stay close together when peddling the red-clay, beautifully carved oil lamps. Their family forms the clay into a flat, tear-shaped basin, a pinch to the sides for the spout, then they heat the dirt until it dries and hardens, then they etch the sides. The lamps are an authentic souvenir, the word that means to remember to return. They are not simply a tourist trinket but are also purchased by the locals to be filled with oil at dusk and lit. The lamps are riddled with the contradiction that defines India, extraordinary beauty alongside great ugliness. In spite of the fact that the lamps are the product of child labor, they are quite lovely, the size of the palm of a hand.

Lalitha and Kamala are in the middle of their workday, calling out to passersby in Kannada, of course, but also in a lilting English. "Pree-tee lights. Buy one. Buy two. Pree-tee lights. So little rupee. Pree-tee lights."

But one on one they're less talkative and protective in a different way from Preeti and her sisters.

Yes, they say, they like making the lamps. They are glad to be with their family. When they are older, what they'd like most is "to have a real shopping store, with a door and sign that says, 'Souvenirs, Little Lamps and Pretty Things, Made by Two Sisters.' "

This much they'll say comfortably. Yet, when asked if they'd like to return to school, they become defensive.

"We need to work," Lalitha says. "We need money."

"Do you miss anything about school?" I asked Kamala.

"I was pretty smart," she replied.

The difficulty is in translation. Not the translation that Prabhakar Kudva provided for me when he took the words from the tapes in Kannada and typed them into English, or even the translation involved in breaking down the expressions cast over the features in the girls' photographs. But translating what the girls mean when they say "I was smart" or "it is good." For example, it was good for Lalitha and Kamala to be back with their family, good by any definition, probably. But I wish they could have a life that combines the benefits and promise of school and the ability to be reunited with their parents.

Then there's this: I'm not Indian. I am a Greek-American woman staring into a life already exotic—that Greek word whose prefix exo, outside, I always hear spoken in my grandmother's voice. Exo, where I'll always be in relation to what it means to be a girl in Bangalore in an orphanage for mostly Sri Lankan refugee children or selling earthenware oil lamps on a street in Bangalore and hoping to make enough money to help feed my family for the night. It's all exotic to me—where it's taking place, and how little interior access and emotional knowledge I have to it. What could I expect my life to look like from such a vantage, and how much more would have to happen before I would call out in a child's voice "not fair"? Because from where I sit, it's not. India is a country that has intrigued me for as long as I can remember precisely because it is such a mosaic of contradictions—the colored chalk drawings that ornament the doorsteps of Indian homes during religious holidays, the expensive fireworks displays, which I have been told by Indian friends shame any Fourth of July display witnessed here in the States. Those fireworks are manufactured in sweatshops and by children, often easily identified as fireworks factory workers by their missing digits, the pawlike look of their mangled hands that assemble the brilliant and vivid tassels of light set off for *Holi:* Festival of Color, a festival that seems utterly life affirming. It is an event that, though religious, has a whimsical, frivolous element in the color sprayed all through the country. The Festival of Fire. The little mirrors sewn into colorful tapestries of fabric for dowry offerings. The joie de vivre of the whole death-clotted landscape. The practical, earnest children, in a country where childhood is a treacherous time; one slip and the streets rise up and swallow you.

What I felt then, when I first heard the stories, comes back to me as I involve myself in the process of transcribing, translating, interpreting their experiences. I have a sense of immaturity, my own. I felt and still feel self-conscious trying to tell you about five girls, two sets of sisters whose lives touched at an intersection and then forked into different and possibly unhappy endings. I feel foolish in the face of their calm, their lack of melodrama or blame. They seem like small adults easing me into acknowledging the ugly truths of the world, suggesting that it isn't what they want—it's only what they have, and some days it's nearly enough. Or, in the words of Pratibha—twenty-seven years my junior and certainly wiser—*things aren't bad today.*

NOTES

1. For more information on Bangalore, see the *My Bangalore* website at <http://www.webhead.com/www/india/india2.html.>.

2. For more examples of Indian folktales, see Narayan (1989) and Flueckiger (1996).

3. For more on Indian women and the women's movement of India, see Dhruvarajan (1989); Engels (1996); Jeffery and Roger (1996); Joshi and Liddle (1986); and Kishwar and Vanita (1984).

4. For graphs and statistics on hunger in Third World countries, see Foster (1992) and Zwingle (1998).

WORKS CITED

Arnold, Fred, Kim Minja Choe, and T. K. Roy. 1998. "Son Preference, the Family-Building Process and Child Mortality in India." *Population Studies* 6: 34–78.

Asthana, Pratima. 1974. *Women's Movement in India*. Bangalore: Vikas.

Dhruvarajan, Vanaja. 1989. *Hindu Women & The Power of Ideology*. Granby, Conn.: Bergin and Garvey.

Engels, Dagmar. 1996. *Beyond Purdah: Women in Bengal 1890–1939.* Bangalore: Oxford University Press.

Flueckiger, Joyce Burkhaltar. 1996. *Gender and Genre in the Folklore of Middle India.* New York: Cornell University Press.

Foster, Phillips. 1992. *The World Food Problem: Tackling the Cases of Undernutrition in the Third World.* New York: Lynne Reinner.

Goldstein, Rhoda L. 1972. *Indian Women in Transition: A Bangalore Case Study.* West Orange, N.J.: Scarecrow.

Jeffery, Patricia, and Jeffery Roger. 1996. *Don't Marry Me to a Plowman: Women's Everyday Lives in Rural India.* Boulder, Colo.: Westview.

Joshi, Rama, and Joanna Liddle. 1986. *Daughters of Independence: Gender, Caste and Class in India, Kali for Women.* New Delhi, India: Chamach Press.

Kapur, Akash. 1998. "Learning to Survive." *Atlantic Monthly* (September): 40–45.

Kishwar, Madhu, and Ruth Vanita. 1984. *In Search of Answers, Indian Women's Voices from Manushi.* London: Zed.

My Bangalore. Available at <http://webhead.com/www/india/india2.html>.

Narayan, Kirin. 1989. *Storytellers, Saints and Scoundrels, Folk Narrative in Hindu Religious Teaching.* Philadelphia: University of Pennsylvania Press.

Seethalakshmi, Shiva. 1999. "Reading Away, The Poverty Within One Sir Lankan Refugee Orphanage." *The Times of India,* Bangalore edition, January 26: A7–A8.

Zwingle, Erla. 1996. "Women and Population." *National Geographic* (October): 23–31.

· 8 ·

Afia's Story

A Guide to Survival

Afia Begum, Najma Habib, and Rebecca Sultana

$\mathcal{L}$iving in Bangladesh, I have always admired the young girls who work as maids, nannies, and, more recently, as garment workers. I have witnessed from afar their daily struggle to cling to whatever dignity they have left as they eke out a living. Their struggle appears even more surreal now, when I am able to juxtapose their lives' stories with those of others in one of the richest countries in the world, the U.S. A recent addition to the common sights on the streets of Bangladesh are the groups of young girls, all garment workers, in colorful dresses waiting for their bus rides early in the morning and then again for the ride back home late at night.

My friend Najma Habib, a working woman herself, has worked with the helpless and the destitute. Employed at a nongovernmental organization, Najma has worked at the grassroots level with indigent women. Her organization buys handmade crafts directly from these women, eliminating the third-party buyer. This allows the poorer party to keep more of the profit. In the course of her work, Najma has achieved an expertise in relating with women from poorer classes and gaining their trust. Typically, these women prefer to keep a disdainful distance from women like Najma or myself, who are educated, economically stable, and often unaware of the plight of those from the other side of the economic divide. Not many women from the more affluent sections of society would take the time to work for the economic well-being of these women. Of course, there are the members of clubs and institutions claiming to be helping the destitute, but rarely do they come to know the poor personally. Najma's job has led her to gain a closer proximity to them. She became the trusted intermediary for this discussion when she met Afia Begum, a young garment worker in Bangladesh. Najma and I had a tacit agreement that, while she would talk to the girl, I would put her words to paper. I could not have written this chapter nor learned as much without my friend's contribution.

It was impractical to set up an interview on the premises of Afia's workplace. Given the negative publicity that garment factory owners have had over many unfortunate incidents and the repercussions on garment-importing countries, many owners do not allow their workers to be polled or interviewed. Najma, however, was fortunate enough to take some photographs of Afia and her colleagues in their workplace with the promise that the well-being of the factory would not be jeopardized. The meeting finally took place in a friend's house. Afia had worked earlier as a maid for this friend and still maintained contact with the family, becoming, in the process, almost like a family member. Until recently, being a live-in maid was one of the few work options for most rural and uneducated young girls coming to the city. Now, with the increase of garment factories and the demand for more workers, women and young girls are opting for jobs that pay more, let them control their own destiny, and, for once, let them become dependent on themselves. This is a better option than toiling at menial household work, which frequently provokes rebukes or even physical infliction of pain for work not well done. But female garment workers are not entirely free from harassment themselves. Often they are paid much less than male workers, work for longer periods, and usually work in conditions that are anything but healthy. The concomitant, substantial increase in salary, however, is a matter of survival for these young women, many of them single mothers or young girls thrust out into the working world by a desperate family in need of financial help (Chaudhuri and Majumder 1991, 3).

Afia works in a garment factory in Dhaka, the capital of Bangladesh. She comes from a village in Comilla, a district to the southeast of Dhaka. Her father, Abdur Rahman, is a tenant farmer.[1] She has six siblings and is the oldest of the daughters; hence, she had to take over much of her mother's responsibilities early in her life. Afia grew up like many other village girls, helping her mother take care of the family. She learned to cook and clean, keep house, and tend to the smaller children. The only schooling she received was very elementary. Almost all village children start school only to drop out as they, too, start to contribute to the family income. Enrollment in schools is lower for girls than for boys, and girls' dropout rates are higher. Some possible contributing factors are the girls' early marriages and limited opportunities for employment (Ahmad et al.

Afia takes a break from work to pose for the camera.
(Photo by Najma Habib.)

1985, 85). Girls who get a year or two of schooling remain barely literate. Afia's ability to read and write is, therefore, remarkable, and it has
come to good use in her work at the factory.

School, although free at the primary level, is a luxury, especially
when a girl's help is seen as more important in the house. Children of
the relatively wealthy, rural, middle-class families are more fortunate.
Girls might finish high school, while boys progress to college. Had Afia
remained in the village, her lifestyle, though not her status, would have
been much different. Women's lives, especially in the rural areas, remain
centered on their traditional roles of being a wife, mother, sister, or
daughter. They have limited access to markets, productive services, education, health care, and local government. This lack of opportunity con-
tributes to high fertility patterns, which then diminish family well-being

and contribute to the malnutrition and generally poor health of the children. Because 82 percent of women live in the rural areas, such health issues have far-reaching effects on the educational and other national development goals of Bangladesh.[2] In the face of such a crisis, the government and various nongovernmental organizations (NGOs) are working at the grassroots level to bring access to health care, education, and training for improved productivity by these women. Among such assistance, microlending programs are having tremendous effects in reversing the hopeless conditions for these women, giving them access to loans from $75 to $125 to start their own small businesses. While many economists believe that long-term employment provides more security and higher returns than microenterprise activities, traditions in Bangladesh often inhibit a woman's ability to obtain employment outside the home.[3]

About 70 percent of rural women, such as Afia, live in small cultivator, tenant, and landless households. Among these women, many work as part-time or seasonal laborers, usually in postharvest activities. Twenty percent of the women, mostly from landless households, depend on casual labor and other sources of irregular income. The remaining 10 percent of women are from households mainly in the professional, trading, or large-scale landowning categories; they usually do not work outside the home.[4] Women from the landless families usually work in the wealthier houses by helping in the hoarding and storing of grain, or cleaning and cooking. With fewer jobs available within agriculture, more men and women are seeking work elsewhere. When the man of the house can no longer support his family on his own, women and often children have to seek means for their own subsistence (Feldman and McCarthy 1992, 114). Women who migrate to cities in search of work rely mostly on domestic and traditional jobs. Beginning in the 1980s, they increasingly worked in manufacturing jobs, especially in the readymade garment industry, bringing substantial changes not only in terms of their salaries but to the social structure of the country as well.

Bangladesh, a small country in South Asia, is predominantly Muslim. Social structure is strictly patriarchal, and women are supposed to be secluded. However, for the educated and urban population, modernity has prompted women to work outside of home, usually in conservative workplaces such as government, health care, and teaching. Even though urban women enjoy more physical freedom than was traditional and have the opportunity to pursue a professional career, they still move in a different social world from their husbands. Whether at their professions or in social gatherings, women segregate themselves away from the men. For the poorer, mainly rural classes, necessity has a way of overlooking these social conventions. Women working on agricultural fields, construction sites, or as sweepers in streets and buildings are common sights.

According to a study published in the newspaper *The Independent,* there are more than 840,000 people working in about 3,000 factories in Dhaka and other cities in Bangladesh.[5] Of these workers, about 80 percent are female. Yet, women workers are paid less than their male co-workers and have to work in conditions precarious to their well-being both physically and emotionally. According to another article in the same newspaper and substantiated in a workshop arranged by the British Council, Dhaka, women workers are often sexually harassed and propositioned by their male counterparts and superiors. ActionAid Bangladesh, a UK-based development organization, found in an investigation of ninety-three garment factories that about 20 percent of the unmarried female workers are enticed into sexual relationships with their coworkers or superiors. Many of these women are ignorant of safe-sex practices, exposing themselves to the dangers of acquiring STDs or AIDS, thus threatening the overall health situation of Bangladesh (*The Independent* 16).[6] The most vulnerable among the garment workers are "helpers," women who are paid relatively little and are thus likely to succumb to financial enticements. Maintaining such relationships, the study revealed, with timekeepers, security guards, and men in charge of a floor in the factory guarantee the uninterrupted flow of income even when the worker might have to take time off in case of sickness. Since about 75 percent of the female and 50 percent of male workers come from a rural background of absolute poverty, such enticements are hard to reject. Many are reluctant to speak out for fear of losing their jobs. Dr. Nafeeser Rahman, head of the Disability and AIDS Coordination Unit of ActionAid, has already warned of dire health consequences (*The Independent* 16).

Since the revelation of such information—in a country where such relationships are still considered taboo subjects—garment workers, in general, are seen as a morally degenerate group. This is unfair to and grossly untrue of the majority of the women workers. Such interpolation becomes harmful to these women when they lose their jobs and have to find alternate work. Their previous employment as garment factory workers makes it difficult for them to later get jobs as maids or personal caregivers.

Afia's present position is remarkable, as she defies the staggering odds against her. Her story becomes even more remarkable considering how much she has already experienced of life. At fifteen, Afia was married; indeed, most village girls are married by the time they are seventeen and go to live in their husband's home. Marriages are a long process of contracts, fact finding, and, finally, agreement between two families. In many instances, especially among the not so educated or the very conservative, the girl is not even personally informed of what is going on. But it is not possible to remain unapprised of what is taking place, what with the matchmaker and relatives who start to stop by. Once the girl gets a hint of what the parents are involved in, she might start to daydream of her yet-not-seen Prince Charming. Because of the cultural ideals associated with female deference, however, it is considered indelicate for a girl to show interest in her own marriage. Although Afia had to formally give her consent to marry, she lacked any power to intervene or disagree with any decision.

Marriage proposals are conveyed by other family members to the parents or the guardian of the girl. In Afia's case, her uncle arranged the match. It is not uncommon for the matchmaker to conceal a damaging fact about either party. Once married, the young girl finds herself in a position of subordination to not only the men in the groom's family but also the older women, who usually include the mother-in-law and sisters-in-law within the extended family. The custom of exogamy, or marrying outside the home village, heightens the isolation of the new bride. Marriage marks the transition from childhood to womanhood as the young girl learns to be submissive, learning how to do what will please the family and proving her worth through obedience, hard work, good temper, and modest behavior. She will spend most of her time with the other female members of the household, and it is they who may be most sharply critical.

Marriages are described as tests of fate. In cases where the relationships do not work out, fate is blamed. Divorce rates are low compared to western standards—not always because the marriages turn out to be happy ones, but because divorce or separations are rarely favored. Girls are encouraged to endure whatever fate holds for them. If a man divorces his wife, she has no option but to return to her father's home. Relatively well-to-do families attempt to marry off the young girl again, but a family already reeling from the financial toll of paying the dowry has little prospect for a second marriage. Therefore, economy plays a part in marriages; poverty may cause a man to walk away, divorce his wife, and marry again. There are more divorces in poor families than among the urban and middle classes. The fact that the marriage was arranged by others and not the couples themselves does not have any bearing on the outcome.

Arranged marriage is a misunderstood concept to westerners. These marriages are not forced, but in a situation where there is no love relationship, matchmakers, usually parents, step in and choose a mate for their offspring. The ideal of an arranged marriage is to make a fully suitable match, in terms of class, community, education, temperament, and personality, as well as fusing an individual and a household interest. Once the marriage is agreed upon between the two families, the engaged couple can socialize through chaperoned, and in rare cases unchaperoned, meetings. As a happily married woman of eleven years, I have no complaint about how I was married. For most women in Bangladesh and in many Asian countries, this is how marriages take place. In a social situation where interaction of the opposite sexes, apart from a professional context, is not common, such a tradition is a logical one. Soon after I graduated from college with a masters degree, my parents asked me, through a friend of mine (as parents usually will not talk about these subjects directly with their children), whether there was anyone I would like to wed. Since I was more involved with my books than in a social life, I was not romantically involved with anyone, and considering how shy I was there was not a chance of that happening either. Getting the go-ahead, my parents started the elaborate procedure of the marriage with my future husband, whom they had already selected. They had anticipated, correctly, that their daughter would not choose a mate for herself. But if I had chosen to remain unmarried, I could have done so, despite my parents' protests. They would have cried, begged, and been mortified, but they would not have forced me into a situation that would affect the rest of my life. But then, I was too docile a daughter to go against parental wishes and societal conventions.

When a young girl does fall in love with a man and expresses her desire for marriage, her choice may be met with disapproval. Parents might be dissatisfied with the choice of their daughter's mate because of his economic or social status, being less educated than the girl herself, or simply because she chose to select her mate herself, a duty entrusted to the elders. When children grow up and indicate that they have minds of their own and are determined to do something, however, parents often relent. Sometimes the endings are not as happy, especially when a girl might come from a family socially or economically superior to the man's. The girl eventually gives in to parental pressure. It is difficult for a girl, who has lived a fiercely protected life with these parents, to want to emotionally hurt them. In cases where the girl elopes, she loses not only her immediate family but the extended family as well. That is a risk many girls will not take and one that is unthinkable in the rural areas, although legends and folklore abound in Bengali literature—usually with tragic results. In the rural and more conservative population, there are no premarriage meetings and often no acknowledging of the girl's wishes. Afia saw her husband for the first time on her wedding night.

Afia's marriage did not work out. It was painful for her to recount a past she would rather forget. "My husband's name was Kashem Ali. The only thing I knew about him was that he worked in Dhaka and that he came from a family that owned land, although he himself did not work on it." A married woman, even educated and urban, usually does not say her husband's name out loud but refers to him as her child's father. Since Afia is no longer married, she talked about Kashem as just another person. "I was not fated to have a family of my own," she said simply. Acceptance of fate can be fatalistic, inhibiting, or an easy way out of a painful situation. Acknowledgment of fate is often ingrained into a young girl's mind.

As a girl child, Afia always knew that she would be married one day. In Islam, marriage is an obligation. Having a marriageable yet unmarried daughter is extremely undesirable for a father, so a family attempts to marry off a girl, even at the high cost of a dowry that many can ill afford.[7] In contrast, the groom has to agree on a bride's price, usually with a written agreement of a particular sum of money. But the sum is typically deferred with the understanding it can be claimed by the wife in the event of divorce. In Afia's case, she entered into marriage with no independent economic assets of her own.[8]

Afia was married with whatever celebration her father could afford, which was not much. Kashem was working at a textile factory in Dhaka. As he shared his housing with his coworkers, he could not take his bride to live there. He would, therefore, come and visit her only on weekends at her father's house. Afia remembered that every time Kashem came for a visit, the entire household was thrown into a frenzy. Sons-in-law hold a peculiar position of adulation in a girl's family. There is a term in Bengali—*Jamai aadar*—to denote the kind of adulation deserving a son-in-law. This is not due to parents losing a daughter and gaining a new son, but, more importantly, for ensuring the daughter's happiness by placating her husband. Like any other young bride, Afia anticipated her husband's visits with expectations of soon going to his place. It was difficult to make Afia talk about that stage. A girl will not talk about such intimate details unless with a very close friend, and Najma was hardly that at the early stage of their knowing each other. Three months after their marriage, Afia did leave her father's to be with her parents-in-law, who were in another village in Comilla. "I was given four saris. I wore one of those for the occasion." Afia never once said Kashem's name aloud even though he was no longer her husband.

In extended families, which are strictly maintained in rural societies, a married son generally lives in his parents' household during his father's lifetime. Even though sons may build separate houses for their nuclear families, they remain under their fathers' authority, and the wives under that of their mothers-in-law. It was only natural that Afia should be living with her in-laws while Kashem worked in Dhaka. The couple's last phase of the journey to his home was a ride on a rickshaw. As Afia neared her husband's place, covered and veiled, she could hear music, which her mother-in-law had arranged to be played to welcome her. She felt like a new bride again. Kashem's family home was larger than Afia's father's, and her in-laws seemed financially better off than her own family. "I imagined my days of poverty and little food were finally over," Afia told Najma. By that time, she was already pregnant. As a new bride, the first few days were spent inside, where she remained appropriately dressed while relatives poured in to get a glimpse of the new addition to the family. Two days after her coming she was told by her husband's niece, perhaps inadvertently, that Kashem was already married and that his wife lived with their eight-year-old daughter. A young girl's dreams were shattered. Afia remembered being stunned for a long period before she regained her feelings of hurt and betrayal. "I never stopped crying for the remainder of my stay there." Incapable of doing anything on her own, she refused food and continued her days like that for a week. She then told her husband that she wanted to go to her parents'. Most village girls, already with so few expectations from life, would not make such a statement.

Conventionally, a woman looks to her father or brothers if her marriage fails. The male family members will either try to reason it out with her or finally represent her in a village court. However, the extent to which a woman can depend on her family for help varies much according to class. In most cases, however, the family will try to convince the girl to continue the relationship rather than leave. This reflects the strong bias in gender construction in which the only party to come out badly is the girl (White 1992, 112). Afia's father was poor and the family could mobilize little social pressure on her behalf. Afia's journey turned into a one-way journey home.

Afia gave birth to a daughter while living at her parents' home. When her daughter was one and a half years old, Afia left her daughter with her mother in Comilla and decided to leave for Dhaka. Since neither Afia's brothers nor her father were able to provide well for both her and her child, Afia had to find a means to survive by herself. "I just couldn't sit around doing nothing and being a burden to my father. There was not much in the village that I could do. Everyone else was like me, looking for work." Usually it is through someone already working in the cities that girls can find out about work outside of the village. Afia initially worked as a maid, and finally found work in a garment factory. Now, she works as a sewing-machine operator for ten hours a day and earns Taka 1,000 a month.[9] She spends Tk 100 for her rent of a room that she shares with other factory girls, sends Tk 400 for her daughter, and needs the rest for food and her upkeep. Since she cannot yet save any of her earnings, she is contemplating starting on a second job, possibly as a cook. Maybe she could then save some money. "Perhaps it would come to good use"; Afia smiled as she thought about that. Najma was happy to see that Afia was, after all, still young at heart. It would be nice to use the money for something besides basic survival.

When asked about her future, Afia is philosophical. She has sworn off marriage. Her only aspiration is now for her daughter. She wants to earn enough so that she can provide her daughter an education that will allow her to escape her mother's plight. "I miss her so much, although I know she is well taken care of." Afia expresses another fear that lurked in the young mother's heart: "Sometimes I wonder if she will love me as a mother. I'm not there when she needs me." But she understands that it would have been impossible to work full-time and take care of a child. When asked about her daughter, Afia's eyes mist over, yet her voice remains firm. She will not let her daughter go through the same predicament as hers. "I've realized that I can live alone. Now I can shape up my daughter's future my own way. But sometimes I feel that she has missed out having a father becsuse of my stubbornness. But I will teach

Women garment workers waiting for the bus to work. Females usually travel in groups for safety. (Photo by Najma Habib.)

her how to survive." Not having known comfort in her own life, Afia does not expect much out of life for herself as long as she can leave something for her daughter. Right now, working in the garment factory could be the best thing that has happened to her so far, as is true for thousands of young girls. The garment industry is the first industrial sector that has provided employment to such a large number of women outside the home. Women are benefiting from the increased wages, greater freedom, and higher status through their employment (Bangladesh Unnayan Parishad 1990, 2).

For Bangladesh, exportation of garments provides nearly 70 percent of the country's total export earning and is a source of income that the country can ill afford to lose. However, working conditions are still far from desirable, especially for very young workers.[10] At one time, young children under fourteen were employed to help in jobs such as threading, collecting, or running errands. The threat of a consumer boycott of their exported products was one reason garment manufacturers in Bangladesh decided to put an end to the employment of children in their factories. But boycotting the country, stopping imports, or shutting down the factories because of such practices only hurts the ones who need help most—the workers themselves. This has become apparent in the recent fiasco over child labor in a Honduran factory that was producing designer labels for talk-show host Kathie Lee Gifford. In the midst of the furor, the factory was forced to close down, resulting in all the workers losing their jobs. I wonder how many of them found work later (*Sweatshop Watch* 2).[11] If the Bangladesh factories were to close down, all these young girls and underage workers would be thrown out on the streets without a day's income to buy food. Desperate situations call for desperate measures. Many of these children would be forced to turn to stealing, picking pockets, or working at menial jobs that are even more back breaking. The girls might go back to cleaning other people's houses or, worse, be forced into prostitution. At least, by sewing clothes they are earning four times as much and can maintain a sense of dignity (BUP, 1990, 3).

In Bangladesh, steps are already being taken to rectify these ills. In a memorandum signed by the Bangladesh Garments Manufacturers and Exporters Association (BGMEA), the International Labor Organization (ILO), and UNICEF on July 4, 1995, child workers below fourteen years of age are now put in school programs until they turn fourteen (BGMEA 1992, 3). They then are provided the option of returning to the workplace as skilled laborers. When these underaged workers were initially turned out by the factory owners for fear of western boycott, an already precarious situation was made worse for these children as they found themselves near starvation-level poverty, with 30–50 percent of the family income gone. Now the retrenched children, while being educated in schools to read and write, receive Taka 300 per month and are given vocational training as well. A total of 9,743 former child workers of the garment industries have been attending 353 schools run by non-governmental and governmental agencies, as agreed to under the memorandum.[12] Work has been going on in other sectors too. Hostels are being built for affordable housing, adult education is being provided for women workers, and basic health care is being provided by nongovernmental agencies.

Although much has been done about women workers, much remains to be done. Studies have found poor health conditions for female and male employees. Women workers regularly suffer through occupational hazards that lead to physical ailments. Women typically work from twelve to thirteen hours per day, seven days a week, doing, on average, seventy-eight hours of overtime work, while also bearing the burden of household chores and bringing up children. Travel to and from the

Garment workers at Afia's workplace. (Photo by Najma Habib.)

workplace is fraught with danger as they find themselves traveling alone late at night (Chaudhuri and Majumder 1991, 4).

Nari Uddag Kendra, a women's welfare group, with joint collaboration of Canadian International Development Agency (CIDA), surveyed 1,720 garment workers, of whom 1,337 were female and 383 male, from forty-three factories in the cities of Dhaka, Chittagong, Narayanganj, Tongi, and Savar. The women interviewed worked in sewing operations, helping with finishing, cutting, supervising, and quality control. They were queried on issues of women's health, conditions of livelihood, effect of working conditions, and the availability of proper medical attention. Sixty-eight percent of the female workers questioned and 54 percent of male workers reported that their health deteriorated at work. Their conditions were exacerbated by their standing for a prolonged period of time, not being able to urinate as often as needed to, irregular eating and drinking habits while at work, and improper ventilation of the workplace. The problems arising from such conditions can

Workers in the button section of a garment factory. (Photo by Najma Habib.)

range from specific to general, such as lethargy and weakness, gastric ul-
cers, chest and back pain, eye problems, fever, menstrual problems,
headaches, joint pains, and skin irritations. To improve the conditions of
workers' health, 38 percent of the owners will pay for medical treatment
for the workers only when needed, but 34 percent would like to place
permanent medical staff at their factories; 18 percent are willing to pay
only for medicine, while 8 percent will pay regular medical allowances.
NUK (Nari Uddag Kendra—the Organization for the Development of
Women), on its own, has undertaken a number of initiatives to help improve the condition of women garment workers. It has already built four
hostels in Dhaka that provide less expensive housing for women. The
organization has also started evening classes to teach some of the younger
workers how to read and write and also to make them aware of their
rights. With the collaboration of some factory owners, NUK has arranged for doctors to visit the workers in the factories and hostels. Joint
living in hostels has added to the safety of the young girls as they constantly put themselves in danger because they return from work late at
night. Now, they travel to and from work together.[13]

The introduction of female labor has far-reaching consequences not only in gender relations but also in social construction.[14] With the development of the garment industry, a growing number of young, mostly unmarried women has joined the work force, resulting in the redefinition and reshaping of appropriate female behavior and a reconsideration of family status. More women are now visible in the public places than they were a decade ago. Men and women working together have forced greater interaction between the genders. This interaction has led women to seek "new patterns of urban migration, collective living arrangements, the unaccompanied use of public transportation, increased market activity, new consumption patterns, and new forms of political expression" (Feldman and McCarthy 1992, 118). Although these young working women are endowed with more economic stability and independence, they also have to face the brunt of the disdain from religious fundamentalists, who see such freedom as a decline in the societal norms (Feldman and McCarthy 1983, 951).

Aware of the darker side of such work, Najma asks Afia if she fears for herself and sees herself as being exploited. Afia shakes her head. "I'm fortunate that I don't have to provide for a husband and a large family, so financial enticement doesn't bother me, but I do feel I deserve more for the work that I do." She does acknowledge that by the end of the day she is extremely tired. How does she not get hopelessly dejected as most young girls do? Najma's eyes meet with those of Afia for a while, and they both understand. It's difficult not to be dejected, and maybe she is. But she cannot afford to give up. Her daughter depends on her. Although already she has gone through so much, she is willing to go through more hardship should it be necessary. As Najma prepares to conclude her interview session, she thinks about her meetings with Afia. Najma has mentioned to me repeatedly how impressed she is with Afia and how much she respects the young girl's fortitude. Najma is certain that Afia can prevail. The social and economic conditions around her, however, are difficult to circumvent.

During their meetings and at work, Afia regularly has worn a *shalwar* and *kameez,* a long tunic and loose pants, and covered herself with a matching *orna,* a wide scarf that is used to cover the front of the dress. Comfortable and easy to wear, such dresses were once only worn by the very young before adopting the sari permanently. Now, the style is being worn more and more by young working girls and even older women in the cities. Although the sari is still the proper professional dress for women, the *shalwar* and *kameez* are being recognized, especially by the younger generation, as providing more mobility and freedom in a fast-moving world. A village girl of Afia's age would never wear such an outfit. It is significant that Afia's transformation from a demure country girl to a hard-working factory girl is manifested in her choice of outer garments.

There is something in Afia that commands respect. Although only eighteen, she is already worldly wise. She is young and attractive, and I wonder how she would have fared as a construction worker toiling under the open skies, her work consisting of breaking stones, a hard and laborious task. She is not like the giggly girls who work around her, many of whom are only too eager to flirt with the supervisor. Her demeanor is such that anyone would think twice before approaching her with any indecent proposal. The best thing that has come out of this project is that Najma has gained Afia's friendship in the course of their meetings and talks. With her experiences, Najma is already aware of the desperation of those who live in poverty but also about their determination. Najma has already shared with Afia her knowledge about groups and institutions such as NUK or *Banchte Shekha* (Learning to Live), a development program for women and children that helps women get out of depressing situations through education or by providing them loans. It is, however, up to Afia herself to map her own life.

Sometimes I wonder about Afia's life and mine and Najma's. Each of us is a mother of a daughter; each of us is fiercely protective of her child, for whom each anticipates the best; we each hope our daughter will surpass the mother in achievements. Yet how different our lives are just because of where we were born. At eighteen, Najma and I were best friends at the university, with no cares in the world, taken care of by parents whose only expectation from us was good grades. We graduated, got married, found good jobs, and in the midst of everything we are raising families and attempting to go beyond what we started out to do. Afia, on the other hand, has been through more than that in an even shorter span. Where will her life take her? She is just eighteen, young and pretty. Perhaps she will marry again. Maybe next time, she will marry someone she herself chooses, and, hopefully, her marriage might work out. Whatever happens, she has gained our respect. It is rare to see such strength of character in someone so young.

NOTES

1. In Bangladesh, children's last names do not have to match with those of the fathers.

2. For the latest statistics on Bangladesh and the country's economic conditions, I have consulted a very useful Web site, the official *National Data Bank* of Bangladesh. Accessed on 1 October 1998. Available at: <http://www.bangla.net/ndb/>.

3. Bangladesh Rural Advancement Committee (BRAC) and Grameen Bank are two such programs having great impact on the economic structure of this class. Grameen Bank, a world renowned and well-imitated concept, has turned around the lives of many. For more information on Grameen Bank, see Counts (1996). While running the U.S. Grameen Foundation in Washington, D.C., Counts visited Bangladesh to study Grameen as an American Fulbright scholar and tells in the book how the concept works both in America and in Bangladesh.

4. Information collected from National Data Bank, "Bangladesh: Women's Role in Society." Accessed on 30 October 1998. Available at: <http://lcweb2.loc.gov/cgi-bin>.

5. See Mahbubul Alan's editorial in *The Independent* (Dhaka, Bangladesh). Accessed 20 November 1998. Available at: <http://independent-bangladesh.com/news>.

6. From 1989 until 1996, Bangladesh had about 2.3 million cases of STDs and 95 cases of HIV, 10 of which developed into AIDs and proved fatal (information from *The Independent* Web site).

7. According to Islamic custom, marriage was traditionally accompanied by gifts from the groom's family to the bride's. However, within the past three decades a dowry system has evolved, with a steady inflation in the economic demands made by the groom. For more information on the dowry system, see White (1992).

8. Although, within Islamic law, daughters have the right to inherit the equivalent of half the son's share of the father's property, women customarily waive their land rights to their brothers in exchange for the promise of future economic protection in the event of divorce, abandonment, or other calamity. See Kibria (1995).

9. Taka 1,000 is roughly equivalent to U.S. $25.

10. For information on the achievements of the garment industries in Bangladesh, I have consulted the surveys produced by both Bangladesh Unnayan Parishad (BUP 1990) and Bangladesh Garment Manufacturers and Exporters Association (BGMEA 1992).

11. Also see Gaudiani (1996).

12. See *The Independent* (Dhaka, Bangladesh), July 5, 1998, 10.

13. For more detailed data, see "Health Problems of Women in Garments Industry" in *The Independent* (Dhaka, Bangladesh), July 3, 1998, 1.

14. See Pearson (1988) for her critique of contemporary analyses of the new international division of labor.

WORKS CITED

Ahmad, Q. K., M. A. Khan, S. Khan, and J. A. Rahman, eds. 1985. *Situation of Women in Bangladesh*. Dhaka: Ministry of Social Welfare and Women's Affairs, Government of the People's Republic of Bangladesh.

Alam, Mahbubul. 1997. "Disaster in the Garments Section." *The Independent* (Dhaka, Bangladesh), 3 March: 6.

Bangladesh Garment Manufacturers and Exporters Association (BGMEA). 1992. *The Garment Industry: A Look Ahead at Europe of 1992.* Dhaka: Bangladesh Garment Manufacturers and Exporters Association.

Bangladesh Unnayan Parishad (BUP). 1990. *A Study on Female Garment Workers in Bangladesh: A Draft Report.* Dhaka: Bangladesh Unnayan Parishad.

Chaudhuri, Salma, and Pratima Pal Majumder. 1991. *The Conditions of Garment Workers in Bangladesh: An Appraisal.* Dhaka: Bangladesh Institute of Development Studies.

Counts, Alex. 1996. *Give Us Credit.* New York: Times Books.

"Fair Labor Association—Starvation Wage." 1998. *Sweatshop Watch* 4(3): 1–3. Also available at: <http://www.sweatshopwatch.org/swatch/newsletters/4-3.html>.

Feldman, Shelley, and Florence E. McCarthy. 1983. "Purdah and Changing Patterns of Social Control Among Rural Women in Bangladesh." *Journal of Marriage and the Family* 45(4): 949–59.

———. 1992. In *Unequal Burden: Economic Crises, Persistent Poverty and Women's Work,* ed. Lourdes Beneria. Boulder, Colo.: Westview.

Gaudiani, Claire L. 1996. "Fighting Child Labor." Connecticut College President Writings. Accessed 30 October 1998. Available at: <http://shain.lib.conncoll.edu/ccadmin/gaudiani/writings/fighting.html>.

"Health Problems of Women in Garments Industry." 1998. *The Independent,* 3 July: 1.

The Independent. Available at: <http://independent-bangladesh.com>.

Kibria, Nazli. 1995. "Culture, Social Class, and Income Control in the Lives of Women Garment Workers in Bangladesh." *Gender and Society* 9(3): 289–309.

Pearson, Ruth. 1988. "Female Workers in the First and Third Worlds: The Greening of Women's Labour." In *On Work,* ed. Raymond Edward Pahl. Oxford: Basil Blackwell, 449–66.

White, Sarah C. 1992. *Arguing with the Crocodile: Gender and Class in Bangladesh.* London: Zed Books.

·9·

A Tryst Missed

Girlhood in Pakistan

Mithi, Pomi, Nasima, and Tahera Aftab

$\mathcal{G}$irlhood remains socially taboo in Pakistan as well as in other South Asian societies. Girlhood, for most girls in these countries, is a period of shame and fear. It is a twenty-four-hour, never-ending nightmare for their mothers. It is a war alert for their fathers. It is a threat to the lives of their brothers. For the community and the neighborhood, it is a danger zone. Girls are perceived as a burden for themselves and for the society at large.

With the tradition of early marriages, especially for women, Pakistan, since its creation in 1947, has now produced several generations of women.[1] A girl born in Sindh, Punjab, Balochistan, or in the northwestern provinces of Pakistan is likely to be betrothed by the time she reaches her sixteenth year. Usually a member of a large family, with several young siblings, a "good girl" is in charge of household chores as early as eight or nine years of age. Indeed, she is expected to fill in the role of her mother, who remains occupied either with a child in her womb or one at her breast. A girl who evades domestic jobs and dares to play is not a *naik* (gentle) girl but a shameless creature, compromising the "honor" of her ancestors and bringing "shame" to the family. The code of honor, *ghairat,* is a brutal shield that protects the male honor, circumventing in a tragic manner the life and existence of women and girls. For women (all married females are considered women, with no consideration of age) and girls living in rural and feudal Pakistan, the faintest or even a rumored aversion to this code of honor is tantamount to an encounter with death. Girlhood, therefore, must remain anonymous and taboo. The longer the period of girlhood, the deeper is the agony of the girl's life and darker her destiny.

151

*A girl about ten years old, from Mithi's village, preparing a meal on a
kerosene stove under a thatched roof. (Photo by Tahera Aftab.)*

A female in Pakistan has two stages of her life—a stage of being
married or of being unmarried. Whatever girlhood may mean for girls
elsewhere, in Pakistan for the majority of girls it is mainly a state of
"being unmarried." The status of unmarried is equal to that of being
virgin, hence in common parlance the word for "virgin" and for "unmarried" is the same—*"kunwari."* An unmarried daughter or a sister is
a threat to the lives of the males of the family as they might be forced
into a violent situation to defend their sisters or daughters.

The language of the culture evades the word "girl" or "girlhood."
A well-mannered person will avoid using the word "girl" for females
between the ages of ten and twenty, lest it should be construed as indi-
rectly alluding to the recognition of the grown-up stage of the female
child. The period of girlhood, though evasive and fleeting, is overcast
by fears and delusions. Girlhood remains subdued and suppressed—but
girls' stories must be told to share with readers the oppression that girls
in Pakistan, and in many other countries, confront. I have selected the
life stories of three girls to discuss, each of whom has a different social
background, speaks a different language, and lives in a different environ-

ment. Despite these obvious dissimilarities, a common factor in their lives is their will to survive.

My first story is about Mithi.[2] She was about fifteen years of age when we first met in her one-room, mud-bricked house with a tin roof. Along with some of the students from a women's studies course I was teaching, I visited a peripheral *goth* (village) situated a few miles away from our university campus. Our purpose was to select a team of women and girls from this village and to develop, with their help, a program of awareness about reproductive health and personal hygiene for women and girls.

Upon reaching the village, we found ourselves amid a crowd of women and girls. Most of them were eager to talk but felt shy to start. Soon I noticed a quiet, sullen face of a girl, sitting at a little distance from the crowd. As I tried to approach her, the rest of the women warned me, "No use talking with her. She is *allahwali* (doesn't belong to this world)." I could see a smile on her tense face. It was later on that I was able to know, in bits and pieces, the story of Mithi's life.

It was her elder brother who made me more aware of his sister's story. I knew him because he works as a part-time gardener at the university where I teach. Once he was gone for several weeks. When I asked whether everything was going well with him, he told me his sister was ill again. He said that she was taken to a spiritual healer since the doctors had failed to cure what ailed her. "*Daktaro ney to jawab dediya hai* (the doctors have said the final no)," he said with a sad tone of finality. He volunteered the next information about the ailment. "She is under a spell, possessed by the spirits. So we keep a close surveillance on her."

I know too well what surveillance means when the object of protection is a "possessed woman." I had recently visited some of the spiritual healers, men and women both, in the city of Karachi. Some welcomed me, others shut their doors in my face. I was, however, able to talk to some of the *pakri hui* (possessed) and *saya mein* (under the spell) women or to their chaperones. I heard some of the most gruesome tales of horror, horror committed in the name of treatment.

I asked if it would be possible for me to see his sister, and during this visit Mithi shared her life experiences with me. As if talking in sleep, her dry lips moved, giving out a soliloquy. I marveled at the serenity of her presence, so collected! Where did she learn the art of picking the threads of life and weaving them into patterns afresh? Her slow monologue drilled deep into my very being. I made a feeble effort to catch her train of thoughts. As if in trance, she moved on. "I am sure Mother still loves me. She named me Mithi—the sweet, sugary one! Mithi . . . at the very sound of it my mouth starts churning SALT." With a strange look, Mithi gazed somewhere across the verandah of corrugated tin sheets of her house where she sat resting against the wall. We could not talk much.

Our second meeting took place at least two months later. This time five of my women's studies students visited Mithi. She was pleased to see several younger persons of her age. The rest of the story of Mithi comes out of the pages of my students' journals.

A tale, the kind that Mithi related, is always told in bits and pieces, but not because the woman or the girl telling the story is not coherent. Remember, this woman or girl is virtually picking up tiny bits of glass. One gets hurt when picking up the sharp edges of glass pieces. Recollection is painful. Retelling the story all of a sudden means re-enacting the scenes. The past once again overpowers the survivor, the muscles get limp, the throat is choked, the vision is blurred, the whole being is blocked by a massive volcanic eruption of emotion, a roller-coaster ride. Returning to some form of normalcy, the person's first reaction is to appear distant, dazed. For the onlooker, it is the state of being "possessed."

Mithi says her mother thinks she should forget her past. Her mother says, "We are helpless. We cannot undo it." She alone knows what happened to Mithi on that fateful night, when everyone in the neighborhood was asked to celebrate the election victory of the person who held the ownership rights of the land on which the houses of Mithi and those of her community were raised.

That night the drums were beaten, the loudspeakers boomed the film's songs, rice cooked with meat was brought in huge containers, even iced water was there. Colored buntings gleamed under the light of electric generators. The drums, the loudspeakers, the clanging of aluminum plates in which rice was served, the deafening vibration of the generator, mixed with the unending shrieks of the children and the noise of women's loud gossip; these erased Mithi's voice when she was dragged, struggling like a goat being taken from her neighborhood to the butcher, into the small truck that had unloaded the food for the feast. Before anyone noticed Mithi's absence, she was back.

She was a heap of flesh, meat. Like the goats of her village, Mithi was butchered. Butchered by the man who had organized the feast. His identity did not matter. It does not matter even today. She could not be taken to a doctor or to a hospital. What a shameful thing to do, to let anyone know about a shameful thing! Her mother was sure that if they were in the inner villages, Mithi would have been axed to death as a *kari* (doer of a blackened deed) by her brother or another male of the family. They waited for her next cycle of periods. The missed cycle was the beginning of a new cycle of tortures. Mithi was dragged from place to place, with great secrecy, by her mother. At every new location, she was forced to undergo more tortures to get her insides cleansed.

Her mother remained convinced that if on that ill-omened evening Mithi had not worn her pink dress with mirrors, things would have been different. The scars on her body now frighten Mithi. The family believes that Mithi has "visions" and the spirits possess her. Mithi's own voice is lost in the noise of the new, strange Mithi.

Her mother gazed at Mithi, bowed down, kissed her forehead, and sighed, "Oh, how I wish you were dead the moment you were born."

The story of Mithi doesn't end here. Also, it is not the story of *only* Mithi. Nafisa Shah provides an eyewitness account of the life led by other girls in some parts of Sindh, the area of Pakistan that is Mithi's family's origin. "The birth of a girl is received with a sense of self-pity," she writes. "Girls are a 'blessing,' but they belong to someone else so they are temporary guests in the house of their parents" (1997, 34). Shah continues:

> *Sangawatti* or the politics of marriage may determine the fate of a woman long before her birth. In exchange marriages, if women of productive age are not available, pledges are made in a custom called *paith likhi diyan*—to pledge a pregnancy—in which a woman not yet born is pledged into marriage in the exchange. In Upper Sindh, especially Larkana, the father who makes the transactions prefers to charge half the money for his daughter's bride price and the other half is charged as a *sangh*. The same daughter will return a daughter born to her to the father who will then pass on the daughter to his agnates in the exchange deal. Hence in marriages the capital value of women is valued against an admixture of customs and market forces. (34)

This "temporary guest" status for women remains forever. The parents do not want to spend money on the girls, as they will soon go the homes of their husbands. The husbands and the in-laws never accept a new woman as part of their family. Thus, women and girls are almost

Little girls from Mithi's village. They have never been to school.
(Photo by Tahera Aftab.)

status-less individuals in the patriarchal feudal society of rural Pakistan. Disowned by their own kith and kin, girls develop a lack of self-respect and always consider themselves a burden on their parents. This also adversely impacts their mental and physical well-being. Shireen Rehmatullah, who has long worked in rural Sindh, writes that "traditionally parents do not want to invest in girls' education as they do not find it useful for them. After all, they are *'paraya Dhan'*[3] and will leave the home anyway" (1994, 8).

WHITHER GIRLHOOD? THE STORY OF POMI

More than fifty years have passed since Pakistan emerged as an independent country after fighting a long, drawn-out battle against the colonial hegemony. Freedom, however, has yet to be experienced by a majority of women and girls, particularly those living a life in bondage in tribal rural communities. Here in these villages, cut off from the rest of world, the tribal landlords virtually maintain their own prisons. Tales of physical

Another group of young girls. (Photo by Tahera Aftab.)

torture and abuse of these unfortunate prisoners seldom catch the eye of law enforcement agencies. The slave masters' treatment of their female prisoners crosses all limits of human endurance. Women in rural Pakistan are voiceless and powerless. An uneducated, unskilled woman survives at the mercy of her male providers. The absence or failure of the males of the family to protect and provide for the female members of their family turns many a woman into easy prey for the other males in power. With the emergence of women's groups and their effective advocacy of women's human rights, women are now voicing their resentment toward the abuse that they and their daughters suffer. It will take another fifty years—or even longer—for *some* women to be free as human beings. My next story comes from a rural area of the province of Sindh in Pakistan. (It may be of some interest to know that the girl in my next story and the first woman prime minister of Pakistan come from the same neighborhood.)

The story of Pomi, of the village Kolhipara in Sindh, is reported by a woman activist, Tasneem Bhatti. She visited some of the villages of Sindh's desert, Tharparkar. Tharparkar is almost like a hunting zone for women and girls. The life and honor of men and women here are at the mercy of the feudal masters of the region. It is quite difficult for persons speaking a different dialect to establish a rapport with the local populace. Tasneem Bhatti is a familiar person in this rural area, as she often visits it as a social worker. It was during one such visit to the Nagarparker region that she met with the family of Pomi. Pomi was born in a society wherein the girls open their eyes to confinement. *Waderas* and *patels* (the village chieftains) are the masters of the destiny, and *Bhopas* (Hindu priests-cum-wizards) decide their fate.

Women and girls in Sindh age quickly. Hard labor and poor diet corrode their skin and dwarf their physical existence. Worse than the hard work and malnourishment is the fact that these girls often miss their girlhood. It is not an exaggeration to say that female babies are born into womanhood. Pomi, when Tasneem met her, was a mere eight-year-old child who looked much older than her physical age. Pomi, as Tasneem came to know, went through a familiar cycle of a woman's life in rural Sindh. As a child born into poverty, Pomi had a life that promised little. Her father was a landless laborer, one of many low-caste Hindus, who are social outcasts and are viewed with a unique type of abhorrence. With his small earnings, he could no longer take care of his wife and children and was forced to borrow about three thousand rupees (not more than $80) from the local landlord, the *wadera,* of the village. He could not repay this loan and soon died. The death of the father, the head of the household, was the signal for the vultures to circle their prey—the females of the family. To add to the misery, Pomi's two brothers ran away, leaving the mother and three daughters alone.

Her mother, Bhomi, now a widow, was destitute and wished to repay the "huge debt" that her dead husband had left behind. Failure to repay debt in rural Sindh often results in a virtual imprisonment of the person in debt and of his family. Thus, Bhomi and her daughters now were literally mortgaged with the *wadera.* They worked seventeen to eighteen hours a day in the bondage of their masters, gathering firewood from the jungle, grazing the cattle, tilling the land, cooking, drawing water from the deep wells, and a myriad of other back-breaking jobs.

Pomi's mother, in spite of being blind and old, would wander the countryside, doing whatever she could to mitigate the sufferings of her young daughters. Pomi's sister used to do even more work than her mother or other sister. As if this hard work was not enough, she would also be prey to sexual molestation. The old mother tried to find out a way out of this quagmire, to somehow save her young daughters from perishing in such an appalling situation. No one from the entire vicinity was able to do anything for them, except for silently observing their dilemma.

In the early hours of the calm and peaceful mornings, Pomi used to take out the herd of goats for grazing; her melodious songs used to awaken the sleeping people. Pomi used to hide her anguish behind the folk songs, her recreation being the admiration of the landscape, cattle being her only company.

Much later, Tasneem Bhatti learned that, with the help of some friends, the three women finally bought back their freedom. Bhomi was even able to get her daughters married. I wonder how many girls are lucky enough to have generous friends who will help them buy freedom. Will freedom be available free of cost in the coming millennium? I wish I could be optimistic.

A GIRL WHO MAKES HER DREAM COME TRUE

My last story is about a girl who learned to fight for herself and for others. This is the story of Nasima, a nineteen-year-old living in Old Golimar, a slum of Karachi. Nasima was born to a poor family. Her father works as a hired laborer with petty contractors in the building construction business. He is getting old and very soon will be unable to continue this type of hard work. Nasima has one older and one younger sister. The elder sister has completed high school and now coaches children of the neighborhood; the youngest goes to school. Nasima could not continue her education after her primary school. Nasima's mother used to sew clothes for the women of the neighborhood. The earnings were very modest, as it was a poor slum area. The mother's health was not good, so she could no longer take more orders. After surgery—Nasima referred to it as *bara aprashun* (hysterectomy)—the mother had to stop working on the sewing machine. At this point, Nasima made a decision: she would stop going to school and help the family. Nasima decided to carry on her mother's work, but in a new pattern.

When I met with her in the summer of 1998, Nasima was making stuffed toys from the fabric that she buys from the *lunda bazar,* a market where used clothes, mostly shipped from western countries, are sold. She visits these markets at least twice a month. Her mother always accompanies her on these trips, since it is not safe for a young woman to travel alone and to shop in these markets, Nasima told me. After buying the required fabric, mostly western long dresses, Nasima has to rip the seams of the dresses, wash them, and iron them in order to cut out suitable pieces for her toys. She earns about $30 a month and saves money from her income for the dowry of her elder sister.

At the age of nineteen, Nasima has the wisdom of a mature entrepreneur and businesswoman. The job and the money she earns have given her confidence that is often missing even in school-educated girls of her age. I could see the dynamism in Nasima when she said, "I want to buy a better sewing machine, an all electric-running machine." Nasima has no skilled training in the business that she has created for herself. What survives and sustains her is her conviction and faith in her own potential. She is not worried about the school that she has left or about her incomplete education.

Her main worry is that the area where her family lives suddenly changes into a war zone with gun shootings between the workers of some political parties and the police. Everything comes to a dead stop. Even the shop owners who buy her toys refuse to make payments as they say, "No one is buying toys in Karachi now. There is grief around."

Nasima is a born optimist. She hopes that things will be better tomorrow; that she will save enough for the dowry of her sister and for the new electric sewing machine of her dreams. Has she plans of getting married? Nasima looked puzzled and, with a faint smile on her face, looked at me.

As long as there are Nasimas, girlhood in Pakistan is not completely doomed.

NOTES

Interviews with Mithi and her mother were conducted by the author in June 1997 and July 1998 in Karachi. The interview with Nasima was done by the author on July 18, 1998, in Karachi.

1. For general information about women's lives in Pakistan, see Haeri (1995), Hafeez (1990), Mujtaba (1992), and Yusuf (1992).
2. I am using pseudonyms for the girls I discuss in this chapter.
3. Property or wealth belonging to another person.

WORKS CITED

Bhatti, Tasneem. 1997. "Human Rights Status of Women in Sindh." *Alam-i-Niswan: Pakistan Journal of Women's Studies* 4(2): 87–91.

Haeri, Shahla. 1995. "The Politics of Dishonor: Rape and Power in Pakistan." In *Faith and Women in the Muslim World,* ed. Mahnaz Afkhami. New York: Syracuse University Press, 161–74.

Hafeez, Sabeeha. 1990. *Girlchild in Pakistan: Priority Concerns.* Islamabad: UNICEF.

Mujtaba, Hasan. 1992. "The Living Dead." *Newsline, Special Number: The Private Jails of Sindh* 4(5): 49–58.

Rehmatullah, Shireen. 1994. "Female Literacy: Barriers and Bridges." In *Challenge for Change: Literacy for the Girl of Today, the Woman of Tomorrow,* ed. Tahera Aftab. Karachi: Karachi University Press, 6–12.

Shah, Nafisa. 1997. "A Woman's Sexual Space: Control and Deviance." *Alam-i-Niswan: Pakistan Journal of Women's Studies* 4(2): 31–40.

Yusuf, Zohra. 1992. "A Rising Graph." *Herald* (January): 47–48.

· *10* ·

Horizontal Rain

Road from Sarajevo

Ajla Hodzic

CAR WINDOWS

I'm not very good at telling stories, especially since I have a hard time with beginnings and ends, defining space and time. I also have a tendency to erase chunks from my memory, maybe not a noble habit.

I do remember leaving Sarajevo. I remember many things about Sarajevo, as seen through my twelve-year-old eyes. Many pretty sights, and not so pretty ones, take over my train of thought once in a while, usually at inappropriate times, when I'm struggling to fall asleep or write a paper or follow an important discussion. That's when I press "delete." But for the sake of this story, I will tell you what it is that I remember.

A sheer April morning, 1992. The city bathed in gray, due to this annoying, drizzly rain. My father's waving figure, somewhat crooked and dizzy-looking. I remember the whistling of grenades, snipers. People dragging bags and suitcases, mumbled "goodbyes," stuffed buses; men smoking at the station, showering kisses on their sons' and daughters' faces, trying to escape the notion that this might be the last time they hug. I remember thinking the same thing when my father kissed my eyes and faked a smile. One thought that I savor through the years is his fingers; the stench of nicotine when it mixes with rain.

I remember leaving Sarajevo, tightly packed in a car with my mother, her brother, my aunt, and two cousins. My uncle took off fast and zoomed down the city streets. I remember being sad that I couldn't see out the windows very well. Raindrops were sliding on the windows horizontally, distorting the buildings and the asphalt and the sky. Sarajevo looked like a ruined watercolor painting through those windows. I

163

Ajla with mom and dad at Sarajevo International Airport.
(Photo by Amra Cengic.)

don't remember any sounds. I have this habit of neglecting sounds while thinking.

We drove for a long time. Once in a while I would wiggle my feet and legs just to make sure they were not asleep. I don't remember any conversations, except now and then my mom or my aunt would ask us kids if we were hungry or if we wanted some water, or if we needed to go to the bathroom. We always said we were feeling fine.

The images of the barricades come to me in the clearest flashes. One after another, lined all through the outskirts of the city and further, big piles of sandbags and armed, bearded men, suspiciously eyeing our stuffed, wrinkled figures inside. I remember their huge, dirt-covered hands, clenching shiny automatics, and long necklaces of bullets slung over their uniforms. Little conelike bombs hanging from their belts. Grins spread over their greasy faces, and rain dripping from their beards. I remember being scared but unable to stop staring. Their yellow teeth, signs reading "Serbia," their flags with Cetnik symbols, and heavy, muddy boots . . .

Occasionally, we would pass a barricade of Bosnian Army soldiers, and we would see young men, teenagers, standing around in T-shirts, smoking cheap cigarettes, waving for us to get by. My uncle remarked that they only carried half-automatics or small hand guns. He said that it was a pity they were so young and handsome, that they shouldn't have been standing there in the rain. I remember my mother saying that this was going to last. I was sure she was talking about the war. I knew my father had lied when he said that we would see each other in a week or two, at most.

Arriving at the main barricade set up by the Serbs, we were ordered to pull over. My uncle rolled the window down and offered the man a crippled smile. Then we were ordered to get out of the car. My uncle begged. There are women and children here, I remember him saying. We got out. I remember seeing a young Bosnian girl, straddled by a couple of soldiers. I remember thinking she would have marks on her skin where they had grabbed her arms and thighs. I remember feeling for her because her skirt was ripped. It was a pretty skirt. I don't remember her name. Then, a white car pulled up next to us and a tall, well-dressed man got out. His eyes ran over us but stayed on my uncle. They exchanged a weak greeting, and the next thing I knew I was being ordered to get back in the car and get lost. The tall man was the chief of the barricade, my uncle's friend from work. I remember my uncle saying that we would not have been in the car, especially not in one piece, if he hadn't appeared. Someone said that it was strange how your enemy can save your life. I remember someone talking about mercy. And luck. (Later, we found out that the bus behind us—which was headed for Austria, and which my mother and I almost boarded but couldn't find a spot on because the bus was packed like a matchbox—that bus was emptied, the women raped, their fingers and ears cut as a method of collecting their jewelry. I imagined what it would have been like to be on that bus.)

Some time later I must have fallen asleep, because I don't remember much of the countryside. Occasionally, between dozing off, I saw frames of little, deserted houses, some cattle roaming around, and some yellow and white flowers in the fields. It had stopped raining. It was afternoon. We were close to the Croatian border. Crossing the bridge over Sava, I looked down at the river and tried to figure out if it was brown, green, or blue. I don't remember the color, but I figure it must have been a shade of green. Most rivers I knew were a shade of green. Then, we were in Croatia.

Except that we were nearly in a fatal car crash, I don't remember anything until we arrived in Zagreb. My uncle was passing a van on a two-lane road with a hill in front of us, and a big, blue truck came speeding up the road from the other side. We ended up in a small ditch, luckily, and the truck driver helped us pull the car out and back on the road. He asked if we had just escaped Bosnia "to get killed in Croatia?" He knew by the plates. And we probably seemed very tired.

I remember falling asleep in a hotel in Zagreb and not being very hungry at dinner. I contemplated writing a letter to my best friend in Sarajevo, but my mom said that he probably wouldn't be mad if I didn't write. I just didn't know what to say, so I didn't write the letter.

We drove to Ljubljana, the Slovenian capital, but I don't remember much of our stay there. I remember taking a plane to Istanbul, where my grandparents had moved some time before the whole mess began. I remember that my grandmother cried when she saw us, her "luckies," and I remember her delicious spinach pie. I remember staring at the TV screen, not understanding a single word. I made fun of the way the news reporter spoke. My grandfather said that the people on TV were talking about Bosnia a lot. He asked about Sarajevo, how it looked, how many people died, how we handled the shelter and the snipers, how we managed without much food. I don't remember what the answers were.

ISTANBUL, COCKROACHES

I resisted learning Turkish for a while. I kept reminding my grandfather, when he would try to teach me a word or two he himself barely knew, that we were going home soon, and that there was no need for me to learn another language. After my mother explained to me that we were to stay in Turkey for a long time, she didn't know how long, I picked up a book of my grandfather's. It was an old book, a 1945 edition. I wondered where he had gotten it. He said something about a Turkish guy who studied in Sarajevo, his friend, and how he sent him the book when he returned to Turkey after college. My grandfather said that the man was probably dead now, and let go a short laugh with a slight shake of his head. I rewrote a chapter of the book each day into a little red notebook someone had given me. I remember my mother telling me that rewriting was the best way of learning a language's grammar.

My mother looked for a job, but she couldn't speak Turkish very well, so the jobs offered to her were low-paying ones that she didn't stick with for very long. My grandparents lived off of my grandfather's pension, which he had accumulated in Germany. Since money was an issue of concern, he came home one day from the market and told us we had to leave, that he couldn't afford to feed us anymore. We packed our bags and left. The hotel we stayed at was infested with cockroaches, the toilets wouldn't flush, and the sheets were brown. We couldn't afford a better place because we had spent our money on two plane tickets to Kuala Lumpur. I don't remember why my mother picked Kuala Lumpur, but I think it was the only place that Bosnian refugees were allowed in without a visa at that point. I asked my mom to show me the map of where we were going, and I said that it was too far away. I remember asking if we were going to ever see Dad again.

The day before our flight, my uncle and his wife (who had rented an apartment on their own) came by the hotel to tell us not to be "silly." My grandfather arrived shortly after they left, begging my mother to forgive him, telling her to think of her sick, old mother, and how crushed she would be if we were to board the plane. He said he wouldn't kick us out again. I remember seeing my mother cry hysterically for the first time. I remember crying myself, but I don't remember why.

THE RED SWING

Fall came abruptly. Since my grandparent's apartment was located in one of the bad neighborhoods of Istanbul, we moved to a little village near Izmir, a gigantic palm-tree-lined city on the southwestern coast of the Aegean Sea. My grandfather had bought a small apartment in Izmir, but the building was still being built, so we lived some seventy kilometers outside the city, in a fragile summer house of my grandfather's friend, in the village of Ozdere.

I remember sitting at the beach by myself on chilly September evenings, swinging on a red swing, thinking of my father, remembering the day he went to be drafted but came back home because our army had no weapons to distribute. They had told him they would get back to him. I thought about my mother, how sad she looked, how much weight she had lost, and I wished we could eat something other than rice and eggs.

I started seventh grade in the village middle school there. My Turkish was impossible, except I knew how to buy necessities (bread, eggs, and rice). I could say "apple" too. I had to buy a uniform for school; it was bizarre. A uniform! It turned out to be this tiny, long-sleeved, just-above-the-knees black dress, with a white collar, a nice waistband, and a pair of tight, white socks that came up to my knees. I felt bad that I couldn't wear my ripped Levi's jeans but, after all, it was a small village. My friends taught me how to milk a cow. I remember the thick taste of that milk. That's why I can't drink skim milk anymore. Tastes like water.

I don't remember how, but I started speaking Turkish like I was one of the crowd. I translated the news for the household in the evenings, trying to decrease the number of the dead people I would hear about. I remember my grandfather correcting me once in a while. I guess he could understand some Turkish after all.

Winter in Ozdere is grotesque. The sea was wild and foamy, ubiquitous, the shore washed out, children muddy, and the cattle harder to approach. The rain is warm and sharp on your skin, and the wind, stinging and piercing. I remember packing again, after another of my grandfather's breakdowns, his face deformed in fury as he pushed my mother on the bed and flew out of the room. We then took a bus to a refugee shelter on the outskirts of Istanbul. I drank apricot juice on the bus and threw up in the bathroom of the bus terminal at one of the stops along the way.

The shelter was a barbed-wire pile of aluminum barracks with dirt floors, damp mattresses, ripped blankets. I remember the sticky taste of cold soup we were served the evening we arrived. I remember my mother's black-rimmed eyes. Something I remember too often. I remember the drained faces of the women and fragile bodies of waiflike children running around the camp, covered in mud. I remember mute evenings, when I'd watch the street lights swim in puddles and steam rush from the manholes. The steam was warmer than our barracks, and I often contemplated sleeping on one of those manholes. My mother wouldn't hear of it. She would often cry at my remarks, and I remember feeling guilty and trying to shut my mouth, telling her I that I was sorry if I had said something wrong. She would shake her head, saying it wasn't me. I didn't know what was wrong, then. I thought she was always worried about me getting sick. She would check my forehead countless times a day, and she did it with her mouth. She said that lips were the most sensitive part of one's body to heat. It became a habit with me too. That's how I check for fever now.

After a while we left the camp. I don't know how and why, or what time of the day it was, but the next vivid recollection is my uncle's apartment in Prague. He and his family had moved to Prague around the time I started school in the village. I remember little about them leaving Turkey. I remember, faintly, my grandmother mentioning that she would miss her son or something of the sort, and I felt bad for my grandmother at the time. I wished that she wasn't so old. She was a saint; she never complained about anything.

Prague felt familiar. The buildings smelled the same as those in Sarajevo, from outside and from inside. I saw many statues that reminded me of those in Sarajevan parks and piazzas, but I never knew who the statues represented. Carl's Bridge grew on me. My cousin and I would sneak a peak over painters' shoulders to see what colors they were mixing, admiring all the jewelry and the multicolored bead necklaces. We threw bread at the pigeons, and I took many pictures. Most of those where of the trams. I loved the trams in Prague. They were identical to those in Sarajevo.

Then, I remember sitting at the kitchen table, writing in my diary, and hearing my uncle and my mother quarrel. I remember them yelling; my cousin and I tried not to look at each other. I remember "money" being mentioned frequently, then packing. Packing had become a natural occurrence. We then boarded a plane to Istanbul and took a bus back to the village. I remember thinking that I missed the red swing.

THE MUSIC BOX

Somewhat near the end of the school year, we moved into an apartment in Izmir. I started at another school and finished seventh grade there. My mother couldn't find a job, so I found one. It was barely enough money for toiletries—toothpaste, pads, deodorant, toilet paper. My grandfather would not have even thought to buy these items. We thought ourselves lucky that we had those eggs every day. I worked in a boutique, nine a.m. to nine p.m., six days a week; I fell asleep at work the third day. I scrubbed the floor every day, cleaned the toilets, folded the clothes, sprayed and cleaned the windows, smiled at the customers, always telling them I was fifteen because they would ask how old I was every time. My boss said I couldn't be thirteen. He told me to forget the number thirteen. So I did.

I remember falling asleep as soon as I got home. I remember my feet hurt, and I remember my mother putting some pomade on the blisters. I remember not remembering that summer.

Then, there was eighth grade. My grandfather wouldn't give us money to buy my books or a uniform (those uniforms were more sophisticated than the village-school ones—white blouses, checked shirts, green vests, white socks, navy jackets and bows). He said I should leave school and work. I had almost settled for the idea, but it made me sad. So, I went to the Ministry of Education for that municipality and explained my situation to the minister. He looked at me as if I were a joke, but I got my uniform, my books, and I was back at school. I don't remember much of eighth grade. I know I made a friend. Her name is Senem. I don't know where she is now. I should probably look for her sometime.

What I remember most clearly about eighth grade is early morning walks to school, passing through parks and alleys, the market, sitting beneath the palm trees, the street merchants, and newspaper stands. There were the steamboats and blue buses, the turquoise sea and silver-painted trash cans. I don't remember the winter that year.

In the summer, I worked in a kindergarten. I remember my favorite student. She was five and had the most miraculous wheat-colored curls. She was the best dancer, too. I taught them ballet, drawing, and rhymes. We played in the grass a lot. I remember feeling very tiny back then; I remember thinking that, if I wanted to, I could fit into a music box and become a note. I remember being a child then.

I saw my father that summer. It had been two years. He had managed to leave the army for a month, and he came to Izmir. He didn't recognize me. I remember him staring right through me at the airport, and I remember the tavern we ate dinner at that evening. The next thing I remember is being lonely. My parents returned to Sarajevo together, and I started a boarding school on a scholarship. My grandfather sold the apartment and moved to Ayvalik, a small coastal town some hundred kilometers north of Izmir.

WASTING PAPER

Fatih College was my first real chance. I read many books. I wrote more often, and I felt lonesome and inadequate. I thought of Sarajevo more than ever before. I was happy that I had discovered science. I discussed poetry with my math teacher and didn't sleep very much. I thought it a waste of time. That's probably one of the reasons I am hard to live with now.

Then, there was my first cigarette. Many books, many cigarettes, many hours awake, many math, physics, and chemistry problems. I am a "too much of everything" person. I guess it is considered a weakness. Things become an addiction to me easily.

Toward the end of the school year, my mother came back. She had to climb Mount Igman (one of the mountains surrounding Sarajevo, and the only way out of the city at the time) with a guide, while they were being fired at from the Serb territory. She said she *had* to see me. She also said that she had to get in touch with Dad; he had thought that she wouldn't survive the trip, begging her to stay, but she's stubborn. That's where I get it from.

That summer, my grandfather called from Istanbul, where he had moved again, and asked us if we would like to stay with him. I remember thinking that my grandmother was probably sick again.

I worked in a municipality office as a clerk, dealing with people who came in to ask about property and the legalities of building a house on a certain piece of land. It wasn't a hard job, but I was the youngest one in the office. A fourteen-year-old clerk. Sometimes, they would ask me to make tea and serve it to the staff. I still don't know how to make good Turkish tea. It takes too much time.

I developed an eating disorder. I would devour everything I was served, virtually sweep the table, stuff everything down my throat. I would then attempt to puke in the bathroom and I was successful a few times. It became a bother, so I stopped doing it. Still, I ate as much as I could fit into my growing belly. My mother told my grandma that I was trying to make up with food for what I lacked in my life. Home, father, clothes, stability, I don't know.

While in Istanbul, I got a call from my school telling me about a man who was putting together a show for prime-time television about Bosnia and the war. They asked me if I'd like to help him. Gladly. He lived in America, they said, and he was a professor. I thought that was amazing. He asked me if I would like to study in the United States. Of course. He said that he would keep an eye on my grades, and if I kept up the good work, I might get a call from New York. So I made a promise.

I saw my uncle and his family that summer. They drove from

Prague to Istanbul, and they stayed with us for a little while. Then I went back to school. My grandparents moved back to Izmir, again, and my mother went with them. She found a job with a company where she cooked coffee for the staff and washed the dishes. She's an economist, but her Turkish wouldn't allow her to find a better job.

The second year of high school (which was actually my junior year, because I had skipped the freshman year), my sleeping habits became a problem. I ate too much, read too much, thought too much, and slept too little. I had high blood pressure for no apparent reason, and my teachers thought it best if I became a day student for a while. So I moved in with my grandparents. My mom put me on a diet, which was followed by yet another paranoid scene by my grandfather. He threw us out in the street after he tried to hit my mother, and I punched him in the chest. We had enough money for a bus ride. We stayed with my mother's friend, a Bosnian woman with three kids, for about a month. I missed out on school. I don't remember speaking a single word to anybody during that time. I remember feeling very sick.

My mother's friend and her children ended up going to America. They had a relative who arranged for their trip. They left us the apartment, which belonged to her brother, and my mother kept her job. I went to school and hoped to get my scholarship. Not a word came from New York, though.

My mother went back to Bosnia for good. The Dayton Accord was signed, and the war seemed to be over. I remember watching the news and seeing people celebrate all over Sarajevo, spilling into the streets, singing songs between the skeleton-like buildings. I remember turning the TV off and feeling completely alienated. I didn't know what to make of it.

I became a boarding student again. I wrote in my diary; I had four notebooks completely filled with words. Then, I threw them into a garbage container just off campus. It was a relief. Now, I feel as though I wasted a lot of paper.

One day my English teacher took my class to a "British College Fair." I filled out some applications, roamed around, asked a representative of Luton University for a scholarship. I remember the way he looked at me—as if I was out of my mind—and I remember giving up entirely. I got a call from Luton a week later. All I had to do was prove my eligibility for financial aid. I called my mother and cried on the phone. I made arrangements to go back "home" for the summer. I remember the whirling in my stomach. I started to wonder what it meant to "belong" somewhere, but I don't remember feeling the need to.

BARE POLES

I had never thought the daytime sky could be so dark. Landing at the Sarajevo International Airport, I couldn't see past the thick air around the plane. I remember the severe pain in my stomach as I walked out into the rain. I remember thinking how funny it was that it was raining again. I thought that maybe the rain hadn't stopped since the last time I saw Sarajevo. That thought depressed me. I brushed it off as I was helped by a UN soldier. He said "Welcome" or something of the sort. I said "Thank you," appalled. Who were these people? Does anyone speak Bosnian anymore?

I bummed a cigarette from my dad on the ride to our apartment. The apartment had remained in one piece. I didn't look out the windows of the car this time. I was too scared to do so. It was a foggy sight anyway.

It stopped raining the next day. I walked around the city, feeling as if I was surrounded by ghosts. I saw thin, tired faces, faded smiles, blurred eyes, butchered buildings, cut-up trees, ripped-up playgrounds, morbid jokes. The National Library had been stripped down to bare poles and ashy remains of old manuscripts. I remember the TV-screen image of it burning in great, purple flames, and I remember crying in the middle of the street, just by the river. My parents fell in love in that library.

I remember seeing friends from sixth grade, not recognizing them, asking for directions around the city; the names of the streets were changed. The streets were changed. I couldn't believe I was sixteen.

Being in Sarajevo felt like falling through a time warp. I remember looking at the seesaw in the park. I remember the green slide. There were some new kids running around now. I heard the ringing in my ears as I realized that four years had passed since I slid down that slide and made wreaths with magnolia and poppies.

Just as I was ready to go back to Turkey, graduate from high school, and go to England, I received a phone call from New York. I had to make my decision on the phone because, if I was going to be a senior in Green Meadow Waldorf School, I had to make it to JFK in five days.

SKIPPING

August 20, 1996, I arrived at JFK. I had a host family that was supposed to be waiting for me, but I couldn't find them because the plane landed earlier than the given time. I fished for my name on one of the boards people were holding and wondered if there was a smoking section anywhere around. There wasn't. So I waited for my host family and tried to picture what they looked like. I didn't know much about them. Actually, I didn't know anything except the names of their children. I sat around, slightly lost, but not nervous or scared. I remember thinking it was strange that I felt comfortable in that blue-tiled room. I remember feeling somewhat lonely at times, but I also remember skipping the thought.

And there they were. I remember we hugged. I was hungry. My host mother gave me a banana. I remember having a good feeling about the whole situation. The children were beautiful.

I remember the sun spilling all over me, biting my face and eyes, as we walked out into the parking lot. I remember a blue Toyota. I remember feeling slightly nauseous, but trying to smile and say something.

I remember it wasn't raining. Then, I remember falling asleep in the car on the way to a place.

water green

often
i dream
in a language different
from the one i
speak
to you

language
learned
before crawling
or footsteps

it smells
of fried eggplant
my mother
serves
with goat cheese

tastes
like tiles
of old bridges
in my broken
city

color of
a tart apple
(water green)
from my grandmother's
garden

thick
like the scorched smell
of coffee beans
in ovens
of old Bascarsija

and sometimes
hard
to remember
like an old song never
fully memorized

   —Ajla Hodzic

· 11 ·

Charley Lauren's Story

Growing Up in the Shadow of Mental Illness

Charley Lauren Ortman and Patricia E. Ortman

*S*urely if there is hell on earth, one part of it is inhabited by those unfortunate souls caught in the grip of mental illnesses. These invidious disorders clearly inflict a stranglehold on the lives of their victims; without intervention these diseases also invade, paralyze, and destroy the lives of all who care about them. Although we know this to be the case, and without losing sympathy for the primary victims, all too little attention has been paid to these secondary victims, especially the children of those with mental disorders.

It appears that no one seems to know how many children in the United States are living with mentally ill parents. It is unclear why this information has not been obtained (or estimated) by any official sources. That fact, in itself, may suggest the status of this group. Why has no one thought to ask? Doesn't it matter? Don't these children matter? Shouldn't we be doing something to help them? How can we do that if we don't know how many there are, who and where they are? In light of this, then, it is only possible to extrapolate, from other known statistics, some very rough estimates of the total number of children—girls and boys—who may be living in this situation.

About 20 percent of new mothers suffer from postpartum depression (Papalia and Olds 1995, 170). That means that, for some part of their lives, about one-fifth of all children in the United States—roughly half of them girls—live with a mother who is depressed. Although the risks to children are not extreme if these cases do not turn into chronic depression (defined as depression lasting for more than six months), children of depressed mothers (or fathers, if they are the primary caregiver) are at risk of various emotional and cognitive disturbances, including behavioral problems and poor school performance, as well as eventual depression themselves (Papalia and Olds 1995, 170). Since women suffer from depression disproportionately to men in any event, there may be a higher risk for girls than for boys to eventually develop depressive symptomology (Sue, Sue, and Sue 1990, 334).

Unfortunately, however, parents do not suffer only from depression. Many parents suffer from alcohol and drug abuse; eating, anxiety, and personality disorders; some suffer from schizophrenia. Often parents have more than one illness at a time. The National Institute of Mental Health (NIHM) claims that 10 percent of the American population suffers some disability from a diagnosable mental illness in any given year (1998, 1). Since this includes all cases, it is hard to say how many may be active parents, but even a small percentage of 26.8 million people (approximately 10 percent of the total U.S. population) would seem to suggest that many children have parents who are at best somewhat disabled from a mental illness in any one year.

NIMH also claims that of this 10 percent, 5 million are American adults who suffer from the most severe mental illnesses: schizophrenia, manic-depressive illness, major depression, panic disorder, and obsessive-compulsive disorder (1998, 1). If we say that only half of these individuals are of parenting age (2.5 million), only half of them actually have children (and only one) (1.25 million), and only half of those are girls, then minimally we are talking about approximately 625,000 girls living with at least one parent who is *severely* mentally ill in any given year. This is a vast number of girls, and still does not include those whose parents abuse drugs and alcohol—a mental disorder according to the American Psychological Association's classification system but not mentioned in NIMH's list of most severe mental illnesses. How do these children cope? What is being done for them? How do these parents cope? What is being done for them, as parents? These kinds of questions are just now being brought to light and investigated.

In a 1993 study in Grand Rapids, Michigan, Vanharen et al. "investigated to what extent the children of psychiatrically ill adult patients are identified and referred to mental health services" (1993, 678). They found that forty-seven of the one hundred patients in a local hospital who were interviewed had school-aged children. Of these forty-seven, nineteen had children (at least one) who had received assistance from a mental health professional. However, only four of the mental health patients had been treated by a psychiatrist who had even inquired about the mental health of their children; and in only one case did the psychiatrist refer the child for professional care. The other children were referred by their parents themselves or by a community agency (678–79).

In 1994, the State of New York released the findings of a Task Force on Mentally Ill Parents with Young Children, which found that the needs of mentally ill parents and their children have been neglected by public policy makers at all levels (Blanch, Nicholson, and Purcell 1994). A 1996 case study of a chronically mentally ill mother of two also highlights the "unaddressed policy questions and unmet service needs of mentally ill parents and their children" (Nicholson, Geller, and Fisher 1996, 497). Although not reflecting the U.S. system, it is interesting to note that a 1996 study of mentally ill parents in Denmark brought out the lack of assistance in that country as well to parents in their roles as parents, with respect to their children, and thus to the children themselves (Wang and Goldschmidt 1996).

It seems, then, that children with mentally ill parents may be, at the present time, a relatively invisible and neglected population not only in the United States but also throughout the world. The following is the story of one girl's life and experiences. It is, in part, the story of a child whose mother was mentally ill for most of the child's young life. It is a tragic story for all concerned, ending in the divorce of her parents. But this particular little girl was also very lucky, for she had many people in her life who cared about her and made sure she got taken care of. Many, maybe most, children are not so fortunate. Therefore, I believe that this story may also be inspiring, for it exemplifies many things: the emotional duress mental illness causes others, the extraordinary commitment to mental health that must be exhibited, and the prodigious amount of energy that must be expended by a large number of people in order to win any battle against mental illness; but also one child's resourcefulness and resilience in coping and her abiding trust and faith in both her parents. Perhaps it also demonstrates in some small way the absolute power of love, which may in fact be the only heaven we have on earth.

CHARLEY LAUREN'S STORY

Charley Lauren Ortman is my niece. She was twelve years old in November 1999. She and her two brothers (Andrew, age seventeen, and Dylan, age nine) live in Maryland, splitting their time between their now-divorced parents: Charles, my brother, and Ellen, their mother. Charley's father, a Korean linguist, has been in the Air Force for nineteen years and maintains a residence at Ft. Meade. Her mother, a waitress and restaurant manager, lives in the nearby town of Laurel.

Charley was born at Bethesda Naval Medical Center in Washington, D.C., on November 20, 1987, eight months after her parents were married. This was her mother's second marriage. She and Charles had met and married in a bit of a whirlwind, caught up with falling in love and ignoring my advice to go more slowly. Although Ellen was cute, charming, and witty and my brother generally good-natured and easygoing, I could see trouble brewing in the combination of what appeared to be Ellen's lack of self-esteem and need to be in control and Charles's tendency to be overbearing and somewhat thoughtless. Charles adopted Ellen's son, Andrew, from her first marriage, and so, within much too short a time, they became a family of four. On the way home from the hospital, Charley's parents stopped by our home to show her to my husband and me. At that time, we agreed to be her guardians.

In the course of his service, Charles had to return to duty in Korea when Charley was only a few months old. His family went with him. They returned for a visit when Charley was about a year and a half; her independent nature was already clear. At that time she kept many of her small treasures in her diaper, which she called her "pockie" (pocket), and was fiercely protective of them. She appeared securely attached to both her parents, a fact I believe contributed significantly to her ability to cope as her home life worsened, and was developmentally on track, even precocious.

Her parents were in marriage counseling and it appeared that their marital difficulties, which had developed almost immediately, were on their way to a possible resolution. Unfortunately, Ellen's bulimia, which she had suffered from since adolescence (some thirteen years) had not come to light and was not being treated. She was also pregnant again and concerned that she "didn't have the energy" to have another child at that time, but was unable to consider the possibility of an abortion.

Back in Korea, both the pregnancy and birth were difficult. Charley was just a few months over two years old when Dylan was born. Although Charley doesn't remember much about Korea, she does remember feeling happy then, and has a picture in her mind of sitting under a tree near her family's apartment at OSAN Air Force Base, waiting for the ice-cream truck.

But the stresses of living in a foreign country with two small children and an infant, combined with ongoing marital problems, a breakdown in the marriage counseling, and her still untreated bulimia, caused Ellen to begin slipping into depression. It seems likely, in retrospect, that she suffered from an undiagnosed case of postpartum depression. Our family was unaware of the severity of the situation, and thus unable to provide either guidance or assistance.

Charles and Ellen did not return to the United States until Charley was about three and a half. She continued to do very well. She was loving, outgoing, sociable, and still fiercely independent. It was clear to anyone who saw Ellen, though, that she was in bad shape. Initially we assumed that the stress of traveling and relocating was the major cause of her problems and that she would get better once the family had settled into housing and life had achieved some normalcy. Ellen, too, was aware that she wasn't doing well. She recognized that she was having a hard time caring about anything, including herself, but she believed that she could handle the problems she was experiencing on her own and did not seek therapy.

Over the next three years, Ellen's condition deteriorated into chronic clinical depression, anxiety with accompanying panic attacks, and both bulimia and anorexia nervosa. She briefly saw a therapist. She periodically took drugs to combat both her depression and her anxiety. The side effects of both were undesirable. She would attempt to give them up only, of course, to have the symptoms roar back with the same or greater ferocity. Eventually, her weight hovered between eighty-five and ninety pounds; generally, she was too weak to move around much except to go from the bed to the couch and then back to the bed, so, while Charles was at work, the children fended for themselves or Andrew cared for the younger ones. Ellen was frequently hospitalized—on two occasions for several weeks, each time near death—only because Charles physically picked her up out of the bed and brought her in. On several occasions in the hospital, laxatives were discovered hidden in her bedding. Twice she went to her mother's home in Texas for a few weeks, coming back when she had gained a few pounds, which she quickly shed upon returning. While Ellen was hospitalized and in Texas, Charles's parents helped care for the children. Although encouraged to do so, Ellen never stayed in Texas long enough to become completely well. Almost inevitably, she returned with great anger toward her mother.

In fact, as is usually the case with clinically depressed people, she was angry at almost everyone almost all the time, including and especially her husband and her children. In her anger, she became abusive, often seeking to blame Charles for her problems. On these occasions, she frequently drew him into arguments and spoke so hurtfully to him that he would eventually lose his temper and become verbally abusive himself. This made him feel bad about himself; he learned to try to avoid these situations. The better he became at avoiding these arguments, the sicker Ellen became. And although she could be very loving and affectionate to her children, she often railed at and excoriated them for the smallest infraction. Andrew passively accepted her abuse; Charley Lauren put up some initial resistance but then broke down in tears; Dylan fought back. Eventually, all the children began simply to ignore her. This provided them with some limited degree of pyschic protection, but caused Ellen to become even angrier.

Charley Lauren's first vivid memories stem from this time in her life. They are of her parents fighting. She doesn't remember her mother ever *not* being sick. Although the children frequently visited their mother while she was hospitalized, Charley remembers, and only vaguely, doing it once. She believes that she was about five or six. As she says, her mother was "really thin" and "scared me."

Ellen's behavior eventually completely frustrated, angered, and exhausted everyone who cared about her. Charles especially couldn't understand why she would do nothing to help herself, why she would want to die, and why she would want her children to watch her do so. He didn't want her to die because he loved her; also, he felt obligated to do whatever he could to prevent that from happening for his children's sake. Ellen couldn't find the will to do anything for or about herself. And then suddenly, amid all of this, Charles's father unexpectedly died from heart failure. This crushed them both, causing Charles to be even less able to cope with Ellen's apparent unwillingness to live, and Ellen, since she regarded Charles's father as more of a father to her than her own, to have even less desire to live.

Under these circumstances, Charles and Ellen separated and reunited on a number of occasions, with one or the other of them moving out of the home for a few weeks or months at a time, but always moving back in as they struggled to make their marriage work under debilitating circumstances, as well as care for their children. It is an understatement that the children were not receiving good parenting at the time; it

verged on barely adequate and was sometimes abusive and often ne-
glectful.

The situation, especially Ellen's apparent recalcitrance with respect
to eating and her frequent near-brushes with death, was anxiety pro-
voking for everyone in the extended family. I was worried not only
about Ellen herself but also about the effects of both her and Charles's
behavior on the children, and so the children were brought, at my insistence, to see a therapist to try to help them understand that they were
not responsible for either their mother's illnesses or their parents' inabil-
ity to create a stable relationship. The therapist didn't see fit to recom-
mend seeing them more than once even when apprised of their living
situation. He seemed to believe that they didn't need help in coping. I
disagreed, for it was clear to me that the children were exhibiting symptoms of stress. My husband and I could do little except retrieve Charley
Lauren as often as possible for an overnight or weekend visit to provide
her with some relief from the situation. I was glad for her sake to note
that Charley had developed a very strong friendship with a neighborhood girl and spent most of her free time with her and her family, thus
finding refuge from the ongoing misery at her own home.

Unfortuntely, when Charley was seven, her father was recalled to
Korea; he had been unable to postpone his return. Given Ellen's continuing precarious condition, the family was relocated to Wisconsin (where
they all wanted to be) in order to be near the paternal relatives, who
would help with their caretaking while Charles was gone. At this point,
Charles and Ellen decided on a divorce. At Ellen's insistence, she would
take care of the children in spite of her ongoing and serious conditions.
Charles agreed to let Ellen have custody of the children on the condition
that she obtain therapy both for herself and for the children. He reasoned
that if Ellen could not get well to save herself, perhaps she would be able
to get well for the sake of her children if he took himself "out of the
equation." By this time, he also agreed with me that the children clearly
needed help in coping with the ongoing stress of their mother's illness,
as well as the idea of divorce. He purchased a home for them and enrolled the children in school. Ellen found a job. Charles reported to
Korea in early August. Until their home was ready, the family stayed
with the paternal grandmother. They moved in to their own home at
the end of September 1995.

It soon became apparent that the responsibilities of caring for her
children and a home were overwhelming for Ellen, and the situation

rapidly deteriorated. She quickly lost her job and seldom ventured out of the house. After an initial visit to a therapist, she did not seek therapy either for herself or for the children. The children missed more and more school, and Andrew assumed much of the child care, including the preparation of meals. It appeared that the children were taking turns staying home, as the attendance pattern indicated that a different pair of children attended each day.

The children's paternal relatives were in a constant state of anxiety about the well-being of Charley and her two brothers. Requests to Ellen that she follow up on therapy both for herself and her children were not acted upon. Visits to the home throughout November and December indicated that the family was living in the living room and kitchen, "camped out" because, despite regular monthly payments from Charles, who was sending almost his entire paycheck, Ellen was unable to manage her financial resources and had shut off the rest of the house to save on the heating bill. The house was filthy, in disarray, and smelled of vomit. Phone calls to the home often temporarily interrupted abusive verbal battles between Dylan and Ellen.

The situation was untenable. Ellen was unable to take positive action on behalf of herself or her children. She was also unable to acknowledge that this was the case and to ask for appropriate help. We were all terrified; she was "going down" and taking the kids with her. By the end of December, it had become clear to everyone that, whether she knew it or not, liked it or not, agreed to it or not, Ellen's only chance of getting well was to be relieved of all responsibilities except that of getting well. The children would have to be removed from her care. However, paternal relatives were afraid to take such action themselves because of Ellen's instability. The children's grandmother was fearful that she might get scared of losing her children completely and try to run away with them. But the children's school was getting more and more concerned because of the spotty attendance records and because Andrew was getting into fights; they were prepared to notify the local social services to request the children's removal from the home. Since Charles had been kept apprised of the situation and knew of the progressively more desperate circumstances of his family's lives and the rapidity with which the situation was becoming critical, he applied for compassionate leave to come back to the States to attend to the situation. The Air Force granted it, but would not let him come back until March 1, 1996. During January and February, the paternal relatives regularly retrieved the children from their mother's home, as they had been doing for the previous three months, to provide some semblance of normalcy and stability for them, and tried to keep Ellen calm so that she would not do anything foolish or dangerous.

Upon their father's return, the children were removed legally from their mother's home and placed in the temporary custody of their paternal relatives and into therapy. Charley Lauren and her younger brother, Dylan, stayed with their grandmother, and Andrew with an aunt and uncle. Ellen was sent, once again, to her mother's in Texas, which is where she wanted to go, to seek treatment and hopefully this time to finally get well. After a month of leave, Charles returned to Korea to finish his tour of duty.

Charley Lauren doesn't remember much about what it was like during the few months of living with her brothers and mother, except that she lived right across the road from her friend Sarah, so she could walk over to her house. Once again, she spent a lot of time with a friend. She remembers her mother being too weak to cook and fighting with Andrew a lot. She remembers her mother "getting dressed up" and sitting and talking to some people at the kitchen table. In a picture she later drew for her therapist, she depicted four children swirling around and around inside of a house and a man on the outside walking toward it. Charley explained that this was a man "from Maryland" who was coming to save the children. Her therapist believed that this was an accurate depiction of her experience of her life during that time, as well as her experience of being "saved" by her father, for in fact Charley Lauren felt relieved when her father returned and relieved to be taken care of. She also felt sad that her mother had to leave and, she says, she "cried and cried." However, she wanted her mother to get better and believed that she would, so she tried to be patient. It was a relief and "fun" to be in a calm household with only her grandmother, uncle, and younger brother and no fighting. She felt better about school and signed up for art. She enjoyed going to the therapist, who she felt was very helpful. She learned that she wasn't responsible for either her mother's illness or her parents' divorce. She believed that Ellen's mother could make Ellen eat and go to a therapist and that then Ellen would get well.

At the end of July, Charles returned to the States and he and Ellen finalized the divorce. The children were placed into joint custody of the parents, with Charles having primary placement and Ellen having visitation, provided she got and continued to receive therapy in Maryland, where the family would be resituated until Charles's tour of duty was over.

Charley then returned to Maryland with her father and brothers in the fall of 1996. The children continued in therapy in Maryland for another year and a half, gradually increasing the length of time between visits. For a while, Charley worried that her mother might not come back at all and had a hard time concentrating at school, but Ellen was finally able to return to Maryland in early November; however, she lived too far from the children to see them on a regular basis until March 1997. At that time, she was well enough to secure a full-time job near her family, purchase a car, and rent her own home; the children began visiting her regularly and then, with the children's therapist's agreement, they began dividing their time between their parents' homes equally. Both Ellen and the entire familial situation have since stabilized, and Charles and Ellen have developed a good working relationship around the care of their children.

Charley Lauren didn't learn that the nature of her mother's illness was mental until sometime in the early winter of 1996, shortly after her mother had returned to Maryland but before she was seeing the children on a regular basis. The children were still worried about her and still did not accept the divorce. Charley had come to spend the weekend with me and had brought up the topic of the divorce. She was angry, saying that she didn't understand why people got divorced, that she thought it was wrong, a sin, and asked me what I thought. I told her that I didn't think it was a sin, but that it was an unfortunate thing resulting from people making a bad mistake in who they married, but that people were human and human beings made mistakes, sometimes bad ones. I explained that sometimes people, like her parents, shouldn't get married in the first place because they simply aren't suited for each other, but that that happens. I also told her that her mother's mental illnesses were also a problem because people with mental illnesses usually don't form good relationships with other people. In order to establish positive relationships, you must first have a good relationship with yourself; mentally ill people don't have that.

Poor Charley's eyes widened in shock. She burst out saying, "Do you mean my mother was *mentally* ill?" and she started crying. I was shocked because I didn't know she didn't know. Sounding betrayed, she demanded, "How come no one ever told us?!" I told her that I was terribly sorry, but that I assumed that by this time she had been told, or else figured it out, but also that it was never anyone's intention to keep it a secret from her or her brothers; apparently it somehow had just never come up before. Everyone just always talked about Ellen being sick, so apparently the children just always assumed it was entirely and purely physical. We hugged each other and cried together because it was sad and painful. Then I explained the nature of her mother's mental illnesses. I told her that I believed it was better for her parents to be divorced because, no matter what they did, they couldn't figure out how to get along, and that their constant fighting was hurting everyone. In the long run, everyone—including Charley and her mother—would see that it was the best solution.

After our conversation, Charley talked with her mom and, although she doesn't remember the conversation or telling me, sometime afterward she told me that her mother told her that she couldn't make herself eat because she didn't feel that she was worthy of feeding or keeping alive.

Charley Lauren started middle school (seventh grade) last fall. As I said, she has spent time alone with my husband and me, including overnight visits, since she was about four, and we have always had a good relationship. We have talked about everything from movies to sex. She is a sociable, intelligent, articulate young woman who continues to exhibit a great deal of independence and who has a variety of interests. She is always "up" for doing new things, for having an adventure. The following is what Charley Lauren has to say about herself, her life, and life as a girl. She had just finished the fifth grade at the time of this interview.

I would describe myself as a loving, caring person who doesn't judge people by how they look or the color of their skin. I judge people by what they're like, how they behave. If they're nice I'll be their friend, but if they are mean or bad-hearted, I won't. So, I try to get to know people before I make up my mind about them.

Friends have been important to me since I was very little. Not only do I just like people a lot, but they have helped me to cope with the difficulties of life. I make friends wherever I go, and so I have a lot of them. When I was little, before we moved to Wisconsin for the year I was in third grade, my best friend was Helen, but she moved back to West Virginia when her father was released from the Army. I haven't heard from her since. I missed her for a long time and didn't have a best friend, but my dad promised me that someday we would try to find her and go visit. I hope we do that someday. Helen was very important to me when I was little because when things were in an uproar at my house, I could always go there. Her house was usually calm and her parents got along. I spent a *lot* of time with Helen and her family before they moved away, including whole weekends when I would go with them to visit their grandparents in the country in West Virginia. Going to Helen's house was the main way I coped with the chaos at my house. I would just get away from it all at Helen's. When she moved, I spent more time with my friend Jackie.

About a year after we moved back to Ft. Meade, I got a new best friend, a girl named Sam, short for Samantha, but she also moved back to Texas. We liked the fact that we both had "boy" names.

In Wisconsin I have many friends—Sarah Nemec, the Griffith twins, Jessica and Jennifer, and the Bietka girls, Jessica, Joanne, and Jasmine. When I'm at Sarah's, we ride her horses, feed their calves, pet her gerbils, things like that, that you do on a farm. With the Griffith girls, I ride their four wheelers, play hide and seek, read, and just kid each other a lot. Sarah lives across the road from the house we lived in when I was here for third grade, and I would go to her house when things got to be too much for me at mine.

I think my friends would describe me as nice, caring, kind, the same way I would describe myself. If you asked me if I was smart, I would say yes, but that isn't one of the things I would think of off the top of my head. I would also say that I am athletic. I have very strong legs and I like volleyball, basketball, football, especially swimming, and, most especially, horseback riding. [Her father notes also that she is good at baseball and "has a hell of an arm."] I love horses and now take riding lessons once a week. If I could I would own all the horses in the world—feed them, ride them—just have them!

Another thing I really *love* to do is read. Whenever I'm bored, I just pick up a book and I can read a book through just nonstop. So I would also describe myself as a great reader. One of my all-time favorite books is *Unicorns and Other Mythological Creatures*. It tells the stories of the sphinx, the phoenix, and imaginary creatures like that. I love those kinds of stories, and I love horse stories. Right now I'm reading *The Horse Whisperer*. Reading was another way I escaped when things got too rough for me, but I also really do just love to do it anyhow.

I am a girl, but it's hard to say what being a girl or being a boy means these days. Neither one is really clear to me because, even if you're a girl, sometimes you like "boy" stuff, like football and things, and sometimes you like "girl" stuff, like singing and dancing. For boys, it's the same way. There seem to be "boy" things and "girl" things, but both boys and girls can do all of them. I don't know what makes these things "girl" or "boy" things. Maybe it came from Adam and Eve. Maybe if Adam did something first that became a "boy" thing and if Eve did something first that became a "girl" thing," but it's not true, because boys and girls can each do everything.

The only real difference that I see between boys and girls is in looks, just looks. When girls mature, they get breasts and boys don't. And boys have penises and girls have vaginas, but that's about all. You can't even tell from hair, because girls can have short hair and boys can have long, so there really doesn't seem to be any differences except looks.

However, all my friends are girls, so maybe that's a difference. They wouldn't have to be, but they just are. Girls have girls for friends and boys have boys for friends, although some girls don't like girls and just hang around with boys. And some people are sexist—some girls don't like boys just because they are boys and some boys don't like girls just because they are girls. Some girls don't like girls, just because they are girls. I think that that's wrong. It's just like judging people on the basis of their race. I learned not to do that partly from reading about history and how white people treated black people. People who do either one are wrong to do that.

When I get together with my friends, we talk about getting mature and what that means, how our bodies are and will be, how we should act when we're mature, what other kids are like and how they act. When I'm with people who I know well, I'm myself; I don't act different from myself. Most girls these days think they have to be what others want them to be. They have to have the right style clothes and do what other kids and their parents want them to do. They live under a lot of pressure trying to be what everyone else wants them to do or be.

For example, sometimes girls who have boyfriends will say, "I have a boyfriend and you don't." And that's supposed to make you think you should have a boyfriend, too, but I think that that's stupid. I'm not going to have a boyfriend until I'm fifteen or sixteen because I don't want to have a boyfriend until I know someone really, really well for a long time. This kind of pressure happens not only in fifth grade but even younger. It can happen to boys, too. Girls can have girlfriends instead of boyfriends as well as girl friends. And boys, too, they can have boys for friends or they can have boyfriends.

Sometimes parents want their daughters to be perfect and sometimes both girls and boys have parents who are just lousy or don't really care. Parents may want their kid to be a doctor, which is okay, or a physical therapist, or something, but maybe a kid wants to be a singer or something. It's a lot of pressure. I tell them that they have to be themselves and be who they are and not what everyone else wants them to be. I think that that's what happened to my mom. She just lost herself. She didn't know who she was and so she just got sick.

I think that I have a good sense of myself and am not easily influenced or pressured by others in that way. I'm more confident that I'm able to stand up to the pressure. I'm not sure how I got that way. Sometimes it just comes to me while I'm sleeping, "Hey, I'm going to ignore people who pressure me." Actually, I think everyone has been that way, but they lose themselves and then can't find themselves. And actually I think that my family and my friends all have helped me stay this way. For instance, Grandma says, "Words *can* hurt, but they really *can't*." And my dad says, "If it's okay to hit then it's okay to be hit, but you shouldn't do it." And my mom says, "It's okay to be different but everyone's really the same." So I learn from lots of people in my family.

I have also learned from my friends. For instance, in my third grade class there was this girl named Libby. She was a member of this little group of kids; she was being nice to me, and we started to be friends. Then her group of kids said, "Oh, you're hanging around with Charley. She's stupid." Then Libby started being mean to me. So I thought, "Well, I shouldn't have been friends with you in the first place if that's how you are," and I didn't care.

The same kind of thing happened when I was in fifth grade with a girl named Vanessa. She was nice to me sometimes and mean to me other times. This boy named Isaiah made fun of me, and Vanessa made fun of me, so I ignored her and stopped being friends with her.

When my parents first got divorced, I was upset. I didn't want them to get divorced. It made me feel different, like I was the only one from a divorced family. But then I realized that half the kids I knew have parents who were divorced, and I didn't feel different anymore. Then I understood that my parents' divorce was actually for the best. They couldn't get along. When they were married, I would dread going home from school because I knew that when I got there they would probably be screaming and yelling and mom would be crying. Sometimes I would ask them to stop, and sometimes I would just go straight up to my room, slam my door, or just leave and go to my friend's house for a few hours to get away from all the fighting. I looked forward to seeing them when they weren't fighting, but it didn't seem like that happened very much. It seemed like they were fighting most of the time and blaming it on us. I remember one time when I sat down in my little rocking chair and screamed at them to stop. They didn't pay any attention. I felt ignored, like I wasn't even there, like I could curl up in a little ball and disappear. That hurt a lot. They got divorced so they wouldn't continue to hurt us. So it's for the best. Now they get along better.

I don't really remember what my mom was like before she got sick, and the whole time she was sick, I was sad and worried. I felt scared every day. I guess I was sad and worried and scared for years. I thought that I would wake up one day, and she wouldn't be there. I felt really bad when she was really sick and couldn't get out of bed or even walk around, when she would collapse. Now I'm just thankful and grateful that she lived. I think it was a miracle that she survived. She has a job now and can go outside and walk around and have a normal life. The way I picture it she was going down the road of life and it divided. One road led to death and the other led to life. My mom found all the strength she had to live and so she did. I'm grateful that her mother forced her to eat three meals a day and keep them down. Before she was all better and came back out to Maryland, I really missed her and worried about her a lot. I had a hard time concentrating in school almost that whole year because I kept thinking about her and wondering when she was coming, *if* she was coming. That was fourth grade. But since she's been here and gotten well, life's a lot easier and happier. Most of the time, she's actually pretty calm. It's a relief. I can concentrate on other things, including school, because I'm not always worrying about her. Like I said, I'm just grateful she's alive.

I believe that this experience made me smarter and made me believe that God helps those who help themselves. For a while, before my mom came back out to Maryland and we were waiting for her, I began to doubt Him or Her. The whole time before that, I just trusted and believed that mom would be okay and come back. But she kept not coming back, and I began to doubt. When she showed up, I believed again.

I would tell kids with parents who have mental illnesses that it's okay, it's not their fault, that they should believe in God and their par-

The authors, Charley Lauren and Patricia Ortman, on Patricia Ortman's Washington, D.C., front porch. (Photo by Charles Ortman.)

ents, that their parent will probably heal, like my mom did. They should try not to worry too much. They should learn to accept the way life has to be, get used to it because it's probably for the better, like I got used to the divorce.

Now I would describe my relationships with my parents and my brothers as a tight bond. I feel like I have that with all of them even though I get mad at my brothers a lot. I don't get mad at my parents much. My dad hasn't changed that much over the years but he is calmer, less worried and excitable than he used to be. One of the best things about him is that he lets my friends stay over a lot. But I don't like that he has a bad temper and he gave it to me! I can get grumpy too.

My mom has changed a *lot*. She can do more things and now she knows what to do. She knows us and she can help us. She is an adult. She's stable and she functions! She's very, very nice to me. About the only problem I have with her is that she asks us to have our rooms in perfect shape and I'm only human. I can't do that. No one can!

My big brother, Andrew, is never around much anymore to help me like he used to be, but when he is, he's nice to me. Dylan plays around too much, hits, and doesn't really listen, but he can understand me better 'cause he's almost my same age. I love them all very much and what's most important to me these days is to be able to go home to a house which is not all worked up, a family which isn't always mad, which is stable and calm. Both Dylan and my mom can both get all worked up about what I think are unimportant things pretty easily, so it's good to have them mostly calm.

When I grow up, I would like to be either a veterinarian, probably a large animal vet, or a therapist, the kind who talks with people to help them figure out their problems, like the therapists I had. It was fun going to see them and they helped me a lot. If I do that, I will get a Ph.D. I plan to have a husband and two or three kids, a dog or two, some cats, some birds, and four or five horses. If I didn't want to do that, I might try to become a singer like my idol Trisha Yearwood, but I don't want to be moving around like she does all the time.

Life for me right now is easy. I have money, a house, food, a good family life. I have everything I need and am a happy young woman because of that. This hasn't always been true, so I am thankful for it now.

WORKS CITED

Blanch, Andrea K., Joanne Nicholson, and James Purcell. 1994. "Parents with Severe Mental Illness and Their Children: The Need for Human Services Integration." *Journal of Mental Health Administration* 21(4): 388–96.

National Institute of Mental Health (NIMH). 1998. *Mental Illness in America: The National Institute of Mental Health Agenda*. Accessed on 6 August. Available at: <http://www.nimh.nih.gov/research/amer. htm>.

Nicholson, Joanne, Jeffrey L. Geller, and William H. Fisher. 1996. " 'Sylvia Frumkin' Has a Baby: A Case Study for Policymakers." *Psychiatric Services* 47(5): 497–501.

Papalia, Diane, and Sally Olds. 1995. *Human Development*. 6th ed. New York: McGraw-Hill.

Sue, David, Derald Sue, and Stanley Sue. 1990. *Understanding Abnormal Behavior*. 3d ed. Boston: Houghton Mifflin.

Vanharen, James, Catherine LaRoche, Marsha Heyman, Albert Massabki, and Lois Colle. 1993. "Have the Invisible Children Become Visible?" *Canadian Journal of Psychiatry* 38(10): 678–80.

Wang, Anne-Rose, and V. V. Goldschmidt. 1996. "Interviews with Psychiatric Inpatients About Professional Intervention with Regard to Their Children." *Acta Psychiatrica Scandinavia* 93(1): 7–61.

About the Contributors

Tahera Aftab is professor of history and director of women's studies at Karachi University, Pakistan. The founding editor of *the Pakistan Journal of Women's Studies: Alam-e-Niswan,* she is also the president of Pakistan Association of Women's Studies. She edited *Literacy for the Girl of Today, the Woman of Tomorrow* (University of Karachi Press, 1995).

Mah-Rukh Ali was born in Oslo in 1982 to highly educated Pakistani parents who had immigrated to Norway. When Mah-Rukh was twelve, she started contributing to *Samora,* a Norwegian magazine that fights racism. At fifteen, she published *Den sure virkelighteten* [*The Bitter Reality*], a nonfiction book intended to stir public debate in Norway about racism and that is excerpted here in translation. She is currently finishing her secondary education, traveling extensively throughout Norway to discuss her book, and writing a regular column for a leading national newspaper, *Klassekampen,* while increasingly involving herself in socialist politics.

Ayanna Anamoor is a seventeen-year-old Muslim from Somalia who came to Canada as a political refugee. She is hiding for fear of reprisals for having given birth to a child, Jasmine, as a single young woman. She would like to become a nurse.

Afia Begum comes from a village in Comilla, about three hundred miles from the capital of Bangladesh. Daughter of a landless farmer, she is the oldest of the girls among six siblings. Married at fifteen, she was divorced three months later. To support herself and her daughter, Afia traveled to the city and worked as a maid. She later started working at a garment factory. Now she is financially independent and sends home money for her daughter and her family. Despite innumerable problems facing her and her family, Afia works to make the best of her situation.

195

Joy Ekema-Agbaw was born in Yaounde, Cameroon, lived there for three years, and now resides in Pennsylvania. She is eleven years old and in sixth grade. She loves writing poetry, reading, bike riding, and traveling. She hopes to become a poet. She speaks English and some Pidgin English.

Susan Frazier-Kouassi is a social psychologist who has worked both in the United States and West Africa in academic and government settings. She currently serves as the executive secretary of an international nongovernmental organization, the Institute for Education of Women in Africa and the Diaspora, based in Abidjan, Côte d'Ivoire.

Najma Habib manages a project in upgrading the quality of English teaching in elementary schools in Bangladesh. The project is funded by Britain's Department for International Development and is implemented through the British Council in Chittagong, Bangladesh. She previously worked as an information officer at the NGO called Corr—The Jute Works, which is a fair trade organization marketing handmade products produced by 6,500 rural women in Bangladesh. She has also worked as a research assistant for ECOTA, an association of development agencies engaged with craft and indigent producer welfare activities. With them, she has conducted research on issues of dowry, divorce, and income-generating activities in a village in Gazipur, Bangladesh. Four of her case studies on the lifestyles of rural women artisans were published by the International Federation of Alternative Trade (IFAT).

Ajla Hodzic was born in Sarajevo, the capital of Bosnia and Herzegovina. She left for Turkey with her mother at the beginning of the war in Bosnia in 1992. She lived in Turkey for three and a half years, with the exception of a month and a half in Prague. In 1996, she came to the United States to continue her education. Currently she is a student at Wellesley College in Massachusetts.

Sherrie A. Inness is associate professor of English at Miami University. Her research interests include girls' literature and culture, popular culture, cooking culture, and gender studies. She has authored three books—*Intimate Communities: Representation and Social Transformation in Women's College Fiction, 1895–1910* (Bowling Green, 1995); *The Lesbian Menace: Ideology, Identity, and the Representation of Lesbian Life* (University of Massachusetts Press, 1997); *Tough Girls: Women Warriors and Wonder Women in Popular Culture* (University of Pennsylvania Press, 1999), and edited five—*Nancy Drew and Company: Culture, Gender, and Girls' Series* (Bowling Green, 1997); *Breaking Boundaries: New Perspectives on Regional Writing* (University of Iowa Press, 1997); *Delinquents and Debutantes: Twentieth-Century American Girls' Cultures* (New York University Press, 1998); *Millennium Girls: Today's Girls Around the World* (Rowman & Littlefield, 1998); and *Kitchen Culture: Women, Gender, and Cooking* (University of Pennsylvania Press, 2000).

Ariana-Sophia M. Kartsonis is a half-first, half-second generation Greek-American born in Salt Lake City, Utah, and currently completing an MFA degree. Her work has appeared in *International Quarterly, So to Speak, 13th Moon, Hayden's Ferry Review, Painted Bride Quarterly,* and *Amaranth.*

K. Limakatso Kendall earned a Ph.D. in drama and is a writer, teacher, and researcher in performance studies and English. She is fifty-three years old and lived in Lesotho from 1992 to 1994, in South Africa from 1995 to 1998, and has recently returned to the United States. She is the editor of Mpho Nthunya's autobiography, *Singing Away the Hunger: the Autobiography of an African Woman* (Indiana University Press, 1997), and is the author of numerous articles and short stories.

Manko Kendall was born in Lesotho, lived for four years in South Africa, and now lives in Texas. She is in the sixth grade. She loves computers, drawing, math, reading, designing clothes, and TV. She plans to become a doctor. She speaks Sesotho, Zulu, Afrikaans, English, and a little bit of Spanish.

Palesa Kendall was born in Lesotho, lived for four years in South Africa, and now lives in Texas. She is in the sixth grade. She enjoys music, dancing, judo, swimming, and bike riding. She hopes to have a career helping people who have something wrong with their brains. She speaks Sesotho, Zulu, Afrikaans, English, and some American Sign Language.

Bosson Caroline Kouassiaman is a fifteen-year-old, Ivorian-American young woman born in Boston, Massachusetts. She has lived in the United States, Cameroon, Côte d'Ivoire, and Burkina Faso, and has attended schools in the American, British, and French educational systems. In addition to volunteer work on the pediatric oncology floor of the C. S. Mott Children's Hospital at the University of Michigan Medical Center, she pursues interests in writing, fashion designing, and music.

Patricia E. Ortman is associate professor of psychology and human development at Mount Vernon College in Washington, D.C. Her research interests include feminist pedagogy, gender equity, and women's spiritual growth and development. Among her publications are "A Feminist Approach to Teaching Learning Theory with Educational Applications" (*Teaching of Psychology,* 1993); and "Continuing the Journey Toward Gender Equity" (*Educational Researcher,* 1994), coauthored with Dr. S. Klein et al. She is a member of the National Gender Equity Expert Panel of the U.S. Department of Education as well as on the advisory board and a faculty member of the Ford Foundation–funded gender equity teaching conference for education professors held at Marymount College in 1999.

Charley Lauren Ortman is a sixth grader in Fort Meade, Maryland. She is eleven years old and has lived in Fort Meade for the past three years. She has also lived in Wisconsin and South Korea. She loves animals and takes horseback riding lessons once a week; she is learning to jump and looks forward to owning her own horse one day and participating in equestrian jumping competitions. She also loves to read, listen to music, and play with her friends. When she grows up, she wants to be either a veterinarian or a children's psychotherapist.

Elisabeth Sandberg is professor of English and chair of humanities at Woodbury University in Burbank, California. She was born in Oslo in 1951 and immigrated to the United States in 1979. Her research interests focus on nineteenth- and twentieth-century American fiction, gender and sexuality, and ethnicity. She has presented numerous papers and published articles, especially on Jo Sinclair.

Rebecca Sultana is a Ph.D. candidate at Texas Christian University. Her field of study is the literature of contemporary first-generation immigrant writers in the United States. She is also interested in postcolonial studies, cultural studies, immigrant literature, and South Asian women's literature. Prior to coming to the United States in 1992, she has taught in the English Department at Chittagong University, Bangladesh. She will be teaching at East West University in Dhaka, Bangladesh, when she returns home this fall.

Lisa B. Thompson is a Ph.D. student at Stanford University's program in modern thought and literature. Currently a dissertation fellow at the Institute for Research on Women and Gender, she is also a teaching fellow at Stanford's Center for Comparative Studies in Race and Ethnicity. Her play, *Single Black Female,* recently debuted at Theater Rhinoceros in San Francisco. Thompson will complete her dissertation, "Show and Tell: Representations of Black Middle-Class Sexuality in Contemporary Narrative and Performance," as a Smith College Mendenhall fellow next year.

Wendy M. Thompson is an eighteen-year-old poet/militant feminist who is a volunteer from the Health Initiatives for Youth, a San Francisco–based organization that deals with young queer and HIV + people in the inner city. She will be attending the University of California, Santa Barbara, where she will major in Women's Studies. In her future, she hopes to become an activist and an advocate for young (queer) women of color.

Merlinda Weinberg is a Ph.D. student at the Ontario Institute for Studies in Education at the University of Toronto. For twenty-five years, she was a social worker, manager, consultant, and educator specializing in work with youth and their families before she decided to obtain a doctorate in sociology and equity studies.

Vivian Yenika-Agbaw is an assistant professor of children's and young adult literature at Bloomsburg University. A native of Cameroon, she has lived with her family in Pennsylvania since 1991. Her research interests include postcolonial literature, social issues in adolescent literature, and the role of critical literacy in literature. She has published numerous articles, poetry, and short stories in international, national, and regional journals.